SEARCH

If you're searching

- for the right mind-set and skills to succeed in your studies and relationships,
- for inspiration and strategies to sustain your confidence and reduce stress,
- for advance warning about the things and people that might sandbag you and how to avoid them,

then you've found the right book.

"As a second-semester freshman in college, I was amazed at how many tips, suggestions, life lessons, and college hacks that I had yet to discover. Reading this book was enjoyable just as much as it was beneficial."
Anthea, Georgia College & State University student

"Dr. Duffey and Dr. Roquemore have managed to condense years of experience with college students into this immensely helpful resource. Students and parents often do not know what they do not know. This book will help them anticipate and plan for many issues they might not have otherwise considered. I cannot recommend this book highly enough."
Stephen Wilson, PsyD, Director of Counseling Services, GCSU

"As a retired K-12 educator and father of two sons, one a recent college graduate and the other a college sophomore, I found Search: A Guide for College and Life *one of the most helpful and detailed resources for navigating college and life experiences. This guide offers students, parents, and professors significant insight into the challenges that young people face as they search for their ultimate purpose in life and provides practical, real-world and clinically-proven tools to assist them during the difficult and complex journey into adulthood. I recommend this guide without reservation!"*
L. Michael Newton, EdD Retired K-12 School Superintendent

SEARCH

A GUIDE FOR COLLEGE AND LIFE

Barbara Roquemore EdD
Jeff Duffey MD

SEARCH: *A Guide for College and Life*
by Barbara Roquemore EdD and Jeff Duffey MD

Copyright 2020 by Cairde, Karuna & Hedd Publishing, LLC

All rights reserved. No part of this book may be reproduced, distributed, or transmitted in any form or by any means, including photocopying, recording, or other electronic or mechanical methods, without the prior written permission of the publisher, except in the case of brief quotations embodied in critical reviews and certain other noncommercial uses permitted by copyright law. Write to Cairde, Karuna & Hedd Publishing, 2841 Middlecreek Way, Cumming, Georgia 30041

www.searchaguideforcollegeandlife.com

Cover by Anisha Umêlec / 99designs
99designs.com/profiles/anisha
Interior Design by Sue Balcer of Just Your Type Desktop Publishing
www.JustYourType.biz
Index written by Carol Roberts of Roberts Indexing Services
www.robertsindexing.com

First Edition 2020
ISBN 978-0-9862583-2-9
Library of Congress Control Number 2020901935

URLs are provided for informational purposes only and their mention should not be considered a recommendation. The author is not responsible for the content of these sites. See the disclaimer for more details

*To the students, faculty, and staff of
Georgia College and State University*

Contents

Preface 12
Acknowledgments 14

1   ASSESSING YOURSELF 1
    Recognizing Vulnerabilities 1
    Recognizing Strengths 4
    Cherishing Differences 5

2   REMINDING YOURSELF WHY YOU NEED
    TO SUCCEED IN COLLEGE 7
    Avoiding the consequences of not having enough money 7
    Having the possessions and pursuing the activities you want .. 11
    Keeping or improving your social position 12
    Being competent so you can adapt to the future 13
    Understanding yourself 15
    Developing a compelling life-purpose worthy of yourself 17

3   GRASPING THE IMPORTANCE OF TIME
    MANAGEMENT 21
    Using Mindfulness for Perspective and Renewal 22
    Prioritizing 24
    Organizing Your Time 25
    Organizing Your Workspace 28
    Mapping Out Your Daily Journey 28
    Creating Some Daily Habits 29
    Selecting Courses and Registering 29
    Selecting Teachers 32
    Planning the sequence of your courses 33
    Developing a Strategic Plan for the Semester 34

4	ESTABLISHING A WORKABLE ENVIRONMENT	37
	Staying Safe	37
	Living in a Residence Hall	45
	Living off-campus	47
	Living at home	50
	Educating yourself about weapons on campus	52
	Having a car on campus	53
	Deciding whether to have pets	53
5	PREVENTING HEALTH PITFALLS	59
	Eating	59
	Sleeping	62
	Maintaining Physical Health	65
6	AVOIDING FINANCIAL PITFALLS	75
	Managing money	75
	Saving money on expenses	77
	Minimizing Student Loan Expense	80
	Working	81
7	BELONGING TO THE COLLEGE COMMUNITY	87
	Thinking about diversity	87
	Reviewing basic manners	89
	Socializing	90
	Understanding Social Groups	92
	Surviving Spring Break	96
	Dealing with social media	101
	Working with Systems	103
8	CONSTRUCTING EFFECTIVE MINDSETS	105
	Understanding the Importance of Mindsets	105

Using a 'Cold Hard Realities' Mindset for Motivation 108
Using A Brain-centered Mindset in your Academics 119

9 TWEAKING YOUR ACADEMIC SKILLSET 127
Finding Potential Helpers 127
Discovering Helpful Applications and Websites 128
Getting at the Mechanics 130
Buying Textbooks 131
Making the Most of the Classroom Experience 132
Reading 137

10 ENHANCING RELATIONSHIP SKILLS AND RELATIONSHIPS 141
Considering Family 141
Adjusting to Roommates 143
Analyzing Peer Relationships 144
Improving Dating Relationships 147
Memorizing a Mnemonic Device for Assessing Your Date—the Eight Ps 150
Coping with Stalkers and Unwanted Attention 153
Getting Serious or Breaking Up? 159

11 STRATEGIZING TO MEET THE CHALLENGES THAT ARISE AS THE COLLEGE YEARS UNFOLD 161
Entering the Middle Phase-The 4 Ss 161
Wandering in the Wisdom Wilderness 164
Reflecting on the End Phase 167

12 RECOGNIZING WHAT HELPS FIRST-GENERATION COLLEGE STUDENTS WILL ALSO HELP YOU 169

13	IMPROVING YOUR WELL-BEING	179
	Learning More about Mental Health	179
	Identifying Specific Coping Techniques	180
	Developing Healthy Mental and Physical Habits	182
	Feeling Suicidal	184
	Surviving a Loss by Suicide	190
	Getting Help	190
14	SUMMING IT UP WITH AN EQUATION AND FINAL MNEMONIC	193

APPENDIX OF RESOURCES	195
A-1 Resources to Help You Plan What to do for a Living	197
Some Statistics on the Advantages of College	200
A-2 Resources Concerning Diversity	209
A-3 More General Resources for Wellness	213
A-4 Symptom-Targeted Resources	215
A-5 Resources to Help you Size Up Impediments to Well-being and Success	217
Gambling that what you don't know won't hurt you	221
Tobacco	222
Alcohol	222
Marijuana	223
Kratom	223
Psychostimulants	224
Methamphetamine (Meth)	224
Cocaine	225
MDMA	225
Opiates	225
Designer Drugs	226

    A-6 Resources to Give You an Overview of Some Symptom Complexes 227
        The Self-Evaluator 227
        Normal Grief 228
        Adjustment Disorders 229
        Major Depressive Disorder without Psychotic features ..229
        Major Depressive Disorder with Psychotic Features 229
        Overviews of Anxiety 230
        Generalized Anxiety 231
        Social Anxiety 231
        Panic Disorder 231
        Obsessive-Compulsive Disorder 231
        Post-Traumatic Stress Disorder/ Trauma 231
        Attention Deficit Hyperactivity Disorders 232
        Psychosis 232
        Eating Disorders 233
    A-7 Affirmations After a Break-Up 234
    A-8 Items for Your Safety Kit 236
    A-9 Wilfred Bion's Theories about Groups 238
    A-10 Resources to Help Nurture an Openness to Wonder 241

Bibliography 245

References 251

Index 259

About the Authors 273

From the Authors 275

Preface

You won't read this book. Anyway, that's what popular speakers said. You're supposed to be McThinkers who insist everything be short, simple, and easy to understand. We disagreed with them. We saw no shortage of critical thinking, courage, or persistence in the same generation that gave us the Parkland students whose activism formed Never Again MSD. We believe in you. We also know that this book could change your life. We were not going to miss the opportunity to give you a chance to read it.

In college, your search connects with humanity's search for answers to questions about the nature of the human condition and the meaning of life. You join humankind in searching to understand how things work, why we do what we do, and where each of us fits in. You need strategies for this lifelong adventure.

This guidebook's strategies will help you develop confidence as you find your way past the pitfalls of college and life. Whether you use it as a reference guide or read it straight through, it will give you tips and resources to improve your academics. You will feel more prepared to find a meaningful job and pay off student loans.

Whether you are following in your parents' footsteps or blazing a trail as a first-generation college student, these strategies will help you in your search.

Your abilities and identity are not set in stone. You can grow with effort. Use this guide to set new goals, identify specific vulnerabilities, get the best mindset, and improve your studies. Let it help you understand relationships during college and increase your personal growth. This book is a thoughtful, compassionate, open-minded discussion of both the practical and philosophical realities of college and life. Nonstudents will find it relevant, as well.

Gaining skills and factual knowledge are only parts of the college experience. College provides opportunities to explore the nature of the human spirit as it has manifested throughout history.

Use college to discover who you are, as you become an increasingly self-reliant and critical thinker. We hope your spirit will grow as well as your mind, launching you into adulthood.

All the same, facing this can be intimidating— especially if you already feel a bit insecure or lonely. The techniques covered in this book will help you develop confidence for the adventure. You already know you have to work to succeed. This book will show you how.

You are the best judge of whether our suggestions make sense and are correct for your circumstances.

Chapters 3, 4, 5, 6, 10, and 12 will help you in your first days of college, but you don't need to know everything in this book before you start. Note the table of contents for later reference. Some topics will interest you now. Others will interest you later, as different circumstances arise. A quick scan through the first part of section A-5 in the Resource Appendix will give you some ideas about what things are most likely to sidetrack you in college.

If you are not sure about a career or are having any doubts about whether you are ready for college or college makes sense for you, please skip to section A-1 in the Resource Appendix, "Resources to Help You Plan What to do for a Living." There, you will find information and resources to help you consider a variety of careers and options. You will discover jobs that require college, or an alternative to college, or minimal post-high school education.

Mastering the day-to-day practical topics frees you to explore the more philosophical parts of the book. We hope this book will be like a movie you see several times—each time getting something different out of it because you have changed in the interval.

We found we could not write about how to cope with college without writing about how to cope with life. We believe nonstudents will find in this book guidance for similar situations in their own lives.

There are two-year colleges, sometimes called *junior colleges*. There are *four-year colleges*. When a college grows into a university, it has several subdivisions of study. These subdivisions are called *colleges*. A university may have within it a college of education, a college of arts and sciences, a college of engineering, or other colleges representing other fields of study.

We have taken literary liberties in the book for the sake of simplicity and readability. We arbitrarily use the word *college* as though it were interchangeable with the words *junior college*, *four-year college*, and *university*. We do not distinguish between liberal arts, technical, or online colleges, even though the experience of going to each is different. We treat college as if it were a fixed entity. College is rapidly changing.

In each chapter, the book sets out strategies you can use along the course of your search. Here are the chapters and their corresponding strategies:

Chapter 1 - Gauge your readiness for the search before you start.

Chapter 2 - To strengthen your resolve, understand the clear need for your search.

Chapter 3 - Plot your course.

Chapter 4 - Decide on your lodgings.

Chapters 5 and 6 - Develop ways to sustain yourself.

Chapter 7 - Pick the right fellow searchers.

Chapter 8 - Adapt your outlook for the adversities ahead.

Chapters 9/10 – Sharpen the needed skills.

Chapter 11 - Make course corrections.

Chapters 12/13 - Realize your self-efficacy and attend to your needs.

Chapter 14 - Survey where you have been and how you got there.

Appendix of Resources - Learn where to reach out for extra help along the way.

DISCLAIMER

Deciding what to do about college is a complicated process. While the authors expect this book can help you think about many of the issues involved, everyone has unique experiences that affect how he or she reacts. Even though the authors hope you do not have any problems from reading this book, the authors take no responsibility for how this book affects you. The authors take no responsibility for any decisions that you may make after reading it. Read this book at your own risk. Please question everything you read in this book. Ask yourself if our statements ring true to your own experiences and beliefs. Although the authors and publisher of this book have made every effort to ensure the accuracy and completeness of this book, they cannot guarantee or warrant that the contents are accurate or complete. They also cannot be responsible for any of the third-party resources discussed in this book. The information provided in this book is intended to help you make informed decisions about what is best for you. It is not a substitute for medical advice or treatment. The authors cannot give you medical advice and urge you to consult your physician before making any decisions regarding any health-related matters. Of course, you should feel free to discuss anything you read in this book with your physician. Similarly, the information provided in this book is not a substitute for legal advice from a licensed attorney, and you should not consider anything in the book a solicitation of legal advice. If you have any legal questions or concerns, you should consult an attorney who is licensed in your state.

ACKNOWLEDGMENTS

The authors would like to thank Shadisha Bennett-Brodde, Susan Spencer, the other members of the Georgia College and State University Counseling Center, and the Student Health Service for their unique contributions and support. We appreciate all the high school and college students whose reviews of our drafts provided valuable targeted comments.

As college students, our children—Andrew, Christy, Erica, Matthew, and Meghan—brought home to us the raw experience of the challenges of college. Because of them, our patients, and our students, we have had the opportunity to see the college experience from many different viewpoints. We are thankful for their contributions to our understanding.

Next: Strategy 1—Gauge your readiness for the search before you start.

1

Assessing Yourself

RECOGNIZING VULNERABILITIES

By early addressing your vulnerabilities, you may avoid some of their logical outcomes. Do you share any of the susceptibilities of these fictional characters?

Isabelle's parents marveled at her ability to multitask and how it had helped her succeed in academics and extracurriculars. They saw her accomplishments and frenetic activity as a promise of great achievements to come. Isabelle felt the pressure. She took pains to look good on social media but found herself fighting inner doubts about whether it was all worth it. She began feeling fake when she couldn't feel wholehearted anymore about some of the volunteer work she was doing. She felt like she just wanted to "be"— instead of always having to "become." As she watched other first-year students, she realized she envied their genuine enthusiasm that no longer came naturally for her.

High school was harder for Anna because it took longer for her to study than others. Her determination made up for it. She made herself study longer and stay organized. It meant cutting out some extracurriculars. She had no trouble understanding ideas. She found that writing was difficult. When several facts were presented to her, she had trouble remembering them long enough to tie them together into written conclusions. Anna did well in high school. She worries that her determination and willingness to sacrifice extra time will not be enough to make up for the fast pace of reading required in college.

Dan's high school was not that hard. Because his teachers explained the concepts in class, he used his intelligence to pick up the material without having to study. Dan's interests were elsewhere. He crammed and could remember material long enough to do well on the tests but did not retain it because he did not learn it. His grades suggest he knows more than he does. Because it worked in high school, Dan hopes college will also yield to his combination of intelligence, charm, and "academic ingenuity."

Christina has much chaos in her life. She lacks the time and peace of mind that could have made school easier. School cannot be her priority. She sometimes feels like the tension and craziness in the world is an extension of the unpredictability in her family life. She feels like she must be the active adult in her home and the parent to her siblings. Her parents function poorly. Now, their divorce and money worries distract them. She is proud of her reputation as a rational thinker. Her friends don't realize she must fight to focus in class and overcome feeling demoralized. She is puzzled to find herself being the go-to person for other students with problems.

Will, a first-generation college student, knows his family is proud of him but still worries he will become like a stranger to them. His peers and family have been less subtle as they express that he must mistakenly think he is better than them to go to college. Despite his noteworthy academic accomplishments in high school, Will feels pressure to prove himself again academically and justify his decision to take another path. Will feels all this as he faces students who are oblivious to him and make comments that make him feel left out. These students' lack of familiarity with hardship and suffering make them seem immature and silly to him. He feels like he doesn't exactly fit in anywhere anymore and has started somehow feeling fake himself. He wonders when his peers will also begin to see him as a misfit.

Assessing Yourself

Elizabeth has not had tragedy or hardship in her life. She lost one grandmother. Otherwise, her life has been almost idyllic. An essential part of her loving parents' lives, she was cherished and protected from anything that could hurt her. She has benefited from her parents and her faith, which confirmed her worth and contributed to her sense of security. Her parents have ensured that she grew up around people who are like them and who encourage Elizabeth. The flip side of Elizabeth's happy childhood is that it has unintentionally deprived her of the opportunity to develop inner personal strength from overcoming any misfortune. As she finds people who think, act, and believe differently, she feels torn. She wants to understand but is afraid it might somehow change her. She feels homesick and wonders why her roommate feels intimidating to her. She knows of some older graduates of her high school who were equally naïve when they went off to college, drank too much, and got into trouble. She wonders if she can say "no" to herself when her parents are not around to protect her from herself.

Delores is an older student who worked as a server to pay for community college and has just transferred to a four-year school. If she works enough hours to pay for expenses, she might not be able to manage the advanced curriculum her major demands. Delores is afraid she will suffer the same fate as her friend Julie, who had to drop out. Unable to afford health insurance or safe housing, Julie now feels like a zombie because she works long hours in a low-paying job with poor working conditions.

Getting into college surprised Jack. Maybe it was because of a good recommendation from his favorite teacher and his surprising scores on the SAT. Jack knows it wasn't his grades because grades have always been a struggle for him. There were times when teachers gave him latitude. They found him likable and earnestly trying at their course's end. While sincerely wanting to do well in college, he doesn't know how to go about it. No one worked with him on his study skills. Jack knows he needs academic help but isn't sure just what kind and where to find it. Jack remembers his guilt at putting off studying in high school because studying was so frustrating. Fresh in his mind is the dread he would experience as the semester advanced, and he fell further behind. Now Jack feels out of his depth.

Throughout this book, you will find possible ways to surmount these students' vulnerabilities.

RECOGNIZING STRENGTHS

Half-jokingly, someone once said that getting into college requires you to impress colleges with your excellent grades, high test scores, great recommendations, outstanding extracurriculars, and to do life-changing volunteer work. How you meet these arbitrary standards may not reflect your genuine accomplishments and the struggles you overcame. Admissions officers may overlook something you love and do well.

Will Smith said, "The first step is you have to say that you can (Weston n.d. https://wealthygorilla.com/inspirational-quotes-will-smith/)." Make that first step now. Before you go further in the book, write down your significant accomplishments. Did you win a quiet battle within yourself to do something especially hard for you? Were you there for a struggling friend? Does coping with difficult family members come naturally to you? Perhaps, you have managed to form a bond with someone who knows you and believes in you and your abilities to fulfill your dreams. Is there a powerful connection with art, music, literature, or sport that inspires you? Maybe, you have a foundation of belief about which you have deep conviction and commitment. What are the skills, talents, and strength of character that help you each day? Please take a moment to identify each skill and describe it. Take another moment and think about each of your character strengths and how you might use them.

Perhaps there is something different about how you have blended your experiences and talents. Imagine you are a building. What are the beams within yourself that have supported you through school so far?

It may feel unnatural to remember your strengths. Did you have a grandparent whose eyes twinkled when you walked into the room? Look at yourself through those eyes. Consider the people from whom you draw the faith you have in yourself and your future. Who is a model of how to have a purpose beyond yourself and make it despite all the skeptics?

Remember that you are a work in progress.

(Michael F. Myers 1998)

What you try, regardless of your success or failure, provides you an opportunity. You can grow from the challenge, learn, and improve.

CHERISHING DIFFERENCES

If all the keys of a piano were exactly alike, you could only play one note. For a keyboard to be useful, it needs keys that are different from each other. So too, the world benefits from people who are different from each other.

In football, shorter, thinner, faster running backs try to squeeze past much bigger defensive linemen who try to stop them. The physical qualities a coach looks for in a running back are different from what they look for in a lineman. A coach knows that the very smallness that makes it hard for a player to be a blocking lineman may be just what the team needs in a running back. A running back's smallness puts him close to the ground and makes him agile and hard to tackle.

While a coach knows that it takes different kinds of characteristics in his players to make a complete team, he also knows that all of his players need to have self-discipline, a work ethic, and be able to communicate and get along with each other to win.

The running back cherishes those features that make him hard to tackle. He has found his position on the team and does not scold himself for being different from the big linemen who would block him.

Like the football players, you can find your place in life and discover how your differences make you an asset to an employer, a potential partner, your school, organizations, and your community. Like the football players, you will need self-discipline, a work ethic, and an ability to work with others. These are skills that you can learn.

A deficit may become an advantage. Some Australian sheepdogs have defects in the iris of their eyes that make their eyes look like a key-hole. When they look at sheep, their eyes spook the sheep, and the dog can make them turn more easily.

Imagine a tribe of Native Americans camped for the night on the trail. The tribe member who has difficulty deeply sleeping will hear the noise of someone creeping up on the tribe. Differences can be life-saving for others.

By identifying and celebrating your differences, it helps you understand where you can best use them.

Next: Strategy 2 —To strengthen your resolve, understand the clear need for your search.

2

Reminding Yourself Why You Need to Succeed in College

AVOIDING THE CONSEQUENCES OF NOT HAVING ENOUGH MONEY

Some college courses are worth taking for the joy of learning alone. Some classes are impractical but stimulating and undemanding. Taking too many of these may result in an education that does not equip you to earn a living. Expressing yourself by choosing useless classes now may not be worth later losing the freedom to do things you want.

Life is much harder when you are impoverished. Consider integrating a minor you are passionate about with a more practical but slightly less exciting major that qualifies you for a better job or entrance to graduate school. It is crucial that you realize that you need to begin working on this now, and not your senior year.

You may not need to go to college to make a good living if you have gained technical skills from going to technical school. Maybe you have natural musical or athletic talent. Perhaps you can get on-the-job training in a family business or are an entrepreneurial genius with a rich uncle. If you are thinking about going into a technical field, discover your best match by going to the appendix.

We are told some companies take shortcuts and thin out a stack of job applicants by throwing out applications of people without a college education even if the job does not require one. Don't assume that applying for a job that does not require a college education means you are on an equal playing field. Employers know that college graduates have demonstrated an ability to stick with something difficult, to follow instructions, and comply with requirements.

If you do go to college, however—and you do poorly in college—you may lack the skills or credentials needed to have a job that pays enough for you to live independently. This failure puts you at the mercy of others on whom you must then depend. You may have to stay with and listen to well-meaning parents who don't think the way you do. You may find yourself putting up with a bully at work or doing work you don't enjoy. Partners who know their mate does not make enough money to support themselves or leave them are more likely to discount them, mistreat them, and exploit the power imbalance.

When you are dependent on your parents, you find yourself worrying about whether they will continue to support you. You wonder if your parents resent your dependence on them. You think about their health and fear they will become disabled from cancer. You worry they will have an accident or lose their job. You hate to keep asking them for day-to-day expenses or hearing their lectures about spending money on clothes or how you are exhausting their retirement savings. You feel guilty, but the prospect of moving from their lifestyle to what yours would be on your own is paralyzing.

If you do well at college, you have a better chance of creating a functional home, a home where it feels safe to express emotion. You have an opportunity to live without dependency or feeling the despair of powerlessness.

> *The cost of a thing is the amount of what I will call life which is required to be exchanged for it, immediately or in the long run.*
>
> (Henry David Thoreau 1846)

Reminding Yourself Why You Need to Succeed in College

The more you make per hour, the less the amount of your life you have to exchange for something you buy, according to Henry David Thoreau, the American essayist and author of *Walden*. Getting a higher-paying job requiring a higher education means you have a choice to spend less time earning a living and more time living it. If you make $10.00 as a mean hourly wage, then a dollar costs you 6 minutes of your life to earn. If you make $34.48 an hour as a nurse, then a dollar costs you 1.75 minutes of your life to earn. If you make $55.78 an hour as a biochemist, then a dollar costs you 1.08 minutes of your life. If you make $75.12 an hour as a dentist, then a dollar costs you 0.8 minutes of your life—about thirteen percent of the time it takes the ten-dollars-an-hour-worker to earn. The more you earn each hour, the less of your life you have to work to make it. (Check out your future job salary using the Bureau of Labor May 2018 Employment and Wage Estimates US at https://www.bls.gov/oes/current/oes_nat.htm)

If you take the path of least resistance now by not getting an education, it may cost you more effort over your lifetime. With a better paying job, you may be able to amass some money to use to take advantage of breaks to move to a better position or avoid working for someone you don't respect.

If you lack job skills, you may have to take and stay in a job that requires long hours that are scheduled at someone else's convenience. It may not be a job that aligns closely with your values, you enjoy, or provides an opportunity for advancement. You may have to work under harsh working conditions. You may be doing a job that stresses your body and risks your health. Such a job puts your ability to continue to support your family at risk. It also may mean that you are spending more time away from your family because of long hours, a long commute, or mandatory travel.

You may not know how it is to be poor. You may assume that if you were temporarily poor, you would escape it by working harder. Think again. When you are poor, you cannot afford some of the protection you have now. You might now have adequate health insurance from your parents, so health emergencies may not be problems.

When you don't have enough money, one crisis may lead to another like dominoes. Take this sequence of events, for example: If you cannot afford health insurance or work at a job that does not have it, then paying for a health emergency can mean you don't have the rent. So, you let the car insurance lapse. You later get pulled over for a traffic infraction and charged with driving without insurance. You are forced to get a quick loan to pay the fines and your uninsured car's repairs. Your expenses are then more than your monthly income. You miss some payments. Your credit suffers. Life settles down a bit. When you go to get a better job, they check your credit. Someone else with a better credit rating, considered more reliable, gets the job.

Life is unpredictable. You want to have a job that makes enough money, so you don't knock over that first domino.

> *In my family, anything that was considered an educational opportunity, they wanted me to be able to do. I would even say that my parents, and their friends in our community, thought of education as a kind of armor against racism. If you were well-educated and you spoke well, then there was only so much they could do to you.*
>
> (Condoleezza Rice 2010)

The 66th US Secretary of State, Condoleezza Rice, believes that being educated enough that you can get a job that pays a living wage would give you a fighting chance at a good life and more freedom. Without it, as Condoleezza Rice's parents and their friends likely would agree, you are more subject to discrimination, unfairness, and society's mistaken damaging view that a person's worth is based on their wealth. You may find you hold some variation of this view and could end up feeling ashamed and left behind when your peers finish school and get better jobs because they did better in school.

Most of the world does not care whether you have a good life. Many people would believe you did not know much about how the world works if you thought that, just by being born, you would be assured a good life. They would see you as feeling unnecessarily entitled and naïve.

> *I know what it's like to access the privilege of a ZIP Code but also be born in one that could have destined me to something else.*
>
> (Alexandra Ocasio-Cortez 2018)

Look around you at the work-study student checking you into the residence hall, at your server, at the barback, or at the scholarship student who is your student instructor. Many have to pay for much of their college expenses. Alexandra Ocasio-Cortez, US Representative D-NY from the 14th District, had previously worked long hours as a bartender and server during college. Like AOC did, they already know what it is like to be disadvantaged. They had to develop frustration tolerance and self-discipline to make it into college. Imagine how you might feel if you were poor and had a chance to get out of it. Imagine how hard you would be willing to work. Can you compete with their determination?

HAVING THE POSSESSIONS AND PURSUING THE ACTIVITIES YOU WANT

If you use college to develop knowledge, experience, and ability, it may lead to making good money afterward. Besides enabling you to escape financial hardship, this money allows you to travel, eat at better restaurants, live in houses located in safer neighborhoods, and buy "stuff" you or your family want. Success may contribute to your attractiveness to a future mate - or at least to potential in-laws. You will also be able to enjoy going to events with your friends without worrying that you can't afford it. Your children will not have to suffer deprivation.

KEEPING OR IMPROVING YOUR SOCIAL POSITION

Having the right academic credentials and belonging to distinguished college organizations are parts of some social vetting customs. Meeting accomplished influential people and experiencing different social circumstances in college prepare you to handle yourself properly in similar situations in business and life. You learn how the world runs. You will be ready when others probe your working knowledge of art, literature, and the history of humankind. People want to observe if you are a cultured person or just a faker whose illiteracy will embarrass the company or the family you hope to join. You will avoid showing factual ignorance. Not knowing some facts can be as embarrassing as not knowing how to order from the menu or which piece of silverware to use first.

Even people of means, who may choose to use their position to get around some rules, find the conventions involved in keeping social position are inescapable. Keeping social position means preserving social connections and activities, so you avoid exclusion. Without college, this could be uncommonly difficult. Continuing to make the family's hallmark contribution to the community may be almost impossible without succeeding in college. Failing to do this risks your family's position and reputation. You don't want others to think of you as a blemish on the family.

Reminding Yourself Why You Need to Succeed in College

BEING COMPETENT SO YOU CAN ADAPT TO THE FUTURE

To survive, you need to make informed, rational decisions. Making sound decisions requires factual knowledge and critical thinking. You face a *tomorrow* that will be changing exponentially faster.

You have already heard gloomy future forecasts. Before you skip this section, humor us. Study it. You may be alive for a long time. These changes won't just be happening to some abstract hypothetical person. They will be happening to you. You are not preparing just for life as it is now. You are preparing for life as it will be over your lifetime. Not only is knowledge power, but it is also the key to your survival.

The time to come promises social disruption in your lifetime. Climate change will cause the US population to migrate within the country and compete for scarcer resources. Rising ocean levels will force large numbers of families all over the world to retreat from the coasts and leave their flooded islands or countries. Well-trained baby boomers in positions of responsibility will be aging out of the taxable workforce and no longer paying as much tax. The decline in the birthrate and the dramatic increase in the aging population will put added pressure on you, the younger taxpayer, to pay for their healthcare and Social Security. The political power structure will change because of shifts in US and world demographics. Because many jobs will be able to be done remotely, you will be competing for jobs against eager people from all over the world.

Artificial Intelligence and inventions will put pressure on Social Security, Medicare, Medicaid, and the social safety net as many more people lose their jobs. Kai-Fu Lee, the founder of the venture capital firm Sinovation Ventures —a former executive at Apple, SGI, Microsoft, and former president of Google China— stated that robots are likely to replace 50 percent of all jobs in the next decade. (Lee 2017)

Without some intervention, the middle class will continue to disappear. The gap between the upper and the lower class will widen. Futurists suggest that members of the Gen-Z generation (people born 1995-2015) are more likely to change jobs than the generation before them. Futurists believe many of the occupations they will have will involve technology not yet known.

Jack Kelly's article, *Predictions for the Uncharted Job Market of the Future,* is a wake-up call. He states, "The bottom line is that if you have the abilities, focus on science, technology, engineering and mathematics, computer-coding-related careers. If you don't have right-brain dominance, find a skill or profession that cannot be replaced by technology, easily taught to a younger replacement, or shipped to another country." (Kelly 2019)

If there is social unrest, you may quickly need to change locations, jobs, or adjust in-place. To do this effectively, you need the competence education provides.

While this is going on, you may also have to adapt to changes in your parent or partner's health and economic status. Parental illnesses like heart attacks, cancer, or strokes can be as sudden and disruptive as car accidents and divorce.

While at first glance, these problems seem insurmountable, in the United States, nothing is inevitable.

> *The world needs your voice. There is a great power in speaking your truth and standing for something important. Find a message that you must share, and then do it in a way that is authentic to you. My way is using rap, but there are a million different ways to share your message. There is a lot of suffering and injustice in the world, and there is also a great deal of hope. When you step forward and start speaking about what you see and what you want to change, you can begin living in that hope instead of despair.*
>
> (Sonita Alizadeh 2018)

Afghan activist and rapper, Sonita Alizadeh's statements were proven true in the US by the students of Stoneman Douglas High School. Look at what they and other students of your generation did to change the gun laws in Florida after the shooting at their high school. Your country and your world need you. Your unique gifts and competence can make a difference. You <u>can</u> participate in the American story.

Life is empty of constancy and filled with possibility. You need to develop a life-view, worldview, and a self-view that makes for hardiness in the face of adversity. You can prepare for the future by taking college seriously. Oprah Winfrey is often quoted as having said, "The greatest discovery of all time is that a person can change his future by merely changing his attitude." By changing your attitude, you can develop that hardiness in the face of adversity.

UNDERSTANDING YOURSELF

In studying what others have found in their quest to understand the human condition, you discover yourself. From your reading and discussions, you realize the pursuit of knowledge is sacred because men and women have died seeking the truth. You understand the freedom to discuss ideas freely is something for which men and women have had to fight.

You are joining your fellow students and professors in a community that values learning, not merely job preparation. You come to find out that Harry Stack Sullivan, a noted twentieth-century American psychiatrist, was right when he said, "We are all more simply human than otherwise." Understanding others helps you understand yourself. Seeing their passion enables you to find your own. Reading about their efforts to seek an inner coherence helps you with yours. Witnessing the suffering of humankind empowers you to understand your pain and how to cope with it.

The contrasts college provides can also help you understand yourself and your life experience in a new way. For instance, if you have come from a family that did not recognize your worth despite what you did, you will find it validating to see a causal connection between what you do and what happens. For example, anyone correctly answering all the test questions will get 100. Being predictably rewarded for your efforts counters the feeling of helplessness. Being in this environment builds self-confidence and a sense of mastery.

You also observe your friends as they struggle hard to find themselves. You view peers resisting the pervasive, nihilistic messages of cartoons on visual media that exhort everyone to believe that no one has a purpose or belongs. These messages make watching media seem like the only logical way to pass through a dull, finite existence. In college, you learn from how your peers struggle with other issues like victimhood, injustice collecting, people pleasing, procrastination, and impulsivity.

Sometimes your friends don't make it. Over the course of college, you will have the learning experience of seeing friends, whose alcohol and drug use did not seem to be a problem initially, end up dropping out of school.

That is just one way you learn what works and what does not. Through trial and error, you make some mistakes yourself, and you realize you survived them. Outcomes show you what you have to take seriously and what not.

Whom you are becoming begins to feel more like your authentic self. College gives you opportunities to practice at situations you may face later in the workforce. For example, going through recruitment resembles interviewing for a job. Learning to live with a roommate helps prepare you for living with a future mate.

Your beliefs may not have stood out in the past because the people around you shared them. Finding people who hold different ones puts your beliefs in contrast and allows you to see them more clearly. In the same way, material that you read in your courses and opinions voiced in class help you delineate what you believe.

You learn some of the assumptions you made about the world while growing up are mistaken. This realization frees you to change what you do and to see the world differently and not repeat the same painful mistakes. You develop a sense of integrity and peace. You begin to build a compelling vision of what your life could be.

You might be one of the many students whose parents' dreams were crushed by the recession of 2008. You currently have a better economic environment to pursue those or dreams of your own.

By building gradual success in the social situations that college provides, you can reduce your social anxiety and help with loneliness. You learn not only to have compassion for others but also to yourself.

DEVELOPING A COMPELLING LIFE-PURPOSE WORTHY OF YOURSELF

Can you imagine yourself eventually working with others who are solving real problems? Perhaps, you can foresee yourself creating art for beauty or for making a statement. Imagine how proud you would be to be part of a company whose product is changing peoples' lives. Imagine having a meaningful job that stimulates your curiosity. Think about what it might feel like to be part of a project that advances science. How would it feel to look at a newly built building or freshly printed book or recent performance and be able to say you were part of it? Can you see yourself telling your children that your work opened the door for others? College can help you make these happen by providing you the knowledge and skills as well as putting you around professors who also want to work for the common good. Imagine having confidence that you are doing the right thing, making a difference, or contributing to art.

You may be asking yourself how can you make your life a manifestation of love in the world. You may be trying to find out where and how you can apply the skills you have been given to best serve your neighbors as yourself.

An immediately pressing and practical life-purpose may command your attention. Supporting your family or getting out of crippling debt have urgency.

Sometimes the most compelling life-motives are just outside your awareness. These might be to prove something to your skeptics, to be the first in your family to do something, or not to let your parents down. You may unconsciously want to beat your rival, to make your beloved grandma proud, or to outdo your siblings.

You might want to make a short video and leave it on your phone, about why you feel passionate about college, to replay when you need a pep talk from you.

While on *The Late Late Show with James Corden* in early October of 2019 to talk about his book, *Letters From an Astrophysicist*, Neil DeGrasse Tyson spoke about people asking him questions about the meaning of the universe. As well as we can remember, he said that many people believe there is a pre-existing meaning if they could find it. He talked about helping them understand that, independent of whether there is or is not a pre-existing universal meaning, they are free to use their abilities to make meaning and purpose for their own life. He attempted to shift their frame of reference from being the passive receiver of a meaning already there that gives them purpose to becoming an active shaper of their meaning for their own life. He shifted the focus from 'finding' to 'creating'.

Bottom line, you don't have to wait until you understand the universe before you begin to create a purpose for your own life and give it meaning.

Reminding Yourself Why You Need to Succeed in College

You might want to peek ahead to section A-1 in the Resources Appendix to see some statistics comparing those who have graduated from college with those who have not.

College can represent a fresh start and an opportunity to make something out of yourself if you apply yourself. Now, let's look at how.

Next: Strategy 3—Plot your course.

3
Grasping the Importance of Time Management

The University of Rochester Medical Center's Health Encyclopedia notes that the prefrontal cortex of the brain is not fully developed until around twenty-five years of age (URMC Health Encyclopedia 2019). This part of the brain is involved in thinking rationally of long-term consequences, making judgments, inhibiting impulses, and planning. These are mental abilities that you use in time management. Time management involves thinking ahead, saying "no" to yourself and others, and developing plans to avoid long-term consequences and meet goals.

Knowing about this normal developmental limitation is empowering. It means you can anticipate and adjust by deliberately putting some safeguards in place and consciously trying to develop habits and structures that can help you as you do time management. Software programs have failsafe and redundancy expecting people making mistakes. You can expect these limitations too.

Time management is not about getting the most work done to become a joyless, productive robot with good grades. It is about getting the job done most productively, so you have time to do creative and spontaneous activities with friends, hang out with family, or have fun. It's about making changes, so you avoid the stress of getting behind or having to cram. It might be tempting to obsess about time management even to the point of using it to procrastinate. Time management may feel degrading and mechanical at first, but—if you persist— you will eventually find a way that works for you. It beats the alternative.

It will be easier to set limits on yourself and delay immediate satisfaction if you have thought about your goals. Our friend Betty Greene likes to quote David Campbell, Founder of Saks Fifth Avenue, who said that *"discipline* is remembering what you want." First, you need to identify what you passionately want. Developing a compelling vision of what you want may need some quiet time alone, research, and discussion. It boils down to knowing what you want more than immediate pleasure. This knowledge will help you tolerate the frustration of studying hard subjects. It will help you give up something because you want something more. It will bring you back to the books when, like many of us, procrastination has bested you.

USING MINDFULNESS FOR PERSPECTIVE AND RENEWAL

Managing your time involves managing your mind. Being mindful is like pushing the "refresh" button on your computer— it updates you to the very present you are living right now.

The distractingly fast pace of the college environment can make it challenging to receive the lessons it is trying to teach. As a college student, it can seem like everything in your life is somehow measured or judged. Every time you turn around, there is another test. What you write is measured and graded. If you play sports, your performance is measured. Blowing your ever-present grade point average (GPA) can cost you a scholarship, grad school admission, or even delay your graduation. Sometimes the measurement is not in figures but by comparison to other people. That does not count your super-ego, the yardstick in your head constructed from all those judgments you internalized growing up. Then you read this book, which we have filled with many details meant to be about "how to" but, after a while, can feel like "thou shalt." It seems like everyone is "should-ing" on you.

Thankfully, you know you are not omnipotent and shouldn't be expected to do everything. That knowledge allows you to be kind to yourself, give yourself credit for what you did do, and allow yourself a break. Being realistic helps you form achievable goals.

All the same, it is just human nature to worry about the future. Most of the just-mentioned worries were about the future. Other worries stem from losses and past hurts. Worrying about the future and ruminating about past hurts distracts you from what you are experiencing in the immediate present. Instead of thinking about what you are doing, you are worrying about something else. Practicing mindfulness can help this dilemma. Mindfulness is a way of intentionally becoming aware of what you are thinking or feeling in the present. Through learning mindfulness, you notice where you are, what you are doing, and how your body is currently experiencing it.

Mindfulness can help you notice those *nows*, so they don't pass by you. It is easy in all this to forget that life is a gift to be celebrated, not a goal to be achieved or measured.

Mindfulness practice can help you rediscover this and take a vacation from too much goal-directedness. In your stillness, you may find the distractions settle away to uncover essential inner truths that were underneath all along. You can rediscover that happiness has no cause. Happiness is our natural state when our constantly dissatisfied ego does not obstruct us.

By being mindful, you save yourself from a too great insistence on relevance— which philosophers have recognized is the surest road to irrelevance. You come into the *now* and get out of the future or past. You may find there are mindfulness groups at your counseling center or off-campus. Here are some sources of information:

http://www.apa.org/monitor/2012/07-08/ce-corner.aspx

https://www.helpguide.org/harvard/benefits-of-mindfulness.htm

https://www.mindfulschools.org/about-mindfulness/research/

There are various mindfulness phone apps, YouTube meditation videos, and websites with libraries of meditations on different topics. You can go to http://mindfulnesshabit.com/10mm to get the 10-*Minute Mindfulness Quick Start Guide.*

You will discover a meditation you can use in the shower at https://www.mindbodygreen.com/0-26626/heres-a-5minute-meditation-you-can-do-in-the-shower.html.

When you are mindful of *now*, intentionally look for things that make you feel grateful. Cultivating this habit of continually orientating yourself toward gratefulness in daily life will help your resilience and energy as you go through the day's tasks.

PRIORITIZING

Consider when your mind is most fresh and try to study your problematic subjects then. If you find you are often putting off studying a specific subject because it is hard, then you should consider asking for help with understanding the concepts or new ways of approaching the material. Find out what your school's educational services office offers. Maybe your high school instruction was weak in that area. If you are allowed to study some during slow periods of your job, those times might be ideal for studying something that comes quickly for you or needs less complex thinking.

Some days you may not have time to do all the assignments you feel you need to do. Saying *yes* to one task means saying *no* to many others. In setting priorities, ask yourself which tasks would hurt you the most if you did not do them. Knowing the task's due dates will help with this. You might make a timeline or look at a calendar you use as a central place you write all your deadlines.

Finishing first the most demanding and consequential tasks frees you to do the others with less worry.

In college, you don't have a mother there to keep you from giving up on challenging tasks. Getting yourself to do frustrating things takes practice. It's just human to be discouraged and beat yourself up about failing in it. Former President Obama said he had a plaque made on his desk that said, "Hard things are hard" after being told that by a senior advisor during a heated discussion. (Obama 2016)

With practice, doing frustrating things gets more manageable, and you gain confidence. Samuel Beckett wrote, "Ever tried. Ever failed. No matter. Try again. Fail again. Fail better." You may have to fail better a few times before you feel like you are succeeding. Persist.

To help you see the light at the tunnel, try to remember that what you know, who you are, and what you can do is always evolving. That means that something you have difficulty with now might be simple when you return to the task knowing more or having practiced at it. School is no different.

Time management is also about not doing tasks that are of little value or consequence. By doing less busywork, you have the time to do the jobs that make a difference. On the other hand, some teachers give out what to you seems like busywork but count it as the main part of the grade. Ask to make sure before you give it a lower priority.

ORGANIZING YOUR TIME

Depending on where you live, your week might includ commuting, walking to class, labs, class, Internet course time, and dedicated study breaks. We recommend you spend two to three hours of study time for each classroom hour. You may go to work, organized group activities, sports, campus events, entertainment, or hang out.

You will have activities of daily living like cooking, eating, cleaning up, grooming, grocery shopping, laundry, exercising, and sleeping.

During the first ordinary week of school, use a notepad or your cell phone's task list app to write down what you do and when you do it. Use the results to determine the time tasks and travel will take. Notice where there are locations you might sit and study between events. Ask yourself, "Where do I have smaller gaps?"

As you go through the week, pay attention to how your body and brain are feeling. Note the times you believe your mind is 'full,' and you are tired. That will help you know to plan to study at other times. Can you take advantage of your surroundings to rest? Is there a place you could sit for five minutes and listen to music on your earbuds? Maybe, that place is on a campus shuttle. You may realize you are exhausted after your job, but you feel fresh during a gap in your class schedule. Find an empty classroom where you could squeeze in twenty minutes to study, take a break, or get your blood sugar back up with a snack.

Some tasks are mechanical, and you may do them while you are waiting in line or for the class to start instead of using the time to check Instagram.

Usually— on the first day of class— your teacher will give you a syllabus that will spell out the content of the course and due dates for projects, papers, tests, midterms, and final exams. Use the syllabi from your courses to put due dates in your master calendar—which is the one central place you put all your activities. Look then at the closest due dates to help you plan out your weekly schedule.

You could put your tasks into different categories. You might categorize things according to how hard they are and try to do the hardest things when you are most rested. You might categorize items according to how long you expect them to take and then look at the blocks of time where they might fit. A more common way that people categorize tasks is according to how soon they need to do things and how important they are. The readings, homework, and quizzes due the current week would fall into the category of *soon and important*. You may need to do laundry by next week that would fall into the category of *soon but not so important*. Then your long-term, more significant projects that may count for a good percentage of your grade would be considered *long-term but important*. Other items that are not that important and not due that soon then fall into *long-term and not important*. Often these are the activities you would like to do if you had the time but are not crucial to your success. By categorizing your tasks, you are better able to prioritize how you are going to spend your time and determine the sequence of your activities. You may want to read more about this way of categorizing tasks, referred to by some as the Eisenhower Matrix, by reading *The Seven Habits of Highly Effective People: Powerful Lessons in Personal Change* by Steven Covey(Covey1989) or reading an article about the Eisenhower Matrix by Cathy Goddard at http://www.lighthousevisionary.com/eisenhower-matrix-a-productivity-tool-to-get-things-done/

Use your semester planner to see what parts of your semester have many assignments due at the same time. Estimate how soon you have to start on those tasks to avoid getting overwhelmed and behind. These busy times usually come at midterm and the week or two before finals when papers and projects come due. In your plans, be sensible about how fast you study and your willingness to get up early.

If you suspect that procrastination will be a problem, don't put off reading these helpful tips from the Academic Skills Center study library of the California Polytechnic State University at San Luis Obispo, California. http://sas.calpoly.edu/asc/ssl.html. The study center library also has useful discussions of note-taking and several forms to use to set up your schedules. You may also find weekly, monthly, daily, and hourly worksheets at http://www.worksheetworks.com

Routinely ask yourself, "What study tasks do I need to accomplish during this block of time?" Don't just tell yourself your goal is to study math for two hours. At the end of the block, note where you need to pick up the next time you are on that subject and what you will need to study. It will help you focus more quickly when you return. If you have difficulty in keeping track of how much time has elapsed, consider buying a *Time Timer* at https://www.Autism-Products.com. *The Visual Timer-Countdown* app by Christoph Wiesner from the Google Play Store gives you a visual representation of the time remaining.

ORGANIZING YOUR WORKSPACE

A structure can free you from the confusion and distraction of clutter. After you have set up a regular place to study, clear your desk, so only one task is facing you. Consider downloading brown noise to play in your earbuds. You may find eight hours of brown noise on YouTube at https://www.youtube.com/watch?v=RqzGzwTY-6w. Make sure the lighting, chair, and keyboard height promote studying for long periods. Use a plastic container or accordion paper file to hold file folders that keep track of your papers.

MAPPING OUT YOUR DAILY JOURNEY

Take some time to study a map of your campus. Find quiet places. Look for areas where you could vent some restlessness, or feel safe and serene. Estimate the distances you may have to walk between classes, rest rooms, food sellers, parking, and shuttle stops. Ask upper-level students where the best parking spots are at given times.

CREATING SOME DAILY HABITS

If you repeatedly try to do tasks as well as you can <u>reasonably</u> do them, then doing your best will become your default position by habit. Multitasking is a low focus/high-efficiency mode that may be natural to you. It may not result in your best work. Multi-task selectively. When possible, do one thing at a time. That will allow you to concentrate better and do your best. It has been shown to make a difference in your brain's capacity to retain what you learn. Lump similar tasks into the same time slot. Deliberately set aside some specific times to check your emails and social media. Work hard at not checking between those times. Set *do not disturb* hours for your phone. When you study, you need short breaks every fifteen minutes to consolidate what you have learned.

Note your transitions from one activity to another. It is easy then to waste time by overextending the break and delaying starting the next.

After dinner, put together a 'to-do' list for the following day. Keep the 'to-do' list in your planner for each day. You may worry about what you have to do the next day. Making a list may give your brain closure and allow it to let that worry go. Later in the evening, quickly review what you did that day and give yourself credit for what you tried to do. Make a habit of asking yourself if you might benefit from help or networking with a particular task. *Geekly Hub* "connects students and educators in online collaboration and productivity space." They connect you with tutors and provide scheduling help at https://geeklyhub.com/

SELECTING COURSES AND REGISTERING

Mistakes in registration and course selection are among the costliest mistakes you will make. They cost you time, money, stress and may dead-end you.

Working with your advisor, you should develop a "Program of Study." A "Program of Study" is a form that outlines the courses that you take to complete your coursework. You sign the form, and your advisor signs the form. This form is approved by the department chair and the dean of your college. The form is sent to the registrar's office and serves as a contract between you and the college. It stipulates that when you complete the courses with the minimum grade point average set by the college, you are eligible for a diploma from that college. Check in the appendix for a sample of a "Program of Study." Please note that each college may have a different name for this form.

College is much harder than high school. Don't overload your class schedule for the first semester. If you make the mistake of overloading yourself, the time pressure will last all the semester. You may then have to forgo more things you would like to do or risk a lower grade point average.

There are several factors to consider in course selection. You likely have a defined time of four years to take all of your core courses, and there may be an even shorter period to accomplish any prerequisites to be accepted in your major. Whether the course is a required course for your major is the first question you should ask. If you don't know what your major is, then you should select courses that are part of the core requirements for graduation. Meet early with your advisor, who can help you pick classes and create a tentative schedule. Not all advisors are created equal. Check out everything your advisor tells you. Accepting that you have to go through the aggravation of looking for written confirmation may save you time and money later.

Many courses have prerequisites so that you have to take courses in a particular sequence. It would help if you looked at what times of year the college offers these courses, so you don't have to wait a semester for one to be available. As soon as you can, get started on courses that are part of long sequences.

Ask yourself what time of day you are best. Try to schedule classes around that time of day, if possible. Look at comments about the instructor on the Internet and then talk to others who have had them. Look at past grade distributions to see if students do poorly in their class. If you are picking electives, don't accidentally select a difficult course that you don't have to take. Space out your challenging classes if you can. Ask upper-level students in your major about the *killer courses*. Plan to have a smaller course-load when you take them.

Get up early on the day of registration. Be prepared and at your computer well before the moment the online registration opens. You might drive to a local café that has Wi-Fi since it may have less chance of crashing from overuse like the residence hall's might. If you are going to use public Wi-Fi, you will need to have done a trial run earlier to make sure you know the sequence to get on that Wi-Fi system. Wofford College suggests students check to see if there are any holds on their registration (perhaps due to payment issues or parking tickets) and that passwords work. This preparation may seem obsessive, but each second counts because there will be hundreds of other students trying to register at the same time. Realize that your college may give other students preference over first-year students. Have plans A, B, C, and D ready to use.

What unusual situations do you expect? Do you have a double major? Some courses don't easily fit into the abbreviated format of a Maymester or summer school term. Take these courses during the regular year if you can. Find out if your scholarship program covers summer courses and if summer tuition is costlier per hour.

The College Level Examination Program, CLEP, gives subject-specific tests. If a student does well enough on the test, they can earn college credit on an introductory course. You could save money by taking the CLEP exam instead of the course. Are there courses you could CLEP?

If you have a language or math disability, you may be able to take alternatives if you get accommodations through your college's disabilities services. Find this out soon because you can't assume getting accommodations is straightforward, speedy, or effortless.

If you pay close attention to course planning, it sets the stage for a manageable workload. It makes time management less difficult for the entire semester.

SELECTING TEACHERS

Having face-to-face classroom interaction with a teacher is becoming a luxury. Please take advantage of this opportunity when you have it. Satisfy your intellectual curiosity. Question your professor about the topics that interest you in their field. See past them— as the person who makes the tests and awards your grades— to the person who chose a lifework in their subject.

Various people may teach college courses. These include professors, assistant professors, associate professors, adjunct professors who come from outside the college, graduate students, and student instructors. When you are registering for courses, you may be able to look up your potential professors at *USA College Today Uloop*. Other apps also rate your professors. Remember that a professor that is well-liked because they are easy may not be the one to teach you the most. When you listen to students talk about not getting the grade they deserve, remember existing studies suggest that people who are not experts on their subject have a more difficult time in accurately assessing their abilities (Kruger, Justin; Dunning, David 1999).

You may have little control, but try to get the best teacher you can. Maybe the best teacher of that subject only teaches it in the spring. Talk to other students who have taken the course before you— perhaps a fraternity brother or sorority sister. It may feel intimidating to approach an upper-level student you don't know with a question. Remember, they were in your shoes once and may be happy to vent some about their course experience. Look to find past students in organizations related to the subject you are taking. If you are about to take French, look for a list of students in the French club.

PLANNING THE SEQUENCE OF YOUR COURSES

If you take English Composition first, it will help you in every other class that requires writing papers. If you take a speech course, it will help you with subsequent presentations. We assume you know your way around Microsoft Office or similar software programs. Otherwise, a practical IT course might save you future aggravation and wasted time floundering around as we do.

After you know your courses, talk with other students in your major about the listed professors, and try to pick the professors that are best at working with students and teaching their subjects. Sought-after professors' classes fill quickly.

Try using your school's website to learn the details about the majors it offers and the courses needed for those majors. Look at the prerequisites for upper-level courses. Study the sequence of courses you have to pursue and start taking those prerequisites early. If you don't manage the easy things and you fail to pay close attention to these details first, you may delay your graduation.

Core classes may not tell you what your major is like, but if you are taking your major courses and feel your discipline gets you down, maybe you need to reconsider your major. Look in the index to find where the topic of finding a major occurs throughout the book in different contexts.

If there is a chance you may transfer to another school, you want to consider taking courses that count at the future school. Don't try to second-guess how the future school regards the first school's specific courses. Multiple unknowns go into each school's complex decision-making. Take the necessary time to study the technical details in the future school's documents about each course. Making a mistaken assumption here may cost you lost effort and money.

If you are planning to study abroad, find out if you need to get any language requirements completed before you go. Ask about course requirements for your major and find out if you have to finish some before your trip. Consider how the study abroad experience will enhance your major area of study. Explore how your career will benefit from the study abroad experience.

DEVELOPING A STRATEGIC PLAN FOR THE SEMESTER

Course selection is just one semester-level consideration. Others include surprise events in your semester like getting the flu, major friend drama, a money problem, or an academic setback. To prepare, you need to identify and improve your support system in advance. You can then better manage these schedule disruptions.

In your time management, remember to set aside time for renewal, so you don't burn out. Also, by not overcommitting, you give yourself some gaps in case something goes wrong, like getting sick. Don't miss class unless it is an emergency.

Throughout the semester, keep an eye out for official emails from the college and read them carefully. If you have special needs, then check in with the disabilities department early and make sure you have the accommodations ahead of time. Look at your email every morning and every night to check for canceled classes from your professors.

When you have a semester-long project, make some deadlines of your own. Have certain phases completed before the actual deadline. By starting early and allowing yourself enough time to complete a task, you don't have to pull an all-nighter. You avoid having to do too many tasks at once. It allows time for disasters, so you can still have results that reflect what you can produce when not pressured.

> *The difference between involvement and commitment is like ham and eggs. The chicken is involved; the pig is committed.*
> –Martina Navratilova
> https://www.brainyquote.com/quotes/martina_navratilova_159092

When Martina referenced this version of the Aesop Fable, she could have been talking about Greek-letter organizations. Sororities and fraternities are serious about their requirements. They are looking for more than just involvement. You must ask yourself, "Do I want to be more than peripherally involved?" Sororities and fraternities expect you to attend chapter meetings, participate in service activities, and plan for membership intake. They want you to play a role in membership intake, hold offices, and be a wholehearted *Big* or *Little*. During the year, you must prepare for and attend multiple social functions. Even if there is no abusive hazing, initiation and pledge activities may be mandatory, time-consuming, sleep-depriving, and last for a semester. Saying "no" to your peers when you need time to study is hard, but possibly even harder if you value how others see you in your sorority or fraternity. Understanding how your fraternity or sorority treats those who have dropped out may keep you in. Each campus is different. Explore yours. Weigh the time and financial cost against the benefits of belonging and having opportunities for friendships and a potentially encouraging community. While sororities and fraternities are evaluating you, they are also willing to explain why you should join them. Ask about how they might benefit you individually.

Next: Strategy 4—Decide on your lodgings.

4
Establishing a Workable Environment

STAYING SAFE

When you worry about your safety, it can be challenging to focus on your studies. Feeling prepared might reduce that distraction. You don't have to be paranoid or frightened to be safe— but you do need a cautious mindset. Safety is more than merely having the right equipment. Safety is also about approaching things in specific ways, setting up routines, and being alert to risks. Being safe means being awake and present.

Only party where you can have a trusted buddy within sight of you. Before going out, get it across to your buddy clearly and emphatically that neither of you can leave without having the other with them. Make a plan to address different contingencies and have your buddy say the plan back to you, so you are sure they are on the same page. Recheck your signals just before you go out. Anyone you meet when you are out, that is serious about dating you, will be willing to wait and call you another day. Don't leave with strangers.

Don't drive when you're impaired. Don't ride with impaired drivers. Make a scene if you have to —but exit the car. In a study of causes of mortality among American college students at four-year institutions, within the accident and injury category, alcohol-related vehicular deaths (per 100,00) were 3.37, and alcohol-related nontraffic injuries were 1.49. (Turner, James C.; Leno, E. Victor; Keller, Adrienne 2011)

Breathalyzers are not that expensive. Having an FDA /DOT approved device available can help you settle whether someone is capable of driving or not.

WHEN ON FOOT Find out where others have reported unsafe events on your campus. Go to the US Department of Education Campus Safety and Security website and pull up your school's name. https://ope.ed.gov/campussafety/#/institution/search . Check your college's website or ask your campus safety office if your college has a safety app. Some colleges have programs where work-study students work as drivers to transport students around the campus at night.

Consider getting the Noonlight app offered by SafeTrek for your phone. To use it when you go into a dangerous place, you push the button and keep your finger down until you feel safe. Then you take your finger off and send in a code. Otherwise, the app uses GPS to alert police to your location. It does cost $2.99 a month.

You might also look at other apps like bSafe-Personal Safety app that allows you to activate the personal safety button by voice to your phone in your pocket and alert guardians with your location. It starts a real-time live streaming audio and video recording.

As an alternative, you might also hold your cell phone in your hand in preparation to push 911, which you would have preset. Don't hesitate to call the campus police to escort you if you feel uncomfortable where you are. If you parked in an isolated area, talk with someone on the phone very briefly and tell the listener where you are as you are approaching your car. Stay alert to your surroundings as you do.

Establishing a Workable Environment

When you are off-campus, keep your phone GPS (Global Positioning System) activated. It will be ready if you become lost and need quickly to escape danger.

GET EQUIPPED. Put together an emergency kit. In the appendix, you will find a detailed list of needed items. Update the contact information on your smartphone for the people in your support system. You then know how to reach them in an emergency.

DEVELOP GOOD SAFETY HABITS You can reduce your risks by learning how to do things well that will contribute to your safety. Safety experts stress being aware of your surroundings. Making this automatic requires routine practice. Have fun by pretending you're a secret agent, and you might have to leave immediately. Look for the exits. Watch for people hanging around behaving suspiciously.

Being aware of your surroundings means getting off your cell. If you know you are going to alter your ability to be aware of your surroundings—then your surroundings need to be safe. That means a person has your back who is not high or drinking. If you are in public, watch your drink being poured and carry it with you everywhere you go to avoid being drugged.

USE PLANNING TO AVOID CREATING PROBLEM SITUATIONS. Make a habit of checking your car's gas indicator, so you don't accidentally run out of gas in a dangerous place. Keep your phone charged and consider having a phone charger in your car. Make sure you have money or credit cards in your car trunk and your pocket, so you are not in an emergency without funds. Study the area before you park, so you are not in a poorly lit area or have to walk too far to get to your car in a strange neighborhood. Think ahead of time about paying, so you aren't stuck flashing cash in public. Thieves look for signs of wealth like jewelry and electronics. A GPS, chargers, and cords left visible in your car suggest there is other treasure there. If you are going to be in a hazardous area, consider wearing shoes you can run in and clothes that don't restrict you. Wearing a heavy backpack or carrying too much in your arms makes catching or robbing you less complicated. It bears repeating: Never leave with a stranger.

WHEN YOU MOMENTARILY STOP, YOU ARE VULNERABLE. ANTICIPATE HOW YOU WILL HANDLE SUCH SITUATIONS. Have your keys in your hands before you get to the door. Lock your car, room, or apartment door behind you quickly. Look behind you to make sure no one is about to catch the door as you open it and then force their way inside. Be vigilant at traffic lights. When the hair stands up on the back of your neck, trust the feeling, and do something.

A former police officer, Justin Freeman, wrote an excellent article published in *Business Insider* about what to do in case of robbery, hostage, or kidnapping situations. Here is the link.

http://www.businessinsider.com/how-to-respond-if-somebody-holds-a-gun-to-your-head-2013-12

Guys- if a strange woman is coming on to you who is clearly above your class- ask yourself if she might want your kidneys or be working with a partner to rob you. If it seems too good to be true — it usually is.

GOOD CAR PRACTICES When you reach your parked car, walk around it and look under it to make sure no one is waiting underneath it to cut your Achilles tendon at your ankle and rob you. Look at the backseat as well as both the front and back floorboards to make sure no one is hiding there. If you notice from a distance that your car has something different or broken about it, walk away from the car. Then, get the police or a service station to look at it.

Establishing a Workable Environment

Do not go near the vehicle or accept help from "helpful strangers" who suddenly appear, especially if there is a van nearby.

If you are in your car and someone is following you, drive on main thoroughfares to the nearest police station and flag someone down or walk inside from the curb next to the door. If you are unsure whether someone is following you, consider whether it would be safe to delay going to the police station long enough to take four left turns or four right turns. That maneuver will help you determine if you are being pursued. Do not pull over if someone points to something wrong with your car at an intersection. Instead, go to a service station.

Maintain your car, so you don't become a sitting duck because you have a dead battery, or your vehicle has broken down in a dangerous location. Put up the hood if your car breaks down—but only if you can safely do it. Quickly get back in the car and lock the door behind you. Tell anyone that approaches you to go for help. Don't let them in the car. Barely crack your window only if you have to for them to hear you.

Sometimes the crime happens later when the thief uses information about you that they have found outside your car's locked glove box. They may have used a device to duplicate the car keys you left on your keychain when you had your vehicle repaired or when the key belonged to your apartment's previous owner.

WHERE YOU LIVE Ideally, you will have a peephole on your front door that you can cover. You don't want to answer the door without being able to identify who is there. You don't want people to look inside through the peephole, either. You may want to invest in an inexpensive doorbell camera. You want a door lock that works much better than a chain link. If you are on the first floor, investigate how your windows are locked. Make sure you have a well-lit area around your residence. Don't leave notes on your door that would suggest you are out. Don't post on social media where you are going. Make sure someone picks up your mail and packages when you are away. Never open the door to strangers.

Preserve your privacy by not putting identifying information on your door, leaving sensitive material lying around your house unlocked, or failing to consider what your hacked computer's camera or microphone might record. Keep your contacts up-to-date on the phone, so you will have the right numbers to call in an emergency. If you have an iPhone, take advantage of the emergency contact feature.

You might consider buying a small safe. You could purchase a fake electrical outlet or hairbrush to hide items. A cheap alternative is the inside of a big book you have hollowed out for small items like your medication. Remember, the panic button on your car key might double as an alarm if your car is close to your house.

Your roommates may be accustomed to having their mothers check behind them. The resulting carelessness can create dangerous situations. Remind your roommates not to smoke in bed, overload electric circuits, or leave space heaters and appliances running unattended.

If you or your roommates own a weapon, always use a trigger lock on it.

SEXUAL ASSAULT This section is about being proactive and doing what you can to avoid being a victim. We want to stress that victims of sexual assault are victims and that perpetrators are responsible for the attack and not the victims.

Students interested in pursuing sexual activity are responsible for knowing and abiding by the rules governing sexual consent. Sexual consent is an agreement to participate in sexual activity. Genital touching, oral sex, vaginal or anal penetration—without consent— are sexual assault or rape. State laws vary, but each state sets an age below which a person cannot consent to sex. People who have significant intellectual impairment are also considered unable to consent to sex.

Consent must be given freely without pressure or under the influence of alcohol or drugs. An intoxicated person is considered unable to give consent. At any time, a person can change their mind and reverse their consent. When that happens, <u>you</u> are responsible for stopping.

The person must know what is involved and be informed by you in advance. You can't say you are going to do one thing and do another. If you imply sex is happening with contraception, and it isn't, then it is not informed.

Giving consent is specific. Giving consent to one sexual behavior does not mean your partner has given consent to all behaviors. Planned Parenthood covers many of these same points at https://www.plannedparenthood.org/learn/sex-and-relationships/sexual-consent

You should not manipulate your partner into doing something they don't want to do by making them feel you expect it of them. They should want to do it. You are not allowed to assume their consent because of their past behavior or how they are dressed. Consent has to be clearly communicated in words. Silence is not consent.

"Since college entry, 22% of students reported experiencing at least one incident of sexual assault (defined as sexualized touching, attempted penetration [oral, anal, vaginal, other], or completed penetration). Women and gender-nonconforming students reported the highest rates (28% and 38%, respectively), although men also reported sexual assault (12.5%). Across types of assault and gender groups, incapacitation due to alcohol and drug use and/or other factors was the perpetration method reported most frequently (> 50%); physical force (particularly for completed penetration in women) and verbal coercion were also commonly reported (Mellins CA, Walsh K, Sarvet AL, Wall M, Gilbert L, Santelli JS, et al. (2017) ."

Before you go into a setting, ask others whether the place is known for drugging drinks. Always watch as your drink is being made, and then don't let it out of your sight.

Self-Defense for Women Warriors: A practical approach by Su Ericksen would prove a helpful read for everyone (Ericksen 2016).

What follows here are some things we would like to highlight:

Sexual perpetrators know your brain operates on pattern recognition and has some preconceived notions about how sexual perpetrators look. Ted Bundy, a serial killer, looked like the All-American guy leaving the college library carrying too many heavy books. When girls came to help him, he chloroformed them. Don't be fooled by appearances. Please don't stop to help strangers or get so close that they can grab you. Instead, get out of the area and then ask the police to help them.

If you get some of your peers to sign up with you, you may find a martial art school willing to teach a short private course on self-defense. You don't have to be a black belt to increase your chances of being able to defend yourself.

Predators want to exploit the vulnerable. They are always looking for the straggler, the one a little impaired by alcohol, or the distracted one looking at a cell phone.

You are much more likely to be sexually assaulted by someone you already know— perhaps are even dating. Guys will tell you that they are at the peak of their testosterone years, that alcohol disinhibited them, and that they can't be expected to control themselves because they won't have a fully formed frontal lobe until they are twenty-five. In reality, —sexual assault is never justified.

Know the safe places on your campus and the call box locations.

Establishing a Workable Environment

Animals immediately play dead when a predator is about to eat them. It is a survival reflex because predators don't like to eat dead meat. We have this reflex, too, and it explains why sometimes a strong woman is paralyzed and overcome by a weaker assailant. It also clarifies why you can't trust yourself being bigger and must work at anticipating dangerous situations if you can.

If you have already been the victim of sexual assault, you can reach the National Sexual Assault Telephone Hotline at https://www.rainn.org/about-national-sexual-assault-telephone-hotline. You can contact your campus's Counseling Center or Women's Center.

FORGE is a national transgender anti-violence organization that offers resources and direct services. https://forge-forward.org/about/

For more resources, go to section A-6 in the Appendix of Resources and look under *PTSD/Trauma*.

LIVING IN A RESIDENCE HALL

Please get to know your resident advisor, because you will likely be asking them questions. Before you ask them, however, consider what information you might read that would give you an answer.

At some schools, resident advisors are called community advisors. Not only do they have practical information, informal mentoring, and useful advice to offer you—it is vital that they know who you are. The more knowledgeable they are about you, the more accurately they can make judgments in emergencies, and the better advocate they can be in problem situations. Remember, however; you are not their only resident.

There is an off-to-college checklist of things to bring at http://www.collegebowl.com. Avoid duplication by coordinating with your roommate. Please make an effort from the very beginning to foster effective communication with your roommate by listening to their wishes and being honest about what is important to you about sharable items. Sharable items might include a first aid kit, microwave, toaster oven, coat hangers, dishes, wastebasket, an extension cord with a surge protector, or mini-fridge. Minimize what you have to pack in the car by setting up an order of needed items with the local chain store in your college's town to be ready for pickup on the day of your arrival. You can save space with a shower caddy, a 'closet doubler,' or a bed riser. Over-the-closet-door organizers offer hooks, baskets, or pouches to store accessories, linen, shoes, caps, or other clothing. Consider buying a mini-safe or lockable drawer because some roommates or their friends like to borrow. Bring an umbrella. You may already use a dictionary + thesaurus app or similar purposed websites. Add a dictionary in print form. Get a secure lock for your bicycle if you bring one.

Moving day is an inconvenience. Pack a small bag for items you will need on the first day. If it is practicable, try to pack light by leaving seasonal or questionable items to be picked up on your first trip home after you know how much usable space you have.

Don't assume the residence hall rules are merely common sense. Read them. If you think you could have the DATOM disease (Doesn't Apply to Me)—read them twice. Injustice collecting can waste your valuable time, so save your energy for bigger fights, like with the inscrutable money-hungry vending machines.

Residence hall living gives you a chance to see yourself through other student's eyes. It also teaches tolerance. You learn how to live with people who think, act, and decide differently from you. You can't get away from them most of the time, so it teaches you frustration tolerance as well. When you start to criticize someone, try to remember that you have to see those same people tomorrow—and the next day. Think of a polite way to be assertive. Consider also that your preconceived notions may have led each of you to misunderstand the other's statements or intentions. Our brains use pattern recognition, and sometimes, the patterns aren't correct.

You may see examples of great caring, courage, and sacrifice in your classmates. Pettiness, cattiness, oddness, and self-centeredness also show up in multiple ways when you live with other students. As a result, much could be said about it.

Fortunately, this book is not the only resource to consult about living with other college students. Every college survival handbook will have some similarities and yet offer some individual advice. Two stand out as complementing the practical problem-solving that *Search* has to offer: *The Naked Roommate: And 107 Other Issues You Might Run Into in College* by Harlan Cohen (Cohen 2017) and *Adulting: How to Become a Grown-up in 468 Easy(ish) Steps* by Kelly Williams Brown (Brown 2018). We hope you will add these to your college toolkit. You may find CollegeCompass.co and hercampus.com good digital resources, as well.

LIVING OFF-CAMPUS

If the apartment complex has a website, check it out and look for comments. If it is part of a national company, google that company to investigate its reputation. Ask upper-class students their opinions of the various complexes and what they know about the responsiveness of staff to maintenance issues.

Do the legwork associated with renting an apartment in a particular location. Commute to school during the time of day you will be going. Walk to the closest stores. Talk to the neighbors about the neighborhood's safety and what they know about the apartment complex and management. Consider googling "sexual offenders near me" to see the list. View the apartment in person and take pictures to document its state of repair.

If a student can get drunk at a bar and walk home to your prospective apartment, that apartment will likely be overpriced, rundown, and in demand. If you choose an apartment in that neighborhood, you could be surrounded by students who felt good parking, a safe community, and nearness to the college were less important than avoiding a DUI. Expect noise there some nights of the week. You would do well to get some earplugs because complaining to loud drunken neighbors never works. Remember that colleges can hold up your grades and transcripts until you pay your parking tickets.

When you view the potential apartment, take someone else with you. This person will ideally be a disinterested party with some maintenance background, have experience in renting apartments, and will look at everything with less excitement.

Inspect the smoke detector. Look for mold. Make sure the burners work on the stove. Look for rodent droppings and dead insects. Has there been damage from prior pets or water leaks on the ceiling from someone's tub? Do all the locks work? Is there a deadbolt? Is there a peephole? Is there any evidence of a past break-in? Does the toilet flush fast? Do the drains quickly empty?

Can you hear the people walking around on the floor above? Are you in the flight pattern of the nearby airport? Is it close to a police station, fire station, ambulance service, busy intersection, or train track? Can you smell a nearby restaurant, sewage, or industrial plant? Can you get out if it snows heavily?

Please don't take for granted that things won't go wrong with the apartment or its management. Make sure everything is in writing. Is it a twelve-month lease? The lease should spell out who pays for water, sewage, electricity, cable, Internet, snow removal, yard maintenance, and pest control. The move-in and move-out dates should be specified. The lease should say how much the deposit is and whether they will refund it at the end of the contract. The lease should state what recourse the tenant has in a dispute. It should detail the day of the month the rent is due and the number of days before they will charge a late payment. It should describe when and how you pay the rent. What amenities are guaranteed, and what are the rules for their use? Is there an extra charge?

Some apartment companies have instituted new payment methods using no cash or checks. In these cases, you must use a payment app that sometimes charges a fee as high as $35 a month. That would raise your rent each month without notice of an increase and before your lease expires.

The lease should address specific situations. Is there a separate pet deposit or monthly pet maintenance fee? Are there additional pet apartment cleaning fees? Is the parking included in the rent? Does the lease require you to pay additional separate charges for utilities for the common areas? Any painting or repairs the landlord agrees to do should be written down with a completion date.

Is it possible to stay longer if you need to? How much is the daily charge? Could the landlord evict you if you have not moved out by the date? Are you allowed to sublet, and what are the requirements and restrictions? What are the grounds for breaking the lease, and how much would it cost you?

Are you leasing the apartment jointly and are therefore jointly responsible, or are you leasing it separately? If you are leasing it separately, what part of the expenses falls to you? Is there one person on the lease that is responsible for paying the bill itself?

You can make standing up to your roommates easier by anticipating differences. In most relationships there is a "honeymoon" when it is likely that everyone is getting along. Use this period to resolve some concerns before they grow. Make a roommate agreement and consider having it notarized so you will have something to show a judge if you need to. It should include specifics about how the rent and utilities are paid, how long friends can stay over, limits on partying behavior, late-night noise, and privacy issues. It should cover thermostat guidelines, cleaning responsibilities, the use of the kitchen, and quiet times for study hours.

Keep records of your payments and dates. Take and keep pictures of the place before you moved in. If you have expensive possessions that could be damaged or stolen, low-cost rental insurance might be well worth it. Your bedroom door needs a lock. It would be best if you locked it and the external doors every time you leave the apartment. Resist getting a remote home monitoring system unless you are sure your roommate won't use it to abuse you later. The better you know your future roommates, the less this is a risk.

LIVING AT HOME

If you live at home, your studying is done alone and long before you join your classmates in the classroom. Being a productive college student from home includes marking off clear boundaries. Sometimes those are physical boundaries like your personal study space. You will be doing a good deal of studying at your desk. Is it suitable? Will the lighting hurt your eyes after prolonged reading? Is the chair hard on your back? Is your Wi-Fi fast enough? Will your computer run the programs your Internet courses may require you to buy?

The quietest room in your house with a separate entrance may be your basement. If you could barter with a sibling for a bedroom more conducive to studying, which room would it be?

If you can't carve out a time and suitable place, you may need to study in the library or the student center.

Set some time boundaries by making a weekly schedule and letting your family know what it is. Delineate specific time slots when you will be studying and other slots when you will not be. If you show them that you are studying during study time, your family will be more likely to respect the boundary. Get a "Do Not Disturb" sign for your door.

You have to take possession of your life and your time first, then you can give others time later. Your parents may feel you are too busy for them. When you do have off time, immediately do something together. Making that effort tells them that you meant it when you said you would spend more time with them if you did not have to study. This way, they don't have to keep reassuring themselves. With younger siblings, you may have to be more concrete and set aside a specific time each week dedicated just to them. Siblings may have more patience if they know they can count on that time. You have to prioritize. At the same time, you wish gently to help family members understand that they are responsible for their well-being and not you.

When you feel like procrastinating with your studying, the temptation is readily available to go places with your old high school peer group who may have more free time. You might feel like you need to spend extra time with them to reassure them you haven't become a snobby college student. You are not just saying *no* to the group. You are saying *no* to yourself and having to tolerate the anxiety of possibly being misunderstood.

Another source of peer pressure comes from the new people you meet in college and wanting to belong. You may have fears about them thinking they are superior because they live on campus. Between the two groups and the lack of time, it may take some time to find your niche.

Another boundary you will need to set has to do with what you will and will not do as part of the family. You are benefiting from living with your family. The empty nest problem that your family might have is that their nest is <u>not</u> empty. You are receiving goods and services that cost them. It will help if you acknowledge that by giving something back. You need to pick circumscribed chores that don't take too much time. If the family members often see you studying, they feel better about doing some of your rightful duties. Reward them by letting your family be a part of your success. Share your progress. Show them how the time they freed up for you and the money they gave you made a difference.

Not all multitasking is safe to do while you are commuting by car. If you must listen to something, consider podcasts and class lecture tapes or study tapes you have made from reading aloud as you read the textbook.

A little sunshine helps your vitamin D level and falling asleep at night. Too much commuting-related sun exposure raises skin cancer risk. Consider using sunscreen, driving gloves, long sleeves, and a long bill cap.

Scope out the alternate routes in case there is construction or traffic. Consider carpooling or taking a rider. Survey the school's parking lots to find spots near your classes. Does your school have a parking pass? Always make sure your car is in good repair, but talk in advance with a friend who could help if your car breaks down.

The paradox of living at home is that it appears that you are not launching yourself into adulthood, like people who leave home are. In some ways, it takes many more adult skills to be a capable college student from home. These skills include setting all these boundaries and doing it as diplomatically as possible. It needs even better time management skills and more determination to study. It can feel like you are the only one in college.

EDUCATING YOURSELF ABOUT WEAPONS ON CAMPUS

If your campus allows weapons, you need to know where they are allowed and all the rules concerning them. Please speak with your roommates about their gun-owning status and yours. Make sure every arm has a trigger lock. It is even more critical to lock guns if anyone nearby has had past suicidal thoughts. Take time to educate yourself about how to respond to a suicidal friend. Learn about what to do in case of gun violence on your campus. Identify the nearest emergency room. Check out your college's banned items list.

HAVING A CAR ON CAMPUS

Look into the availability of Uber, Lyft, taxicabs, electric bike rentals, and public transportation. Investigate the feasibility of using a bicycle. Doing this may save you the cost of car payments, parking, insurance, maintenance, repairs, and theft. Your campus may have Zipcar or another car-sharing service. It may be close to one of the major car rental companies that offer hourly car rentals.

With the added convenience and independence of having a car goes the task of saying *no* to fun-loving friends. Deciding against having a car risks injury if you are riding with an impaired driver. Do the planning to avoid having to. Always possess money set aside expressly for public transportation.

If you are thinking about bringing a car to campus, make sure there is enough parking. Ask other students about their experience campus with finding spaces at peak times.

DECIDING WHETHER TO HAVE PETS

OWNING A PET IN COLLEGE Students having pets at college is a rather recent phenomenon. To discover how prevalent the trend of students having a pet in college, Pierson Education conducted a study on one college campus to collect data on college students who have pets. Pierson surveyed people on social media to determine if they have a pet on campus and how many hours they spend with the pet. Pierson wanted to know how much money students spend on their pet and what housing students had. Pierson found that most students owned one pet, and most students lived in a house. The cost of having pets in a month ranged from

$12 to $150. Students spend between one to twenty-four hours a day with their pets.

Fifty-two percent of the students have dogs, nineteen percent have cats, twelve percent have something else, and twelve percent do not have a pet. One college's respondents may not reflect the percentage of pets in another. Nonetheless, it suggests that this may be a growing trend. Also, of the students surveyed, students without pets may not have been interested in pets enough to respond.

For many students, entering college is their first real feeling of freedom. Beyond class time and study time, students can choose many avenues for spending their time.

Pets bring out strong feelings. Many students want to have a pet because they could not have a pet at home. Students who do have a pet may want to take it with them to college. Still other students want to leave their present pet with their parents who had been looking forward to finally having some freedom.

After the daily grind of high school classes, college seems at first filled with free time. It is easy then for students to overestimate the time they have to focus on nonacademic issues and activities, like having a pet.

Most students don't wake up one day and say, "I want a dog.... a cat...a ferret, or other pet." For many students, the companionship can make them feel happy. A pet may give the student the feeling of home and belonging.

Some students do not realize the responsibility of having a pet. Before you make this decision, check out all of the issues that this decision entails. One question that you need to answer- will the college allow students living on campus to have pets? Most of them will not. There are a few universities that designate specific residences as 'pet-friendly.' Some schools allow small rodents, but not snakes. If the college will permit its students to have pets, there is usually a requirement that your roommates agree.

Establishing a Workable Environment

Before you get a pet, think of the pet's needs. Are you willing to have your time eaten away with the care of a pet? Are you ready to afford the financial burden of having a pet, both medical and food? If your pet is left alone for a long time during the day or night, are you willing to deal with the damage a pet can do to electrical cords and computers? Even during stressful course load times, you can't ignore the pet. What will you do if you have the opportunity to go on a weekend trip with friends, or to a ball game that includes travel and game time?

PROS OF HAVING A PET Many studies show that having pets teaches students responsibility. Other studies reveal that having a pet helps some students in relieving stress, depression, and loneliness. Some believe that having a pet enables you to bond with other students who are likeminded about pets. There are times that a college student needs an emotional support animal. Under the Americans with Disabilities and Fair Housing Act, service and support animals must be accommodated if there is a documentation of need. To have a support animal, you must have a documented condition that would require a trained animal to accompany you during your day.

Sometimes coming home to an enthusiastic wagging tail is lifesaving. No one doubts that pets can be wonderful companions that give you a sense of being needed or loved.

According to a 2017 report by the American College Health Association, college students report high rates of stress, loneliness, anxiety, and depression. Studies have shown that pets increase people's levels of oxytocin, a hormone that reduces anxiety and lowers blood pressure, by 300 percent.

CONS OF HAVING A PET Your friends and dates with allergies may not be excited about your pet, and others may not find their dirty habits and noises as amusing as you do.

If you have a dog, you may find yourself torn between wanting to be carefree and timeless and having to get back home. If you don't let your dog out in time, your dog could make a stinky mess, overstretch their bladder, or take their separation anxiety out on your roommate's furniture.

A few incidents later, you find you have developed your own internal "dog bowel/bladder timer" and with it a nagging uneasiness. Even when you guess right how long your dog will last, you have still had to think about it and endure the suspense and your friends' disappointment that you have had to leave early. You aren't free anymore. You're living with time limits now. Your friends know you as the one with the dog. Sometimes you are lucky enough to get your roommate to help out. Do this too often and you feel obliged and they feel resentful.

Your roommates will expect you to vacuum up the pet hair. Your pet will wake you up to let them out. Walking them in early morning bad weather can make you wonder if putting up with the tyranny of pet bladder and bowels is worth it. Consider that having a pet may mean that your life is no longer your own, and you have lost your freedom. You will have to find someone to care for your pet if you have to go out of town. You will be restricted to living in places that allow pets.

Some pet expenses are unpredictable. You may have extra apartment fees, repair or replacement of items they might destroy, and possibly having to rent a more expensive place with a yard. Unexpected visits to the veterinarian when they are sick, surgical fees, and kennel fees when you must make a sudden trip all add up.

"The costs of bringing an animal into your home go far beyond any initial adoption fee, which can vary from nothing at all to hundreds of dollars." (Weliver, 2019)

Establishing a Workable Environment

According to Weliver, here is a breakdown of the average first year of pet ownership for one medium dog:

One-time pet expenses

- Spaying and Neutering: Dog- $200/ Cat- $145
- Initial Medical Exam: Dog-$70/ Cat- $130
- Collar or Leash: Dog- $30/ Cat-$10
- Litter Box: Cat- $25
- Scratching Post: Cat- $30
- Carrying Crate: Dog- $60/ Cat- $40
- Training: Dog- $110

Total One-time Costs: Dog- $565/ Cat $365

Annual pet expenses

- Food: Dog -$120/ Cat- $130
- Annual Medical Exams: Dog- $235/ Cat $130
- Litter: Cat- $200
- Toys and Treats: Dog- $55/ Cat- $25
- License: Dog- $15
- Pet Health Insurance: Dog-$225/ Cat- $175
- Miscellaneous: Dog- $45/ Cat-$30

Total Annual Costs: Dog- $695/ Cat- $705

(Weliver, 2019)

Everyone's situations, values, and resources are different. What is a consideration for others may not be a consideration for you. Please weigh the risks and benefits of pet ownership both to you and the pet.

Next: Strategy 5/6— Develop ways to sustain yourself along the way.

5
Preventing Health Pitfalls

EATING

This link will suggest some useful cooking apps for college students: https://spoonuniversity.com/lifestyle/food-apps-every-college-student-needs

It is easy in college to become too preoccupied with how much you are eating and your body image. It is also easy to fall into bad food habits when you are rushing. You might want to consider Eve Lahijani's advice from her TED talks. Here is her talk, "Trust your hunger and make peace with food": https://www.youtube.com/watch?reload=9&v=Ssr2UDB9EWQ She suggests you rate your actual physical hunger and try to eat before you get too hungry. Then, you pay attention to your body and stop eating before you are too full. Eating in this way more likely results in your putting some moderation in your eating and not letting food tyrannize you.

Consider finding healthy foods you can eat between classes that you can carry with you. You might consider these to put in plastic bags inside your backpack: hard-boiled eggs, olives, bananas, plantains, blueberries, walnuts, almonds, and Greek-style yogurt. You might chop up some vegetables—like carrots, broccoli, cauliflower, or celery— to eat alone or dip into a small plastic container of guacamole. Look for in-season, locally grown, non-GMO fruits. Buy a *Quest* protein bar or put some natural almond butter on cut up celery sticks or put tuna fish in a small container to get protein. If you want only 10 grams of protein at a time, consider *Kind* bars or *Protein One* bars.

Use olive oil whenever you can. Eggs are a good source of protein. Limit your red meat intake to lower your risk of inflammation. You might consider eating *Beyond Meat* or —when eating out—ordering *Impossible Burgers*. Eat your vegetables first, and perhaps you won't have room for the processed food. By eating slowly, you give your brain time to realize you have eaten enough. Plan your meals ahead of time whenever possible. Likely, you have already heard that you will come out better if you enter the grocery store with a full stomach, and you base your shopping list on your week's meal plan.

Your brain, to function at its best, needs for you to stay hydrated. You get shorter as the day goes on as your spinal discs become more dehydrated, so keep drinking for your back's sake too. Remember that coffee and tea are diuretics and result in fluid loss. You need to drink an extra cup of water for each cup of them that you drink. Getting dehydrated can also affect the blood level of medication you are taking. Take a look at the sugar content of energy drinks and fancy coffee drinks to see if they are worth the calories, the sugar rush, and the later sleepiness. When you feel hungry, ask yourself if you are just thirsty.

WebMD's article, *Make a Great Grocery List in Minutes,* offers a blueprint to help you choose healthy food. Go to https://www.webmd.com/food-recipes/guide/grocery-list#1

If you are in a residence hall, you may have no alternative than to buy foods that keep well. Remember that food that keeps well is likely processed, and the potentially beneficial oils are removed, so the food does not become rancid.

Hercampus offers a dorm grocery list here:
https://www.hercampus.com/health/food/only-dorm-grocery-list-you-ll-ever-need

Live on crackers from the vending machine and sodas, and you will have enough sugar that you don't feel like eating a real meal and enough stimulation to get you through the day. Eventually, however, your health will suffer, and your brain will have a harder time studying. Eating fast, cheap, and healthy is not easy. If you cook or would like to learn, Rachel Phipps has clear instructions in her cookbook for college students. Your roommate would be in awe. The title says it all: *Student Eats: Fast, Cheap, Healthy-the Best Tried-and-Tested Recipes for Students* (Phillips 2017).

In *Good and Cheap: Eat Well on $4/Day*, Leanne Brown shows you how to do just that (Brown 2015). She writes about buying in bulk, buying foods that you can use in multiple meals, and always buying eggs.

In her original book, *Making Ends Meet with a Popcorn Popper,* Jacqueline Lucia revealed her techniques for saving money as a suddenly single parent (Lucia 2018). She noted that the cheapest fruit is fruit that is in season, unprepared, and not washed. Ms. Lucia discovered that delis would sell the ends of cheeses for very little. She discussed finding and downloading current coupons. (Google your store and the words "coupon matchups"). She also mentioned ways of getting money from shopping by using www.ebates.com, www.receipthog.com, and www.receiptpal.com.

Don't obsess, but try to avoid processed foods when you can. Michael Pollan, in his book, *Food Rules: An Eater's Manual*, gives you some simple rules to identify processed foods (Pollan 2009). For example, foods that have high fructose corn syrup, unpronounceable ingredients, list sugar in the top three ingredients, and are made in factories. David Perlmutter, MD, and Kristin Loberg discuss the biochemistry behind the importance of avoiding processed foods in their book, *The Grain Brain Whole Life Plan: Boost Performance Lose Weight, and Achieve Optimal Health* (Perlmutter and Loberg 2016). Simply put, processed foods cause inflammation, which impairs your physical and mental health in multiple ways.

The Plant Paradox: The Hidden Dangers in "Healthy" Foods That Cause Disease and Weight Gain by Dr. Steven R. Gundry is a meaningful contribution to an evolving field of study (Gundry 2017). It will help you see how taking care of your gut flora and avoiding lectins is crucial for your life-long physical and mental health. If you lack time to read it now, ask your parents to read it and talk to you about it. It could change their lives as well.

SLEEPING

Not recharging yourself by getting enough restful sleep can cause you to have problems with thinking and memory, as well as motivation and productivity. The National Sleep Foundation states, "… it's important to pay attention to your own individual needs by assessing how you feel on different amounts of sleep." The National Sleep Foundation has a "rule-of-thumb" recommendation that people age 18-25 get from 7-9 hours of sleep and acknowledges that for some people it might be appropriate to get as little as 6 hours a night or as much as 10-11 hours a night. For more details, go to https://www.sleepfoundation.org/articles/how-much-sleep-do-we-really-need

Falling asleep and staying asleep so that you wake up rested is easier if you have developed a sleep routine. Ideally, you would go to bed at the same time each night and get up at the same time each morning, regardless of your class schedule or the weekend.

Andrew J.K. Phillips found that "sleep regularity is positively associated with academic performance." "Irregular sleep/wake patterns are associated with poorer academic performance and delayed circadian and sleep/wake timing (Phillips 2017)." Go to https://www.researchgate.net/publication/317615572

Taking time at the end of the day to hang out with friends or get to know your roommates better is rewarding but try to limit it to weekends, so your grades don't suffer. If you stay up too late and then take a nap the next day, your body metabolizes out part of the sleepiness chemical it needs that night to overcome the alerting effects of the circadian rhythm. Then, you have trouble falling asleep. Try hanging out with your friends during your usual naptime. That keeps you up, and you don't feel as much pressure to hang out late at night.

A good sleep routine would involve removing alerting stimuli (media, tablet, phone, drama queens) so you can settle down. Put your screens in night mode. If you feel overwhelmed by what you need to do the next day, then make a quick list to get some closure, so it doesn't keep going through your mind. Discuss relationship issues earlier in the day when you aren't worn out. You can avoid waking your brain up with bright light by having a dim nightlight in the bathroom. Nightlights also reduce the chance of falls. Don't overdo it with too many. It is better to sleep in a room that is as dark as you safely can get it.

If the room temperature is in the 60s, your sleeping body is better able to perform certain functions. Your feet, on the other hand, need to be warm, so wear socks if they get cold. If you feel like the residence hall mattress is too hard, experiment with a mattress topper. If you are worried about allergens or bed bugs, you might want to buy a 'mattress saver.'

You will also sleep better without external light in the room. You have several options, including ordering blackout blinds such as the "magic blackout blinds" from https://www.dormco.com. As an alternative, you can make curtains from thick fabric heavy enough to cling to the window. You could also use a sleep mask. Walgreens makes one that fits like goggles. Your eyes can then blink more easily. Consider using earplugs, a noise machine, or fan to drown out any noise. Talk with your roommate to make an agreement about 'lights out' and 'noise out' times.

Getting early morning sunlight helps your brain be alert in the morning and go to sleep at night. You can find more health tips and information about sleep difficulties at http://sleepfoundation.org. While many problems with rest are related to bad sleep habits and not having enough time to sleep; sometimes, the problem is the quality of your sleep. Some of the primary sleep problems include excessive daytime sleepiness, REM sleep disorder, obstructive sleep apnea, periodic limb movement disorder, and narcolepsy. Students with ADHD are at higher risk for restless leg syndrome and sleep apnea.

If you have a persistent problem with falling asleep, staying asleep, or waking up earlier than you should, it might be secondary to another physical problem and justifies seeing your physician. Many illnesses have disturbed sleep as a symptom. These include heartburn, asthma, ulcers, fibromyalgia, arthritis, diabetes, heart disease, and anemia, among others.

As of this writing, Nightware, Inc. has not yet launched its app for the Apple Watch that senses you are having a nightmare and awakens you. https://hitconsultant.net/2019/05/24/nightware-fda-breakthrough-status/

Besides coffee and other caffeine-containing drinks, medicines may affect your sleep. You may want to ask your doctor if the medications you are taking can cause problems with sleep. It could also be you are having unsatisfying superficial sleep because a restless four-legged or two-legged bed partner is encroaching on your space. In winter, when you lie down with dogs, you wake up with 'freeze.'

Extended sleep deprivation can sometimes bring on seizures. Plan, so you don't risk putting yourself in that position during exam week.

Preventing Health Pitfalls

There are a variety of remedies for oversleeping. Ask your reliable roommate to see that you are up. If you live alone, you could pay a monthly fee for having Snoozester.com call you multiple times until you tell them you are awake. You can put the alarm on the other side of the room.

If you must have an alarm clock that can be as loud as an ambulance, then check out the YouTube video for the *Screaming Meanie* with your roommates. You could also check out the *Alarmy* (Sleep If U Can) app for your phone, which requires you to take a picture with your phone or do a math problem before its 'annoying' sound stops. It is advertised as the most constantly used alarm clock in the world. The Step Out of Bed app requires you to step out of bed to stop the annoying sound.

Once you are out of bed, immediately make it to discourage you from getting back in it.

MAINTAINING PHYSICAL HEALTH

BE PROACTIVE The summer before college is an appropriate time to talk with your pediatrician about ongoing treatment. If you are getting too old for their practice, ask them for recommendations for physicians. Luckily, you have the Internet to research to find the right doctor for you. Getting a doctor near your home would make sense for you if you live at home or plan to go home often. You may prefer the convenience of having a physician closer to your school. Consider asking the student health service for physician recommendations. You will want to consult the insurance company- if you are insured- about preferred providers, pharmacies, and hospitals near campus. These providers can help you, and your parents, plan for a health emergency. Such a plan should include having a sheet with information about your allergies, surgeries, medication history, injuries, and added health history.

As you move into the US adult medical care system, don't count on it to look out for you. You must look out for yourself and be your own advocate. You must be willing to persist through difficulties with scheduling appointments, filling out forms, dealing with insurance companies, and explaining your situation repeatedly. Don't stop until you have a sense that your provider diagnosed you correctly, and the treatment is appropriate. Remember your goal of having a healthy body and brain with which to study.

Another part of studying is seeing words and hearing the professor. If you notice your roommate has begun to mumble and complain about how loud your media is, go to student health and get them to check for an earwax buildup. Get an eye check-up if you find reading bothers your eyes or gives you a headache. Don't assume your hearing or vision is fine.

PREVENTING INFECTIONS Please ask about updating your shots and vaccinations when you meet with your pediatrician. Doing this is especially important now because you will be in close quarters with many people. You are more at risk for infections. Please, seriously discuss getting injections for flu, meningitis B, measles, and HPV.

First-year students are more likely to have to take the smaller dormitory rooms and tend to associate in groups more than upper-level students who may live off-campus. First-year students are set up to spread viral upper respiratory illness rapidly. You might want to get shower shoes to avoid getting fungal infections.

Recognize the symptoms of mononucleosis in yourself and others to get help quickly and prevent its spread. Mononucleosis is spread by saliva. Infectious saliva can be transmitted by coughing, sneezing, kissing, or by contaminated food, dishes, or eating utensils. It may take four to six weeks from the time of infection to develop symptoms. Some of the symptoms like fatigue, sore throat, and headache resemble other common illnesses. Check for swollen lymph nodes under your arms and on your neck, for fever, and a skin rash. Your spleen may become swollen. Some symptoms appear later. See a doctor to get evaluated.

Your student health center can quickly screen for strep throat and flu. In the beginning, these illnesses may be hard for you to distinguish from a virus or 'stomach bug.' Getting your flu diagnosed early may allow you to take Tamiflu, which could make the symptoms milder and shorten the course of the illness. Some stomach bugs are spread easily by others coughing and sneezing, by touching contaminated surfaces, and by eating food contaminated by someone with the virus.

SEXUAL HEALTH If you are sexually active, you are at risk for sexually transmitted diseases. Not using condoms substantially increases your risk. Learn how to use condoms. Plan to have them available. Know which ones are most effective. Most people would say it is less embarrassing to buy condoms than it is to get treatment for a sexually transmitted disease.

Human papillomavirus (HPV) is a widespread, sexually transmitted disease that significantly increases the risk of cervical cancer. Read more about it at https://www.cdc.gov/std/hpv/stdfact-hpv.htm.

Some strains of gonorrhea are becoming harder to treat with antibiotics. http://www.cidrap.umn.edu/news-perspective/2018/09/experts-brace-more-super-resistant-gonorrhea

If you are a man having sex with men, consider the pros and cons of taking PrEP (pre-exposure prophylaxis, brand name Truvada) to reduce your risk of getting HIV/AIDS. Go to https://www.cdc.gov/hiv/basics/prep.html for more information.

Couples who use the withdrawal method as contraception in order not to get pregnant do not often succeed. The Mayo Clinic staff indicated, "As many as 28 out of 100 women who practice the withdrawal method for one year will get pregnant (Mayo Clinic Staff 2018)."

This government website provides information about various contraceptives: https://www.hhs.gov/opa/performance-measures/index.html.

This website discusses emergency contraception: https://www.webmd.com/sex/birth-control/plan-b#1. Please be aware that using a condom alone is not adequate contraception.

Many insurance plans cover birth control. In many college student health centers, it is possible to get tested as needed for STDs.

If you are in a geographical area that makes it difficult for you to obtain contraception, you can use NURX.com to get a doctor's advice on which method is best for you. You answer some health questions, complete demographic information, and request your order. Then the NURX medical team will review your request and your health history, and a licensed medical provider will write a prescription. NURX will fill and ship the prescription to you. You can also get PrEP through NURX.

Unplanned pregnancy warrants discussion. It is covered in another book by Dr. Duffey— *Exploring Your Unplanned Pregnancy: Single Motherhood, Adoption and Abortion- Questions and Resources* (Duffey 2016)

MINIMIZING YOUR TIME SICK Eat the right amount of the right foods, rest enough, and exercise regularly to reduce the impact of ill health on your college experience. Being proactive about your health by recognizing symptoms of illness and seeking early treatment will often reduce the length of your disease, reduce complications and expenses.

Taking care of yourself benefits your financial as well as your physical health. Paying attention to make sure after you get your hands dirty that you wash them before touching the mucous membranes of your mouth, nose, or eyes will reduce your chance of getting infections. Don't drink or eat after someone else. Don't share eating utensils. If you are eating out, wait until after you have touched the menu to wash your hands.

You are going to be in close contact with others, and this sets you up for exposure to respiratory viruses, viral gastroenteritis—the stomach bug, mononucleosis, pink eye, influenza, and even meningitis. All of these could result in the expense of medical treatment.

By flossing your teeth regularly, you reduce the bacterial spread and the risk of valvular heart disease.

When you Google health questions, use multiple websites. Googling a medical inquiry may surprise you when you turn up severe but infrequent diseases. If you have a cough, you may have a cold, but you will see lung cancer and tuberculosis come up in the search.

Here are some medical websites for you to consider: The National Institutes of Health, Johns Hopkins Medicine Health Library, Cleveland Clinic, Mayo Clinic, Medline Plus, and Family Doctor.org. You may want to check out the Symptomate-Symptom Checker app or other symptom checker apps to get a general idea of what your symptoms may mean, but these apps should not be used to make a diagnosis or be a substitute for medical help.

Locate the student health center. Check out what it offers and how to reach it. Write down and have convenient their phone number as well as the phone numbers for campus security, your doctor, and your local hospital.

MEDICATION When a doctor prescribes a drug, the doctor has decided that the risks of your taking the medication are less than the risks of your continuing to be sick. If you choose not to take the pill, you will not have the drug's side effects, but you risk the consequences of your illness. You are betting that what you don't know won't hurt you. Continuing to be sick, or getting even worse, will possibly affect your ability to study and attend class. If the medication is to help your brain, not taking it will mean you will be trying to study using a suboptimal brain.

Don't assume that you already know the risks in any treatment or medicine your doctor prescribes. Take the initiative to ask your doctor what the medication's common side effects are. Ask them about the more rare but severe side effects. Before you leave the office, you want to know if there is a discontinuation syndrome, how long the medication takes to work, and whether the new drug interacts with your current ones. If you are at risk of getting pregnant, ask your doctor how that would affect you. Read the package insert and talk with the pharmacist to find out if you should take the medication with food. Read what to do if you miss a dose.

Getting a blood level of medication that is effective but not so high that there are too many side effects requires individualizing the dose. Among other things, your doctor has to consider your age, sex, weight, genetic background, general health, and other medications that can affect the blood level. Once you have started, your input about side effects and the response of your symptoms will help your doctor make dose adjustments.

If you expect to need refills of your medication, keep track of how many pills you have, and call and set up an appointment to see your doctor before you run out. Doing this gives your doctor a chance to evaluate your response and adjust the dose. It also avoids having a possible discontinuation syndrome; if you are taking a medication that requires you to gradually taper it off when treatment is complete. Some medicines have to be started at a low dose and steadily increased for them to have their full effect with a minimum of side effects. To kill all of the organisms causing your infection, take the full prescribed course of any antibiotics you have been prescribed, even if the symptoms have gone away.

If you find yourself forgetting to take your pills, use the alarm on your phone, download an app like Medisafe, or set a dedicated alarm clock that goes off when you need to take them. It may help to have your pill-taking associated with your daily routine. Put your pills in a place you will see them. On the other hand, if you take a psychostimulant like Ritalin, Vyvanse, or Adderall, lock it up or hide it in a hollowed-out textbook, a winter coat pocket during the summertime, or a pocket sewn into curtains or a bedspread. If you give one of these drugs to someone else, even without selling it, you are committing a felony, as well as taking the risk they may have a severe adverse reaction.

ACTIVELY PARTICIPATE IN YOUR CARE When you see a doctor, the doctor listens to your description of your current symptoms, reviews your history, examines you, and may do tests to make a working diagnosis. A working diagnosis represents what he believes is the disease process that he feels best explains your symptoms. The prognosis is a prediction about the course of the disease. Prognosis can change with discoveries and changes in your condition.

Sometimes it is obvious what illness you have. For example, if you have a strep throat and your strep screen is positive. Other times there may be several diseases that have symptoms similar to yours. It may be early in the course of your illness, and the full symptom picture may not have emerged. For reasons like these, your doctor relies on the subsequent information you give them about your response to determine if their theory or working diagnosis is correct. The more accurate observer you are of your response and the closer you follow the prescribed treatment, the more accurate your doctor will be able to be in determining any adjustments or rethinking their assumptions about your diagnosis. Your doctor needs you to be a partner in this process, and they expect you to let them know sooner if you are not getting better, have missed pills, are getting worse, or developing allergic symptoms. It follows from this that coming to a scheduled follow-up appointment is vital for your care.

Allergic reactions are not that frequent and usually consist of itchiness, a rash, hives, and some minimal swelling. Not all rashes are drug rashes. Your doctor will want to hear from you immediately and work with you in deciding whether to stop your medication. Your doctor may want to see the rash before considering stopping the medication or treating a reaction. Call your doctor's office and make them understand that it is crucial they call you back soon. If you believe you have an allergic reaction, at the very minimum, it requires a medical provider's prompt attention. If it is rapidly worsening, you need to think seriously about going to the emergency room because you don't want to experience anaphylactic shock.

ANAPHYLACTIC SHOCK The rarer anaphylactic allergic reaction is much more serious. You need to know the symptoms of an anaphylactic reaction so you can seek help <u>immediately</u> —because it is a life-threatening emergency. Time is crucial because your airway will be narrowing, and you will have difficulty breathing. You may feel it like a lump in your throat that makes it difficult to swallow. You may start to wheeze. Other symptoms include breaking out in hives, feeling warm with flushed skin, or looking pale. You may have abdominal pain and associated nausea, vomiting, or diarrhea. You may have a weak or rapid pulse and feel dizzy from the drop in your blood pressure. Your lips and tongue may swell, and your nose may run.

The next time you see your doctor, ask them what they think you should do in case of an anaphylactic reaction and whether they would approve of you using your roommate's EpiPen in case of such an emergency to buy time before you can get to the emergency room.

TIREDNESS is a common complaint among college students. Many illnesses can cause tiredness, but not getting enough rest, eating poorly, overdoing, and being out of shape are common ones. Other non-lifestyle-induced tiredness causes include—but are not limited to-—anemia, viruses, medication side effects, cancer, depression, and chronic anxiety. Chronic tiredness deserves a visit to your doctor.

THE LONG-TERM PERSPECTIVE New York Times's Pagan Kennedy said that when it comes to staying healthy, it is the decisions we make as a collective that matter more than any choice we make on our own (Kennedy 2018). That is to say; your lifetime health will be adversely affected if you and others vote in a way that does nothing about pollution, climate change, or health care.

6

Avoiding Financial Pitfalls

MANAGING MONEY

If you have already completed the Free Application for Federal Student Aid (FAFSA) forms, you likely have begun some discussion with your family about family finances and your family's ability to pay for some of your college expenses. Having taken Thoreau's perspective, you might have discussed how much of their lives they are willing to exchange to pay toward your education.

Ideally, before you get to college, you need to nail down with them the specifics of what they can pay for and how you will pay for the rest. Some credit card companies require a cosigner on credit cards for people below certain ages, so this topic may need to be part of the discussion.

Several websites may help make estimates of college expenses, but the actual costs will depend on the school, the degree you are pursuing, the cost of living near the school, and other things. One website—with helpful articles and figures—comes from The Balance. It is https://www.thebalance.com/understanding-college-tuition-room-and-board-795382.

Eating on the run, being out with friends, and unexpected expenses can so quickly lead to overspending unless you have a budget that makes you think in advance about your expenses. In discussing your finances and in working with your family on setting budget guidelines, it may be helpful to categorize your expenses to see what you can change and what you can't.

A list of expenses might include <u>irregularly occurring fixed costs</u>—like tuition, fees including lab fees, apartment deposit, residence hall room and board, campus parking.

Other <u>fixed expenses occur regularly</u>—like apartment rent, health insurance, dental insurance, rental insurance, car insurance, Internet, and cell phone. By looking at old receipts and calling sellers, you can nail down these numbers.

<u>Nonfixed expenses</u> are harder to predict. You have some non-fixed costs that occur regularly— like groceries, laundry, toiletries, hair care, and gas for commuting,

Other <u>nonfixed expenses arise irregularly</u>—like traveling home, car maintenance, doctors' visits not covered by insurance, dental care, textbooks, computer software programs required for online courses, and restocking your initial school supplies.

You will have <u>one-time start-up expenses</u>—like room furnishings, initial school supplies, electronics, moving expenses, and possibly Greek recruitment. At the end of the year, you may have moving and storage expenses.

You have the most control of your <u>discretionary spending</u>. You may spend money on eating out or entertainment. Entertainment might include travel, dates, sports events, concerts, Greek activities, or other organizational events. Some affairs will require extra clothing.

There are several websites like *NerdWallet* (https://www.nerdwallet.com/blog/finance/budget-worksheet/) that will help you track your expenses and construct a budget. If you prefer to use your phone, there are dedicated apps, like *Mint: Budget, Bills, and Finance tracker*.

If you set up a checking account, find a bank that has branches both at home and at your school. Having a bank at home comes in handy when you are on home visits or have an unexpected need for your family to deposit money in your account.

In the real world, institutions —and their well-meaning employees—don't always process things promptly. It would help if you had a plan B for when your paycheck, scholarship, or loan payment does not come in on time. Some colleges will hold up registration or other activities until you pay them.

Future employers use your credit rating as a measure of your reliability and your good judgment. A poor credit rating could cost you a job. It will close so many doors in your face. You may not be able to buy some items or will have to pay higher interest. For an introduction to credit ratings, you may want to visit Credit.com at https://www.credit.com/credit-scores/what-is-a-good-credit-score/

If you deposit a check in your bank account, the money is not immediately available to pay for a bill—especially if you have not deposited it in the morning. It would help if you allowed some time for the check to clear, so you won't bounce the check and cost yourself extra charges. Ask your bank about their policy.

SAVING MONEY ON EXPENSES

Being a poor student with too many expenses is a grim situation and requires often doing uncomfortable things out of necessity. One is going to a food bank. You can find a food bank close to you at the Feeding America website: www.feedingamerica.org/find-your-local-foodbank. Food banks can be helpful when you have to choose between buying food or paying rent. One day you will make enough and contribute to another food bank, so don't beat yourself up about having to use one.

Go in with someone and share the food you buy in bulk to lower costs. Pay bills online to avoid the cost of stamps. Eat with friends and volunteer to take the leftovers. Carpool to save gas.

Be practical and locate a thrift store near an affluent area and shop for clothes. Goodwill has furniture as well as clothes. If you are careful and know what to look for, you may be able to use pawn shops to buy electronic items.

Working can be a key part of drug and alcohol recovery. Some recovery programs take in donated cars and supervise recovering people as they repair them. These programs then sell the vehicles mainly for the cost of the repairs. If there is such an organization near you, it may save you thousands on a used car.

Instead of buying something with money, try bartering. Exchange your services (like cleaning, cooking, babysitting) for something you want. Move in with an older adult —like your elderly aunt —who needs help or companionship in exchange for not having to pay rent. Move in with a single mother and help with childcare and cooking in exchange for not having to pay rent.

Avoid paying full price by buying used items if they work just as well. Use coupons. Get the grocery store card for discounts. Wait for sales. Buy on layaway. Buy off-season. Buy store brands. Buy generic drugs. Buy at the yard and garage sales. If an item is damaged or dirty, ask the store manager for a discount. Postpone buying until you can pay with cash to avoid interest charges. Ask if there is a discount for paying cash. Pay your credit card down to avoid paying interest. Avoid paying extra expenses for nonessentials like cigarettes and alcohol. Resell suitable used clothing in consignment or thrift stores.

Crackle.com, Pluto.tv, and TubiTV.com have free movies, tv shows, and five channels. Splitting Netflix or Hulu accounts can make these costs only a few dollars a month.

Do things that are entertaining but also free. Take your lunch outside by having a picnic in a local park. Senior art majors and music majors have to display their art or perform their music in public. Often these events are free. Look at the residence bulletin board or the community calendar for free happenings. Sometimes colleges provide resident advisors with food money for residence get-togethers. Browse your town's craft festival. Some colleges offer Fine Films every month or show movies outdoors. At some smaller colleges, professors rotate opening their houses to have students over on Sunday nights. Be a supporter of your college's sports teams by attending the free games. College students may hear about nearby churches that like lots of college students to come to their midweek suppers featuring short programs and free home-cooking. Look for organizations on campus that may have speakers followed by complimentary refreshments. Go to the gym with a friend. Take a stroll through your town's historic district and explore the town's gardens. Play cards or board games. Assemble puzzles. Try out a new recipe. Splurge on some coffee and go to stand-up night or karaoke. Ask your friends to think of you when they have an extra ticket for an activity.

Realize that sometimes you have to spend money to prevent something more expensive from happening. Promptly changing the oil in your car prevents unnecessary wear and tear. Regular dental checkups save money that would be spent later treating dental abscesses. Getting a flu shot saves you the costs of flu medicine, lost work time, missed classes, and those days of being too sick to study. Taking good care of your possessions means you won't have to replace them as frequently. Keeping your vehicle in good repair and full of gas means you are less likely to be stranded in a remote, dangerous place, late to a destination, and trapped paying top dollar for repairs.

Don't be short-sighted. Don't take on extra hours at your job at the risk of dropping your grades and losing a scholarship worth more than you made in working extra. In that case, you would be working even more the next semester to make up for the scholarship you lost. Some schools offer work-study jobs that allow students to work extra sometimes and cut back around academically busy periods.

Finally, you can save money by avoiding the unnecessary extra costs of a DUI, or MIP legal fines for underage drinking. You could anticipate and prevent overdrafts at the bank, credit card late fees, vaping and smoking costs, emergency repairs of poorly maintained vehicles, and the cost of medical bills because of motor vehicle accidents.

MINIMIZING STUDENT LOAN EXPENSE

By carefully planning what your budget will be and working a part-time job, you may be able to avoid taking the full amount of the loan your college has offered you. The federal government may pay the interest on your federal loan while you are in school, but other type loans may charge you interest while you are in school. Then your loan debt when you graduate will include the loan and the interest that has accumulated while you were in school. So, after graduating, the new total amount you will be paying on includes the interest that accrued during college. Some loan programs will allow you to pay off, while you are going to college, the accruing interest. Some financial institutions will give you a discount for having your loan payments deducted automatically from your bank account. It is essential that you know the types of loans you have and how much you owe. It is worth going to this website to read an excellent discussion of student loan issues: https://studentloanhero.com/featured/student-loan-advice-12-experts/ It will offer ideas on how to locate your loan servicers, information on the types of loans, and provide links to other resources.

Please look at the Public Service Loan Forgiveness student loan program to see if it fits your situation. You may be thinking about working in a job that would qualify, but you have to meet all the conditions. For an overview go to https://studentloanhero.com/featured/public-service-loan-forgiveness-do-you-qualify/

How to Graduate College Early: Save Thousands of Dollars and Years of Time by Deciphering the College Credit System by Danny Swirsky comes through on its title's claim (Swirsky 2015). Mr. Swirsky discusses studying for courses on your own and then taking a CLEP test to get credit more cheaply. He explains the least expensive times to take specific courses, where to take courses inexpensively, and how to transfer credits to schools that accept them. Mr. Swirsky talks about when it makes sense to be on campus and when you can best take online courses from home. The author knows because he graduated from college in three and a half years for a fraction of the cost. His Kindle book is worth the price many times over. https://www.amazon.com/How-Graduate-College-Early-Deciphering-ebook/dp/B019WWDW5Q/ref=sr_1_26?keywords=Cryptic+College&qid=1561742339&s=gateway&sr=8-26

WORKING

If you live in a city like San Francisco, where there is a gig economy, you may be able to do short-term gigs by using an app. For example, you can do dog walking using the Rover app. Each gig may be for a few hours or days. Some other examples include delivering lunches to a meeting, working in a warehouse for the day, or babysitting.

When you are brainstorming through the job lists below, ask yourself how much flexibility would you need from your employer because of your school schedule.

Some shift-type jobs are more open to scheduling flexibility, like waitperson, expeditor, food runner, phone sales, customer service representative, delivery worker, restaurant hostess, parking valet, or department store clerk. Some jobs occur on the weekend or at night after classes are over. These include church nursery worker, nightshift grocery stocker, bank nightshift check auditor, night worker at distribution centers like UPS, night-shift nursing home aide, bouncer, night hotel desk clerk, and office cleaner.

Other jobs might have to be done at specific times. These include work in catering, veterinary helper work, work with athletic teams, and working as a wedding photography assistant.

Other jobs may require some on-call duties or more availability at peak times. These include bar-back, babysitter, tech support, dog walker, lifeguard, church youth helper, tutor, resident advisor, and student apartment complex representative.

If you are a resident advisor or a student apartment complex representative, your schedule will revolve around school year activity. They may pay you in free rent.

You will want to check out the specific rules about work-study jobs. Apply early for these jobs because they are likely in demand. Such jobs include tutor, special events worker, library worker, student store clerk, IT tech support, greenhouse helper, clerical assistant, community advisor, receptionist, research assistant, and student instructor.

You might look for jobs from national companies. Consider being the campus rep for a national college textbook company or sports clothing company. For example, Cengage has a Student Ambassador program. You might become a respondent for market research. You could make money by blogging or being an influencer. Look at Fiverr to see if you have any skillsets that are in demand like blogging, creative writing, editing, playing instruments, and others. Upwork.com lists photographer, web searcher, social media manager, illustrator, logo designer, 3-D artist, website developer, editor, creative writer, transcriber, translator, voice work, and article writer among their listed freelance work.

Brainstorm about jobs anywhere in the world that could be done remotely from your laptop. Such jobs might be web design or writing copy. For a small investment in equipment, you could be a spokesperson in YouTube videos. If you have an excellent speaking voice, you may want to record audiobooks. Here is an incredibly helpful article listing eleven other online jobs for college students, like online tutoring, with links to many. http://selfmade-success.com/online-jobs-college-students/

Besides regular jobs, there may be seasonal work in department stores or pick-up jobs like house or pet sitting. You may be able to work for a temporary agency. Some temp agency jobs turn into more permanent part-time jobs. If you work for a health care agency, you could take short-term jobs as a personal companion when you had a gap in your classes or holidays. Church secretaries often know of people in the church who are looking for help with their relatives. It is worth calling the church secretaries in your town to get some leads for this and other possible handy worker jobs needed by older people. If you are handy, look around the neighborhood for houses that need painting, yards that need cutting, and gutters that are full.

It would not hurt to leave your name at the local physical rehab centers or with hospital or nursing home social work department secretaries. There may be patients recovering from surgery who need help with activities of daily living when they go home.

Consider whether your past skillset would qualify you to start your own business as a private personal sports coach, swimming instructor, or music teacher. Could you start a shop on Etsy using your craft skills? Do you enjoy creating online art or video content?

Sometimes employers have identified a need for part-time help or need to have a particular work task done but have not yet advertised for the assignment. It may be so limited in scope or length that they don't want to bother with the expense of advertising. If you walk in their store or doctor's office and ask, they may take a chance on you because it saves them the cost of advertising. They can see you have taken the initiative, have a pleasing manner, speak well, and look able-bodied. If you feel like you need an edge, tell them you will work the first week for free, and they can make their mind up then after seeing your quality work.

If you go to the Chamber of Commerce website for your town, many of the members listed represent local businesses. If there are reasonably large companies on this list, they will have human resource officers. Take the risk of going straight to the HR officer with resume in hand and tell them your skillset and hours you want to work and see what they have. You may be cleaning offices at night before you know it.

Please take advantage of changes associated with the academic year by expecting them to happen and getting prepared for them. When seniors graduate in December or May, positions open. Similarly, if you wait until you are on campus to look for work during the fall semester, early birds may have taken those positions. If you have a twelve-month apartment lease and remain in the town over the summer, you need to consider that, with fewer students, there is less of a need for you. Fewer customers mean fewer tips. You might want to consider a salaried job.

Some of the better-paying student jobs are discussed at the Trade Schools, Colleges, and Universities site: https://www.trade-schools.net/articles/high-paying-student-jobs.asp You may already be familiar with https://www.glassdoor.com and the help they offer with jobs, career advice, and researching companies.

Network with friends to let them know you are looking. Some students who have choice jobs try to give them to their friends and, as a result, others never hear about openings. You also can check out https://www.handshake.com for help with placements.

Be aware of multi-level marketing schemes that prey on college students interested in making money. This article by Dr. Z of the Consultation Tower is an eyeopener. https://consultationtower.com/?p=202

Ask yourself —"What skillsets do I have that can help this employer right now?" Employers are looking for people who are flexible because the job may change depending on who is sick. They like people who don't have to be told what to do and are self-starters. They also want the same people to be able to follow directions and know their place in the hierarchy. They desire people who get along with others and are team players. When you think about your experiences and skills, ask yourself what have you done that shows these qualities. That is what you hope to get across in your interview and resume. You may have demonstrated these qualities in activities other than past jobs. In organizations, school activities, community living, what have you done that illustrates you are a flexible, team player, proactive self-starter who can comply with authority? You need to familiarize yourself with an employer interview technique called the STAR technique. Go to https://www.huffingtonpost.com/alan-carniol/inside-the-star-interview_b_3310122.html for details. In a STAR interview, you are asked to tell a story about your work experience by describing the work situation, the task created by it, the action you took, and the results you achieved.

Employers are now able to use artificial intelligence to review your social media and determine your suitability. At job interviews, employers may employ software that uses camera images to detect lies.

Just as your employer can use technology to find out information about you, you can find out about them. Companies with publicly traded stock usually have sufficient information on the Internet available about their financial well-being, their future projects, the competition they face, and the leaders in their company. Apps like *Seeking Alpha* offer you a way of getting expert opinions about their status. Knowing what a company is facing, you have a better idea of what you can offer them in their efforts. Employers appreciate someone who has done their homework.

Sometimes presenting yourself to employers can be intimidating. Before the interview, affirm what you believe are your strengths, remind yourself that you have a plan B if you are turned down, and don't fall into the trap of seeing your interviewer as an expert on your worthiness for the job.

If your finances don't require you to work, it still may be a good idea to work, preferably at times that don't take away from your studies. When you start to look for work after college, employers may want an applicant to have one to three years of experience. How can you get that experience if you need the experience to get the job first? You may be able partially to solve this difficulty by having several summer jobs or internships in the right field. Without a job history, you will have trouble showcasing the desired qualities and experience. Don't let pride stop you from asking your family for help in making connections if they have them through their work or business contacts.

When you calculate how many hours a week you need to work, remember that your take-home pay is the net result of your gross pay after state taxes, federal taxes, FICA (Federal Insurance Contributions Act), and health insurance have been taken out. The proportion of gross pay that is taken out will vary from state to state, so ask your hirer what is customary for your state.

Next: Strategy 7—Pick the right fellow searchers.

7
Belonging to the College Community

THINKING ABOUT DIVERSITY

If you are lucky, your college has a diverse student body. Diversity makes it possible for you to get to know people who think differently than you do, look different from you, and have different sexuality, gender identity, and gender expression from yours. You may meet people who are different ages than you, have different physical and mental abilities from you, and come from different cultures and economic groups. If you are that lucky person, you will discover that Harry Stack Sullivan- as quoted earlier-was right when he said that we are all more simply human than otherwise. It will help you realize the need to defend human rights because equality is not negotiable.

Some students are not so lucky, and they find themselves moving from a diverse high school to a college that has groups of people who have been around only people like themselves. If you are the unlucky student, then look for support groups that celebrate who you are and your background. Support groups will help you feel validated while you continue an ongoing courageous, thankless process of consciousness-raising in those around you. Remind yourself that your diversity enriches the lives of those around you. They may not recognize it yet, but you spice up their lives. As they witness you standing up for what you believe, they may come to see you —not a victim or a survivor—but a role model of integrity and courage.

If you are one of the students who grew up in a homogenous group, it can feel very threatening to your core sense of security to be exposed to different ways of being and seeing. Understand that your fretful gut response may be to commit yourself even more to what you already think. You may fear that, if you crack open the door in the least to new ideas, everything will fall apart. Welcome to college! Living with the apprehension of confronting what you don't know about is intrinsic to the college experience. Unfortunately, the college experience is scary and mind-blowing at times. You may not know what to think or do, but being kind and actively trying to understand others may help others be compassionate to you in your ignorance and awkwardness toward them. Remember, as Antoine de Saint-Exupery wrote in *The Little Prince*, "It is only with the heart that one can see rightly. What is essential is invisible to the eye (de Saint-Exupery 2015)."

Look past the superficial to experience the other person from your heart. Realize that it is their gift of graciousness toward you that makes dialogue and your growth possible.

Unfortunately, many people do not respect human dignity. Despite never being just, persecution for being different—by awakening you to the transient nature of things and human relationships—may refocus your own life on something bigger than yourself. You are compelled to prune away what is not authentic in search of what cannot be lost. You can begin to reconnect yourself by cultivating or rediscovering the tools that interrupt your clinging to the distractions. These are tools such as study, frequent meditation/prayer, and participation in the community. In this way- if you need to- you can turn your adversity into a return to relevance in your life.

To the heart in you, don't be afraid to feel.
To the sun in you, don't be afraid to shine.
To the love in you, don't be afraid to heal.
To the ocean in you, don't be afraid to rage.
To the silence in you, don't be afraid to break.

—Najwa Zebian, **Mind Platter**

https://www.amazon.com/Mind-Platter-Najwa-Zebian-ebook/dp/B079JGNQYZ/ref=sr_1_1?ie=UTF8&qid=1543338371&sr=8-1&keywords=mind+platter+najwa+zebian

Remarkable diversity resources are in the Appendix of Resources.

REVIEWING BASIC MANNERS

While treating others the way you would like others to treat you is an excellent guideline to follow in interacting with people, some circumstances call for specific etiquette. If you know these specifics already, you also know that sometimes you have to wait politely as an instructor explains something you already know to the class, since not everyone comes with the same background. We are giving you yet another opportunity to show patience to us as you survey what may be familiar ground.

When you meet someone, please give them a firm handshake. Use their preferred pronouns. Come on time and be considerate enough to call if you are running late.

If you are going to someone's house, bring them a small gift. If you pick a food item, be aware of possible food allergies and dietary preferences. If you are thinking about giving alcohol, then you should be certain that no one in their home has a drinking problem.

Commit to developing the habit of actively listening to others. Not only will active listening show proper respect to a boring fellow partygoer, but the practice will also help you in crucial dealings with coworkers, professors, friends, family, and your date. Active listening shows the person talking that you have concentrated on understanding what they are saying and have a response that reflects that understanding. You aren't just waiting for a chance to give your opinion or offer unsolicited advice—like this.

If you are talking to someone at a party and another person comes up, make introductions. Don't interrupt when others are talking. Avoid cursing, gossiping, saying disparaging remarks, or monopolizing the conversation. If someone tells you something in confidence, keep it to yourself, or he or she will think twice before they confide in you again.

Ask questions to determine their interests and talk with them about those interests. Try to find common interests. If you hear a new acquaintance make minor mistakes, it is better not to correct them unless it is a matter of safety.

People in different cultures have different ideas about how much personal space they need. Make a point of observing how close people around you are to each other and try to position yourself accordingly.

At the dinner table, put your napkin on your lap and eat with your mouth closed. Remember that forks go to the left, knives and spoons to the right with the spoon farthest from the plate. As the meal progresses, use utensils from outside the plate inward. Ask for food to be passed to you; don't reach across the table. Wipe your mouth after eating and before picking up the drinking glass. When you leave the gathering, find the host, and thank them.

Whenever you ask for something—say *please*. When someone does something for you—say "thank you." If you have to leave or you accidentally rub against someone—say "excuse me."

SOCIALIZING

The percentage of adults in any one year who have clinically significant social anxiety varies from study to study. Some studies have the rate as high as 7 percent. Some people with social anxiety disorder have a long-standing, excessive fear of being embarrassed in social situations. That leads them to avoid social situations or endure them with intense anxiety. Even if you don't have social anxiety disorder, you may still feel almost panicked about the social circumstances that college can create. That some students start drinking even before the party speaks to how hard it can be.

Here are some possible conversation starters: a comment about the surroundings or situation; a question about how they are associated with the host; small talk about the weather; your adventures and hassles getting there; something you like about the host organization; a favorable opinion that you suspect they share about campus food, classes, or electronics; the latest campus sporting events; a question about upcoming holiday plans; current news you have googled that day; something funny you have seen on the web; requests for advice about their favorite local restaurant; a comment about something you read recently; or an exciting tidbit your professor said. Try to make small talk positive.

Sticking with these first topics will mean your conversation is bland. You have the ball rolling, and you have not hurt their feelings by saying something about politics, race, religion, or sex that might have offended them. After all— you don't know these people yet— you can't assume they think like you or share your world views. That is where listening comes in.

Next, ask them questions about themselves and their experiences. While you should listen to both differences and similarities— you want to stress what you have in common. Listen carefully and find the parts of what they said that would allow you to add to their comments or ask further questions along the same train of thought.

Pay attention to the tone of your voice when you speak, as well as your body language. Do you sound like you know it all? Does your voice betray boredom? If your anxiety results in you talking fast— take a breath and slow down. Leave some space in the conversation for them to say something without having to interrupt you.

Besides listening, look at their facial expressions and body language to see if they are interested or they are distancing themselves or tightening because you have said something awkward. If they seem anxious, put them at ease by telling a funny and slightly self-deprecating story about yourself as a kid in a social situation. Weren't you the kid that got a piece of spinach—just like the spinach in the salad you are eating—stuck between your teeth and no one told you? Telling such a story allows them to be anxious and shows your empathy without being obvious. It shows that you are a strong enough person that you can admit vulnerabilities. If they don't run their tongue over their teeth, you'll know they weren't listening. Also, a genuine smile helps.

For some differently-abled people, socializing may be a more complex problem. Members of the Autistic Self-Advocacy Network have written *Navigating College: A Handbook on Self-Advocacy Written for Autistic Students from Autistic Adults (Latimer et al. 2013)*. It offers frank, practical, and relevant information that would be useful to both student and parent.

UNDERSTANDING SOCIAL GROUPS

> *The truth is: Belonging starts with self-acceptance. Your level of belonging, in fact, can never be greater than your level of self-acceptance, because believing that you're enough is what gives you the courage to be authentic, vulnerable, and imperfect.*
>
> *Brene Brown, author of Braving the Wilderness: The Quest for Belonging and the Courage to Stand Alone*
>
> *Brene Brown explains this in more detail in TED Talks TEDx-Houston June 2010 The Power of Vulnerability*
>
> https://www.ted.com/talks/brene_brown_on_vulnerability

Accepting that you are 'enough' and allowing yourself to be human helps people know you as an individual. Sometimes, however, there are group forces afoot that impact how you are seen and how the group interacts with you. These may have nothing to do with you as an individual. It is important to know about group dynamics because they are as powerful as they are unspoken.

Group theorists talk about the conflict group members feel between wanting to belong and worrying the group will absorb them, and they will lose their identity. This conflict results in the group member vacillating. The group member moves closer and worries about being engulfed then backs off and agonizes about being abandoned by the group.

When a new member comes into a group, the other group members want to know if they care enough about the group to make some self-sacrifice. For example, a new employee might be given the worst hours or have to get the coffee. If they humble themselves and accept the initiation, then the group sees they care about it. If they don't understand this new-member group process, they think things will not change, and they protest the injustice. The group then thinks they don't want to belong to it enough and think they are unique.

In looking at groups that have initiations, notice if the members of the groups that have the hardest initiations aren't the ones that seem most positive about their group. They have to convince themselves that they have not made a mistake and double-down on it being worth it. It would be like buying a pair of glasses that were much too expensive. You would double-down on how unique they were.

When successful people are asked what their secret was, they often say it had to do with <u>consciously choosing</u> to surround themselves with the right people. While you can't get away from being influenced by peers, you can intentionally work to pick peers that reinforce the best in you and share your ideas about what you want to become. In that way, when those around you influence you, it is good influence.

Finding the right peer group is not an easy task, but it is critical. It takes time. Don't rush the process and make a rash decision. You will have to go against some very human tendencies. There is a tendency to feel more comfortable around people who are not as accomplished or have struggles with which you can identify. You might worry less about them rejecting and leaving you. You might feel good about helping them. When you accept them, it may feel like you are accepting those parts of yourself that feel broken. You might also think that, in their position, they might expect less from you. You might want to have an excuse to backslide a while and know they are not going to call you on your maladjusted behavior because they are doing similar things. You might have stereotypes about successful people that make them seem unattractive to you. Because of the awkwardness of doing so many things for the first time, you may not feel very competent and find yourself self-identifying as a loser.

Make up your mind that you will persist at this trial and error process even though you will repeatedly make mistakes and waste time with the wrong groups. If you find you are drowning in a pool of pitiful peers, get out of that peer group and keep looking for one that works. Accept the challenge to be uncomfortable around people who are successful as a trade-off for having their positive influence. The best time to decide about a group is before you get too far into it and begin experiencing the self-deception about having not made a mistake.

The wrong peer group can subtly corrupt your thinking. In looking for a peer group, ask yourself if the members show personal internal strength by tolerating frustration, cooperating, showing kindness, controlling impulsivity, problem-solving, and working toward goals that you value. Have the people in the group showed good judgment? Do they admit their mistakes? Are they in touch with their humanity despite their competence? When you ask these questions about particular groups, you may find the groups that appear as superficially successful and popular groups are not successful in the ways relevant to your values.

Searching for a peer group, you will meet people who are not what they seem. They may treat you better because they consider you their equal and mistreat others. It's helpful to know when someone is lying to you. This website provides some tips on how to tell. https://www.nbcnews.com/better/health/how-tell-if-someone-lying-according-behavioral-experts-ncna786326

Because we are human, we and those around us do wrong. That does not make us evil. M. Scott Peck, M.D., states, "evil is that force, residing either inside or outside of human beings, that seeks to kill life or liveliness. And goodness is its opposite. Goodness is that which promotes life and liveliness (Peck p43)." He notes that "the central defect of the evil is not the sin but the refusal to acknowledge it (ibid p 69)." Evil people scapegoat others because they refuse to tolerate the sense of their wrongdoing, and they blame others and the world. They don't want to be good, but they want very much to look like they are good people to themselves and others. Evil people are trying to convince themselves that they are good even though they have an intolerable nagging sense that they are not.

We bring it up because you are going to run into evil people in various positions where they look like they are righteous. You need to be able to identify them before they stab you in the back. If such people have been a central part of your life already, consider reading Dr. Peck's book, *People of the Lie: The Hope for Healing Human Evil.*

You can find out more about groups and group theory in the appendix.

SURVIVING SPRING BREAK

At the risk of appearing condescending, paranoid, and hysterically parental, we would like to offer you some ideas about spring break, which may not be at all relevant to your circumstances.

You will find other information relevant to spring break in these sections: Staying Safe—Sexual Assault, Maintaining Physical Health—Sexual health, Sizing-up Impediments to Well-being, and Putting together a safety kit.

WHAT TO TAKE ON SPRING BREAK Decide with your traveling companions who will bring these items: Airborne, Benadryl, Neosporin, Lomotil, Tylenol, Aleve, Pepto Bismol, Tums, eyedrops, Band-Aids, sunscreen, sunburn treatment, insect repellant, mosquito bite treatment, food poisoning treatment, chargers, batteries, toilet paper, wipes, tissue, Kindle, Nook, playing cards, rain gear, and board games for rainy days.

If you don't take it, you can't lose it or have it stolen—rings, dress watches, other jewelry, computers, cameras, store credit cards, and other identifying information in your wallet that could be used against you or would be a chore to replace.

Plan for the possibility your luggage may be lost or stolen. Make copies of your passport, credit cards, insurance cards, identifying documents, significant phone numbers-including your MD, family, US Embassy, credit card companies, and school contacts-and addresses. Give copies to your traveling companions. Keep an eye on your luggage and have locks for all of your luggage compartments to lessen the chance of someone putting contraband in it.

Carry on the plane your prescription medication in their original pill bottles. Leave the remainder of your prescription supply safely at home. If you forget your oral contraceptive or other prescription medication, call your home doctor who may be able to call the script into a local chain pharmacy that can transfer the prescription to another branch where you are.

UNDERSTANDING RISK Spring break can be a potentially risky experience. It is possible to overestimate the ability of those around you to maintain their self-control during spring break activities. You may witness substance abuse, violence, and different kinds of impulsive behaviors. No adult from back home is looking, and students assume they will not see the people around them again. Some peers, however, may later parrot what they hear.

Students sometimes feel being wild during spring break is deserved after the frustration of the semester and is a national rite of passage. PubMed Central offers this journal article by C.M. Lee, M.A. Lewis, and C. Neighbors examining spring break alcohol use and related consequences: https://www.ncbi.nlm.nih.gov/pmc/articles/PMC2895976/

SEX What you need with you the most on spring break is to have friends with you who share your values and will work as a group to plan a safe break. If you don't want to have casual sex, don't go with people who do. In this way, you avoid risking being swept along by group mentality. Group mentality can lead to your doing things against your values that you would never do alone. It draws on the human wish to belong and take part. Seeing others' behavior gives unspoken permission to behave the same way. When you add alcohol and are far from home, it can become rather powerful. At that moment, you don't have the benefit of more experienced upperclassmen who would tell you that they learned the hard way the best rule of thumb is not to have sex with strangers.

If you want to have sex— then plan for it. Get STD testing before you go, so if your testing is positive when you return, you will know you have not had the disease from before. Many college student health centers will do STD testing for such illnesses as HIV, HPV, chlamydia, syphilis, and gonorrhea. Have with you the most effective condoms you can get.

If you decide you want a Plan B kit available, to avoid any hassle, order a Plan B kit online before your trip. Avoid being unable to find a Plan B kit there or finding a pharmacy only to realize others have already purchased the last one, and when you fly home, you have passed the time limit for Plan B to be effective. Also, remember that women above a certain weight require a higher dose to get an adequate blood level for it to work. Read the package insert. You may need to buy two packets. You are legally able to get Plan B without a prescription. It may be on the shelf, but if the pharmacy has it behind the counter and you have some difficulty with the assistant giving it to you, ask for the pharmacist. By law, they must provide it to you if you ask for it

Can you trust a sexually aroused drunk person to tell you the truth about their sexual health status and whether they are currently using effective contraception or intend to use contraception through the entire sex act? If you are in Zika-endemic areas, you will also need to ask if a mosquito has bitten them. They could infect you with the Zika virus that can cause grievous congenital disabilities.

NONCONSENSUAL SEX When that person, who was blackout drunk the night before and with whom you had what you thought was enthusiastic consensual sex, wakes up—they will not remember they were also interested in sex. They will only know that someone took advantage of their drunkenness and had sex with them —when they were not legally able to give consent. Whether they were interested in having sex, or whether you were drunk as well, has no relevance. They will remember that it is sexual assault. Take a minute to review the explanation of 'consent' in chapter 4.

Belonging to the College Community

Whether you plan to be sexually active or not, you need to have condoms in case you are sexually assaulted and can convince the assailant to use one. If rape could result in pregnancy, you may want to discuss with your family taking Plan B.

Remember that every phone is a camera. There could be hidden cameras as well. Never allow yourself to be blindfolded. You don't want your picture to show up on a porn-site or social media. Don't set yourself up to be blackmailed. People can take screenshots and video clips of you using Skype. Your webcam can be hacked, so don't undress in front of it. Never allow yourself to be tied up or taken away from the group to "be alone." You should seriously consider planning never being alone when you're far away from home. You should consider never trusting a stranger and always being on your guard.

You can use the Zipit app in response to predators wanting you to participate in sexting by posting pictures of yourself. It has a gallery of images and replies to shut them down.

HAVE A FRANK DISCUSSION AND BUILD A GAME PLAN WITH YOUR TRAVELING COMPANIONS. Together, game out some of the more difficult situations you might face and exit tactics for each. Having maps of the area and a smartphone app that can translate can be crucial if you are in a country where you don't speak the language. Get everyone to agree on having each other's back and specify just what that means. Make sure everyone understands clearly about meeting times and meeting places because mistakes can leave someone alone and vulnerable. Being responsible for showing up at the appointed time where you say you will meet is more important in foreign countries. Nothing beats having one another in view. Stick together. If you can't stay nearby, remain in close touch and have a person responsible for frequently checking on everyone. Have one person who is responsible for gathering up your group to leave. Have a designated driver. Never go anywhere that you don't have transport to leave. Always have cash for a taxi or Uber. We can't say this too much: Never leave with strangers. Don't put yourself in an out-of-view position where you could be physically abducted. Again, if you don't think they will call you back tomorrow—you have not lost anything by not going with them tonight. You want to be safe from kidnapping and to keep your kidneys. You can get an app that will start audio and video recording and alert designated guardians. Never accept an open drink. It could be drugged.

If you find your friends have become too intoxicated and left you in a vulnerable situation, don't panic. Be devious and cunning about how to escape to someone who can help. Do not trust anything you are told by a potential perpetrator, even if you want to believe it.

In a closed compound, there is competition for beach chairs. Early risers may gobble up what palatable food is on the buffet. Appoint the earliest riser in your group to reserve things.

If you are in a compound that has security, it is there because of perceived risk. Don't assume that you know the nature of what you don't know. Ask about what would be involved before you take an excursion.

THINGS TO DO BEFORE YOU GO Before you leave the country, tell your credit card company where you will be going, so they don't turn down your card. Tell others at home where you will be and provide phone numbers. Look at the US Embassy website for information about where you are going. There will be information about needed immunizations, about social unrest, about areas deemed unsafe for tourists, and about health risks. Even in the US, local people may not be excited about having large numbers of young people when past groups have caused property damage.

Do not telegraph where you are and where you aren't by discussing it on social media. The friends of your friends may be people who are not above taking things when they are sure you won't be there. Thieves are aware of holidays and are online looking for opportunities. Even if losing your computer is not financially crippling, it could cost you valuable time and data.

Buy a money belt to reduce your chance of having your pocket picked. Consider using the hotel safe.

UNEXPECTED EVENTS Plan in such a way that you do not have to leave an affair with someone who has been drinking. Have a designated driver if you intend to drink. If you are in a different country, you cannot assume that medical care, legal process, laws, law enforcement systems, incarceration, and human rights are the same. Legal problems have a way of following you home and complicating job prospects. Try not to be in the wrong place at the wrong time. You may be found guilty by association.

You could be surprised when you develop heat exhaustion, dehydration, and pass out from drinking alcohol while on the beach or in a pool or hot tub. Read about more possible surprises at https://www.aquatechutah.com/hot-tub-tips/never-mix-hot-tubs-and-alcohol/

DEALING WITH SOCIAL MEDIA

We can't remind you enough that employers, grad schools, and future social contacts all can potentially see the posted images of what you are doing and read that inappropriate snarky post with the bad grammar and misspelled words. Your life is substantially transparent. Unless you have just emerged from a cave, you already know about Internet privacy, the questionable legitimacy of what you read, and controversies about the importance of image.

Viewing social media leads to comparing your life to the optimally represented lives of others and experiencing lowered self-esteem. We don't have to tell you to be suspicious of the lives people craft online because they are often misrepresentations.

The Internet can be like a carnival's house-of-mirrors. Imagine that you have an accurate mental picture of how you look. Then, you go into the house-of-mirrors and stand in front of a mirror that distorts your image, so you look fat. With an accurate self-view, it may be easier to choose not to accept that image of yourself. You can remind yourself that you are not overweight, and this mirror is distorting you.

On the other hand, if you were unsure of how you looked, you might see this mirror as confirming that you are fat. Having Internet or real-life associates that reflect a distorted image of you because of their prejudice, malice, or envy is like continually having to look into the distorting funhouse mirror.

Take time to examine your beliefs about yourself, so you are less affected by others' distortions of you. Examine the opinions you now hold about yourself that are limiting or are inaccurate and push yourself to discover contrary evidence.

There is a subtle double-message involved in name-calling. When a bully says that you are weak, they are asking you to agree to two assumptions. One assumption is that you are weaker than they are. The less obvious assumption is that you are an unchanging entity and cannot change to become strong. Of the two assumptions, the second is more limiting over time. Don't buy into either one. Some bullies are thrown off their guard when they hear you calmly and respectfully express that you feel sorry for them as you walk away from the discussion.

Bullies are destructive another way. Their hateful behavior can make us hate them. It is another way to take our power by trapping us in a dysfunctional relationship. If we can work our way to being able to forgive them, it unbinds us.

Here is a link about cyberbullying, in case you want to know even more or need help: https://us.ditchthelabel.org/get-help/

Rebecca Lee has written a helpful article explaining digital self-harm and its treatment: https://psychcentral.com/lib/what-is-digital-self-harm/

Here is a link about Internet addiction: https://www.ncbi.nlm.nih.gov/pmc/articles/PMC3480687/

This site discusses some of the studies done examining how Internet pornography affects your brain: https://www.yourbrainonporn.com

You don't have to be on social media to get in trouble with what you say. You may not be able to avoid seeing the same students repeatedly in your major classes—so don't mess up your nest. Also, college students are closely connected. If you have a nasty break-up with someone in a Greek letter organization, it would not be unreasonable to assume that other members of that organization may be frowned on if they remain your friends.

WORKING WITH SYSTEMS

Your college or university is a system. Systems are imperfect because people are imperfect. There is no guarantee they will work in an orderly fashion. When you request something of the system, plan for delays and expect to have to persist multiple times with your application. Prepare to explain patiently in detail, sometimes repeatedly, why you want what you want and what alternatives you have already tried. You may have to educate the other person. Don't wait a long time for something to happen; go back to see if someone has dropped the ball. Remind yourself that this is good practice for postgraduate life.

Upper-level students, since they may need specific courses to graduate on time, go ahead of first-year students.

You may be dealing with college employees who are caught in the middle. They may be between you and the rest of a system that may have different priorities. Clark Kerr, a past-president of the University of California, said, "The university is a series of individual entrepreneurs held together by a common grievance about parking." You can't know whether your campus is involved in power politics where people hold long-standing grudges from past hurts, are cleverly ambitious, have secret alliances, and enjoy wielding power. Please show some kindness and patience to the people who have their ability to help you compromised by the system. Pawns have feelings too.

Next: Strategy 8—Adapt your outlook for the adversities ahead

8

Constructing Effective MindSets

UNDERSTANDING THE IMPORTANCE OF MINDSETS

In his book, *State of Mind 2.0: 11 Lessons of the Most Productive People on the Planet*, Christopher A. Pinckley stresses the importance of setting goals as part of your mindset. He suggests you use your imagination to discover what you are passionate about, are good at, and value (Pinckley 2016).

George Hutton, in *Frame Control: Subconscious Conversational Dominance*, said: "the stronger the idea is in your mind of what you want, the easier it will be to stay on course (Hutton 2015)."

One of our book's developmental editors, Tony Imbesi, put it best when he said, "Once you've decided on a meaningful goal for yourself, you may find the burdens of its difficulty lightened by your passion."

College is hard work and can be frustrating. Knowing the rewards that come from meeting your goals can motivate you to persist in following your life's work. That means you need to figure out your major as soon as you can.

Figuring out your major means having a general idea of what you want to do for a career. There is more about this topic in the resource appendix. We want to mention two resources here. Steppingblocks (https://www.steppingblocks.com/) can be used as a digital career counselor to help you pick a career and a resultant major. On the website *Wait But Why*— in his article *How to Pick a Career (That Actually Fits You)*—Tim Urban offers a thoughtful discussion of career choice and works you through the path toward finding a career that reflects both you and your current realities. https://waitbutwhy.com/2018/04/picking-career.html

Some music majors must take courses in their major all four years to finish on time. It is essential that you determine whether you have chosen a major like this. If you aren't interested in one of those majors, you may have the option of taking the required core courses first. By doing that, you will buy time to decide without wasting effort on courses that won't count to your major.

Don't make the mistake of thinking that knowing your major will just come to you suddenly if you wait patiently. Don't assume that the careers you hear most about are ones you would like or easily be able to do. Not only are new careers being created all the time, but old ones are also disappearing due to technology. Realize you have considerable work to do to gather enough data to make a wise decision about what you want to do for a living. Please don't wait for it to come to you, go to it. Actively seek out the information you need to help make a decision. Talk to students and professors in various majors, search the Internet, go to the career center, and take some vocational tests like the one at http://www.self-directed-search.com/. While you are brooding on all this data, make some daily quiet time to reflect and find inspiration.

If you feel like you have been floating along thinking that one day it will come together for you, you may be accumulating debt while you wait for an answer. Check to see if you are meeting your career milestones. Arizona State University's Career and Professional Development Services has an excellent description of career milestones for students to reference. https://eoss.asu.edu/cs/students/career-milestones

When you can envision your goals, then it is possible to consider behaviors, activities, and friends in relation to how they help or hurt your goals. Experiences become opportunities to learn things that further your goal or chances to see what does not. You might experience being a volunteer, getting involved in a registered student organization, or having a part-time job. How you see things can be shaped by what you expect to see or what you are attending to, based on your broader view of the world and yourself. If you think positively, you will be less likely to view things as problems rather than opportunities. You will be more willing to look for the silver lining in the cloud. You will also see how self-control is not deprivation, but a means to reach your goal. Your goal is not just a goal; it can be a sense of purpose and meaning.

Being in college does not mean you automatically get good grades; it means you have the opportunity to succeed and make good grades. You must do what it takes to earn them yourself or risk having to drop out. You can make college easier by having a plan, by having detailed knowledge of the land mines, by knowing your strengths and weaknesses, by avoiding troublesome situations, by prioritizing, by having a <u>sense of purpose</u> and by recognizing your failings and asking for help.

It is essential to stop and think about the things that you might be doing that could eventually derail you. You can make college easier— by being careful about <u>not doing</u> things that make it more difficult.

All this, including the ability to have patience, takes self-control. Kelly McGonigal, PhD., in her book *The Willpower Instinct*, notes, "Self-control is a better predictor of academic success than intelligence... (McGonigal 2012 p 12)." She notes, "Self-control is like a muscle. It gets tired from use, but regular exercise makes it stronger (ibid p80)." That makes it important for you to be self-aware and avoid things that lower self-control like lack of sleep, stress, or low blood sugar (ibid, p 46-62).

Dr. McGonigal cites the 2007 APA study "Stress in America"(American Psychological Association 2007) as finding that "the most effective stress relievers are exercising or playing sports, praying or attending a religious service, reading, listening to music, spending time with friends or family, getting a massage, going outside for a walk, meditating or doing yoga, and spending time with a creative hobby (ibid p 137)." She notes that having self-compassion after making a mistake is helpful in maintaining self-control, but guilt and self-blame are not (ibid 137-151).

By lowering your stress, you improve your self-control. Dr. McGonigal writes, "What is the main difference between the strategies that work and the strategies that don't? Rather than releasing dopamine and relying on the promise of reward, the real stress relievers boost mood-enhancing brain chemicals like serotonin and GABA, as well as the feel-good hormone oxytocin. They also help shut down the brain's stress response, reduce stress hormones in the body, and induce the healing relaxation response (ibid, p 137-138)."

She states that "Slowing the breath down activates the prefrontal cortex and increases heart rate variability, which helps shift the brain and body from a state of stress to self-control mode. (ibid p 40)" We have found the *Breath Pacer* app, which she mentioned, to be very helpful in doing this. Another way to improve your willpower, Dr. McGonigal asserts, is to be around friends who have good willpower (ibid, p 192- 195).

USING A 'COLD HARD REALITIES' MINDSET FOR MOTIVATION

Besides being inspired by your goals and understanding how to use your willpower, it is essential to have a recognition of the realities in which you will be operating.

YOU MAY NOT LIKE COLLEGE. You could be surprised at how many students don't like college but don't feel like they can talk about it. It is okay not to like college. Many students don't like the lack of privacy, the lack of solitude, the hard work, the performance pressure, the peer pressure, the pretending, the drinking, ever-present roommates, and partying. They are tired of feeling like they must be abnormal if they are the only ones not ecstatic about their college experience.

You don't have to like or appreciate college to succeed at it. You do have to take it seriously, rather than accepting the popular notion that it is a playground to express your newfound freedom. A college education might still be necessary to achieve what you want. Remember, as you make efforts to make college work for you, you don't have to add to all the pressure by expecting yourself always to be happy there.

YOU MAY FIND COLLEGE ANXIETY-PRODUCING. It is normal to be nervous at the thought of facing new situations, but that does not mean you have made a mistake by going. It is possible to confront your fears and to learn how to cope with them. By planning for specific situations that you expect to make you nervous, you can increase your sense of being in control. By practicing, you learn the ways that work for you to distract yourself. You will discover if being active and doing vigorous exercise helps or you prefer something more soothing like a quiet walk or listening to music or using a meditation app. Remember that you may be coming to college alone, but eventually, you will make some friends and develop a support group. Then, you can enlist friends to game out the anxiety-producing situation in advance. You may find that taking a short nap or imagining yourself somewhere else in a calm place works for you. You can experiment with the alternative of focusing intensely on what you are doing right now in the present moment.

Doing the problem-solving work involved in managing your anxiety in college can take time. Discovering the bigger purposes in your going to college will help you persist at it. The opportunities to gradually develop your frustration and anxiety tolerance that college offers you is helpful in later life, where there is less of a safety net.

If you find yourself feeling worse despite your efforts, talk with your resident advisor about possibly seeing a counselor and getting evaluated. Going to college is like working in a car factory on the assembly line. You can't stop the car assembly line until you feel like yourself. The tests, projects, and papers keep coming. So, the sooner you seek help, the sooner you will get back to the assembly line before you get even farther behind and feel even more overwhelmed.

AS PART OF MASTERING COLLEGE, YOU HAVE TO MASTER YOURSELF, OR YOU WILL KEEP GETTING IN YOUR WAY. Someone said the real reason that no one keeps New Year's resolutions is that we don't want anyone telling us what to do- not even ourselves. That is one stumbling block to following anything you have been reading here.

"DATOM Disease" is another stumbling block to doing what you need to do. We are unsure who coined the phrase. DATOM stands for "Doesn't Apply to Me." That rules don't apply to you might have been made more believable if others have helped you get out of the consequences of your misconduct or made exceptions for you in the past. We suspect you have the human tendency not to let anyone tell you what to do. We suspect you possibly believe that rules don't apply to you.

Despite us suspecting this, we, like you, are human. We are now going to tell you some useful facts and practices all the same— because you can't tell us what to do either. Those rules about not handing out unasked-for advice—well, they simply don't apply to us. So—tongue-in-cheek—we give you the following advice.

YOU WILL GET LOST WITHOUT A MORAL COMPASS. As a small child, you thought it was okay to do things as long as you did not get caught. As you grew up, you incorporated things your parents, teachers, and society told you about *right* and *wrong*. Some things weren't accurate, and other items were said to you accurately, but you distorted because your ten-year-old mind didn't grasp it. For example, you may have seen everything in merciless black and white absolutes.

In college, you have opportunities to reexamine for yourself what is right and wrong. The personal ethics you develop by this repeated examination become your moral compass. Working on this will help you establish character that leads to a sense of wholeness. It makes sense that the word *integrity* is derived from the Latin word for wholeness. It is unlikely that you will experience personal wholeness without having integrity. Evidencing integrity leads to others coming to trust you and believe you are honest in what you say and do. Sometimes, to act morally means saying *no* to yourself.

When you say *no* to yourself as part of behaving morally, remember that the integrity you demonstrate is crucial to the trust on which genuine intimacy depends. For example, if you cheat on your partner, you endanger your partner's ability to feel emotionally safe enough and trusting enough to be emotionally close to you.

MANY THINGS AREN'T SIMPLE. It would seem like the world conspires to convince you that things should be simple. When you were a child, your parents tried to simplify complicated things to make them understandable. Your teachers did the same. Every day you find advertisers who want to make your choice of their item simple. Companies need your buying process to be straightforward and not get in the way of your impulse to buy their product. If you don't accept the simple, superficial explanation and take a more detailed look, you often find things are complicated. This recognition may lead to your making a different decision or have more tolerance.

YOU EXIST IN A FUNDAMENTALLY INDIFFERENT WORLD, BUT THAT DOES NOT NECESSARILY MAKE YOU ITS VICTIM. While the world is not out to get you, it does not have your back either. There are likely staff members on your campus who care about you and can help, but the responsibility is on you to seek them out. How you approach them may make a difference in their willingness to offer help, help which they likely are giving out of kindness and not out of obligation.

It may feel odd at first when you realize the average person around you does not know you and is benignly indifferent to you. This realization might be more shocking if you came from a small school environment or a religious school that emphasized caring about each other. It means you have to take care of yourself. Ordinary people do not feel obligated to take care of you— even if you feel entitled. The solution to this is to work at becoming competent living independently.

Fortunately, you don't have to do this all at once, but you do have to learn to ask for specific help from the college staff— like your resident advisor, teacher, counselor, coach, or student instructor. Go to your teacher's office hours, even if it is just to introduce yourself and make small talk. You might tell them your hometown, ask a question about the syllabus, or comment on something that was discussed in class. This information helps them put a face on your name and breaks the ice if you want to talk to them about something later. It enables you to see them as less impersonal and more approachable.

Other people have learned to become competent—and you can become competent too.

If you belong to a minority, you know that some —but not all— people and groups actively discriminate against you and are not merely blindly indifferent to you. You may feel like Dwayne Johnson did— that doors were closed to him, and he had to get through the cracks. Chris Rock said that it was not that minorities have progressed in their abilities, but that majorities have made progress in being able to recognize the abilities that were always there. Unfortunately— because some of the people belonging to these majorities have a long way to go in understanding and practice— as a member of a minority, you sometimes have to be much better than the majority in any area to be recognized. Even then, there is no guarantee. That this injustice remains an unfortunate reality means you still <u>must</u> work harder than is fair.

YOU MAY BELIEVE THAT YOU HAVE A FIXED AMOUNT OF ABILITY AND INTELLIGENCE, BUT THE TRUTH IS THAT YOUR MIND GROWS AS YOU LEARN. What we think and how it affects what we do is predictive of the outcome. Effort changes the brain because it forms new connections. You are the one in control of that. (See chapter 12 for more on the fixed and growth mindsets.)

In *Mindset: The New Psychology of Success,* Carol S. Dweck, Ph.D., discusses how people believing that their abilities can be developed and are not fixed are more likely to succeed. In her book, she introduces the idea of a false growth mindset. This book is well worth your time to read.

In chapter 10, you will find a more detailed discussion of the crucial importance of having a growth mindset, and how it has a bearing on self-efficacy, your ability to believe you can succeed at tasks.

DON'T LET ANYONE TELL YOU THAT BECAUSE OF YOUR GENDER, RACE, OR NATIONALITY THAT YOU CANNOT LEARN SOMETHING. For example, you may remember from the movie *Hidden Figures,* about Katherine Johnson, Mary Jackson, and Dorothy Vaughan. They fought through discrimination to do the complicated math calculations for rocket trajectories in the early days of our country's space program.

> *The most difficult thing—the most difficult walls or obstacles I have ever approached— is my own limited perception of myself. So, I have the power. I'm not giving the power to the man, the woman, society. I have the power of how I can interpret the information coming to me.*
>
> –RuPaul on the Alex Baldwin Show 2018

COLLEGE IS STILL HARD FOR MOST PEOPLE. In general, better-paying jobs require harder academic work. They pay more because fewer people are willing to do what it takes. The scarcity of skilled employees means employers have to compete for a smaller pool and pay more to get them.

Regardless of how excellent your teachers may be, some subjects are just intrinsically hard. Many ideas are intricate, detailed, and hard to comprehend. What makes this so shocking is that media, news, advertising, and entertainment organizations work day and night to make things as simple and easy as possible. Think about how easy it is to buy something with one click or how news is reduced to simple sound bites. Ideas have to be reduced to a few characters and catch your eye in seconds. It can feel like there is something wrong in the natural order of things if something is too hard. It feels almost like it was a natural law that things should be easy and quick.

We hope you have incrementally learned to tolerate more frustration as your parents matched what you could handle at a particular age to what they expected of you. Otherwise, learning frustration tolerance now will be, well, frustrating—okay, very frustrating. So, keep your eye on the prize. Imagine that you already have that great job. Ask yourself, "Would I be willing to lose it to party tonight when studying at this crucial time would lead to me keeping it?"

YOU ARE GOING TO MAKE MISTAKES AND FAIL AT THINGS— BOTH ACADEMIC AND OTHERWISE. In a Harvard University Commencement Address on June 5, 2008, J.K. Rowling said, "It is impossible to live without failing at something unless you live so cautiously that you might as well not have lived at all — in which case, you fail by default." You may find the inspiring video of her address, identified thanks to Wikiquote.org, at Vimeo's website: http://vimeo.com/1711302.

Neuroscientists tell us that our brains are not fully capable of showing mercy until our late twenties. So much of life is about learning through trial and error. Practice does make us better at things. When you fail, try to have mercy on yourself.

If you sense your unmerciful peers are too judgmental, think of what Theodore Roosevelt said about critics: "It is not the critic who counts… The credit belongs to the man who is actually in the arena; whose face is marred by dust and sweat and blood; who, at worst, if he fails, at least fails while daring greatly; so that his place shall never be with those cold and timid souls who know neither victory or defeat." (Roosevelt 1910)

Nikki Giovanni said, "Mistakes are a fact of life. It is the response to the error that counts." (Goodreads 2012) When you fail, please don't make the mistake of seeing your circumstances as never changing or spreading into all of your life. Think about how you can reframe the situation in a way that you can adjust to what has happened. Put the situation into a bigger picture to begin recovering from it.

(If you are wondering what mistakes are most likely to sandbag you in college, you might want to take a peek at A-5 in the Resource Appendix)

ASK YOURSELF HOW YOUR ACTIONS, BOTH POSITIVE AND NEGATIVE, AFFECT OTHERS AND YOU. It is critical that you check your temper and avoid getting a reputation. Walk away from an argument if you feel you might lose control, or it is not a good time. There is especially no point in arguing with people who are "blackout" level drunk. These people are in a pre-anesthetic state and will not remember most or anything of what you say to them. (That includes saying "no" to their unwanted sexual behavior. Don't waste time doing that when you could use that time to be escaping.)

> *It's not an easy journey to get to a place where you forgive people. But it is such a powerful place because it frees you.*
> (Tyler Perry 2010)
> https://www.telegraph.co.uk/culture/film/7956763/Interview-Tyler-Perry-movie-mogul.html

If you understand how freed up forgiving others can be for you, you will likely consider making forgiving others your default position. If you have to battle, pick your battles. Don't be always looking for small slights or minor injustices. Unfailingly, there are petty injustices to collect, and it is often wasteful of time and focus. Remembering your own frailty helps you forgive the human frailty in others.

If you have been traumatized by others, you can improve your resilience by learning to look at the situation from different angles, accepting things that you cannot control, and focusing on recovery. Dr. Dennis Charney, Professor of Psychiatry and Dean of the Icahn School of Medicine, said: "One can reframe, assimilate, accept, and recover (Charney 2019)." By working at being flexible in your thinking, you will be better able to put things behind you to concentrate on your studies.

Remember that, as long as it is not compromising your integrity, there are things with which you can go along without feeling like you are giving in. For example, you can go along with the group's choice of picking a restaurant.

It is possible to stand up for you without bullying. Don't bully. If you have been bullied yourself and feel compelled to intimidate others, you need help. Felicia T. Scott, from her own experience as a bully, offers her helpful thoughts at https://www.essence.com/celebrity/help-bully-four-tips-end-your-bullying-ways/

LEARN TO SET LIMITS ON YOURSELF AND OTHERS WHO WANT YOU TO REGRESS WITH THEM. Imagine for a minute what it would be like if the financial house of cards made up of loans, scholarships, and financially willing family were to collapse because of your regressed behavior. What would you lose, and what would your life be like after that? Don't let the impulses fed from your present emotional state lead to shortsighted decisions. Don't waste time always trying to confirm your worth in the eyes of others. Focus on your goals instead. Keep working at being true to your values.

YOU NEVER WIN AT BEING PERFECT, AND IT COSTS SLEEP, TIME, RELATIONSHIPS, AND JOY. Our society may allow you to admit your mistakes, but it wants you to learn from those mistakes to become perfect. Society makes situations worse by rewarding perfectionism, but— if perfectionism is too big of a problem— please get some help. Try to learn the difference between the situations you have control over and the ones you don't and let yourself have some peace with it. Realize that "just muddling through things" is a life skill and an even bigger life skill is knowing when to let yourself muddle.

LUCK IS NOT A STRATEGY. Believing a combination of luck, intelligence, and finesse will work in this academic environment is short-sighted.

BECAUSE YOU GET AWAY WITH BREAKING THE LAW A FEW TIMES DOESN'T MEAN THAT YOU CAN COUNT ON NEVER GETTING CAUGHT —BECAUSE LAW ENFORCEMENT IS STILL IN TOWN. If you violate the law, don't rely on law enforcement or the court system being sympathetic or seeing things your way. Don't count on having the luck talking your way out of things that you might have had with your family. Remember that your ignorance of the law is no legal excuse. The best way to avoid potential injustice is not to break the law, not to give the appearance of lawbreaking, and not to be around people who do. You don't want to be at the wrong place at the wrong time. If you're going to be a teacher, you may not be allowed a teaching certificate if you have a felony on your record. Remember that your friends might have in their possession drugs or weapons unknown to you.

REALIZE YOU LIVE IN A COMPETITIVE WORLD WHERE OTHERS, SOMETIMES WITH FEWER RESOURCES THAN YOU, ARE WILLING TO WORK VERY HARD TO GET AHEAD. Enduring personal adversities may have forged in them an indomitable will and persistence that has not been required of you yet. These competitors may be as close as your roommate or halfway around the world.

There are many countries with worthy competitors, but we would like to use China as one example. In 2017 it was roughly estimated (in millions) that there were 325.7 people in the USA compared with 1,409.5 (in millions) people in China. The top 1 percent of the brightest people in the USA amounts to 3.257 million people. The top 1 percent of the most intelligent people in China amounts to 14.095 million people. For every one person in the US top 1 percent, China has 4.33 people in their top 1 percent. So, not only does China have more people, but China may have more smart people as well. Imagine what that will mean in your lifetime. The flip side is that learning Mandarin Chinese now might give you an advantage one day.

IF YOU BELONG TO A MINORITY, YOU ALREADY KNOW THAT YOU COULD STILL GET PULLED OVER FOR NO REASON Remember, if you are pulled over while driving, keep both your hands visible on the steering wheel. Comply with the officers' requests as soon as they make them. Ask permission to make any moves to get your license and registration. Explain everything you are going to do before you <u>slowly</u> do it. Make sure you are clearly understood before you do anything. Stay calm and be polite and respectful. It may help you to remember that many officers are human beings who, out of a wish to protect their community, willingly put themselves at risk of being killed and so are already wary as they approach your vehicle. Officers may be trying their best in a situation in which they do not feel as experienced or as well trained as they would like to be. Use a tone of voice that helps put the officer at ease and reflects that you are at ease, even if you are not. It may feel unfair that you have to do all this, but it may save your life. Check out this advice with your family and see what they add to it.

USING A BRAIN-CENTERED MINDSET IN YOUR ACADEMICS

NURTURE YOUR BRAIN Think of yourself as a brain that studies. Your brain is the axe that you need to sharpen. It is your study instrument. You want to do everything you can to have an effective studying brain. You have already read that your brain works better with enough sleep, the right foods, some sunshine, and a daily routine. Right living helps you think rightly. A sober brain is a better brain. Developing healthy habits may take six weeks to feel consolidated—but it is worth the effort. In the long run, it is easier than taking the path of least resistance. Choosing the way of least resistance wastes time spent in self-loathing.

REDUCE DISTRACTING STRESS. Your brain also works better when it is less distracted by stress and anxiety. As part of being a competent, independent person, you will want to develop connections to others who can provide support when fitting. Friends, family, coworkers, classmates, counselors, teachers are all potential members of a support system. The security of knowing they are available can even make you feel confident enough not to need to use them.

Maggie Jackson, the author of *Distracted*, writes about her concern those very connections may be threatened by our digital habits, in her chapter "McThinking and the Future of the Past".

> *Smitten with the virtual, split-split, and nomadic, are we corroding the three pillars of our attention: focus(orienting), judgment (executive function), and awareness (alerting). The costs are steep: we begin to lose trust, depth, and connection in our relations and our thought.*
>
> —Maggie Jackson 2008

Reflexively using your cell phone or computer has far-reaching consequences.

FIND A MENTOR Some of the more successful people in school have taken the time to find a mentor. A mentor is someone off whom they can bounce ideas, from whose experience they can benefit, and on whose strength they can draw. Such a mentor might be a high school coach, your favorite English teacher, your aunt, your friend's mother, a teacher researching your field of interest, or someone in your home community who does what you want to do. If you are in high school as you read this, consider talking with them about this idea before you go off to college. If you are a woman interested in STEM you might be interested in Million Women Mentors, go to https://www.stemconnector.com/services_offered/million-women-mentors/

> *But you can't sit around waiting for a mentor to find you. You have to search for them, and that may mean looking beyond your immediate department or area.*
> –Kate White, 2013

KNOW THE DOWNTIMES There are some occasions when you might not want to count on your brain to be its best. For example, if you have had to make numerous small decisions, your judgment may not be as sound as if you were fresh.

Pretend you are riding in a car and listening to a story on MP3of a young woman in a blue dress walking downstairs. The part of your brain that is imagining that is the same part that is looking at the road. So, you don't drive as well.

There are differences of opinion about the disadvantages of multi-tasking. You may also be aware that researchers believe there is a difference in how the brain learns things it reads in digital media as opposed to print media.

Sometimes you get so obsessed with a problem that you overthink it. You get stuck inside *yesterday*. When you notice that you are experiencing a block, take a break. Sit back, and try to be more on a receiving mode rather than a producing one. See what comes after you have quieted your mind. Try listening to *Weightless* by Marconi Union. https://www.youtube.com/watch?v=UfcAVejslrU

Check to see if you are taking medication—even over-the-counter ones—that impair memory. Marijuana can significantly reduce your memory also.

It is also useful to see yourself as a growing brain that does not have fully developed frontal lobe function. Knowing this allows you to compensate for this lack of full development. Since this part of the brain is involved with planning, you might want to use more planning aids— like wall calendars, phone calendars, or organizers.

Since the frontal lobe is involved with frustration tolerance and impulse control, you could work to enhance the factors that help with controlling your impulses. By doing that, you will avoid setting yourself up to lose your impulse control. Alcoholics Anonymous uses the acronym HALT to describe situations that lower self-control. HALT stands for Hungry, Angry, Lonely, Tired. AA stresses planning, so you don't get in those states. Since members of AA are recovering, they did not include drinking, which is well known to lead to disinhibition and sometimes sexual assault.

KNOW THE TRICKS. On the other hand, try not to make big decisions without sleeping on them. Your sleeping brain is capable of more complex thought. Many people ask their brains to solve a particular problem as they are going to sleep.

Decisions that we make have multiple determinants. Some of those determinants are outside of our conscious awareness. You have an unconscious brain that listens to what you tell it and apparently does not have a way of checking on the accuracy of the data. So, be careful what you tell yourself, especially if you tend automatically to put yourself down without thinking twice about it.

When we write out a spelling word, a set of nerve cells (neurons) fire off. When we write it ten times, then that sequence of neurons has fired off ten times. When neurons fire off together, they wire together. That makes it easier for them to work. Then you find it easier to remember your spelling word. We offer this oversimplification to explain why repeated or practiced behaviors are more likely to occur. Repeatedly pitching a baseball makes it easier to throw, but so does frequently eating forbidden ice cream makes it easier to eat more the next time.

When you start college or come back each year, in some respects, your slate is clean. Wouldn't it be simpler at that time to use this wiring/firing thing to deliberately set up good habits that become easier to do over time?

As a college student who is trying to learn to think for yourself, you are always assessing risks. You are taking a calculated risk that you will be able to pay off your student loan or that you eventually can learn the right things to get an adequate job after graduation. You are risking that you can predict what your professor will put on the test. Just as you cannot live without failing, you cannot live without taking risks. Relax. You will get better at assessing risks as time goes on.

One risk you will be taking is whether you have matched your career interests with your abilities and life situation. Your brain grows as it learns. Your financial limits, however, may not change. As you assess which career to risk your time and money on pursuing, the more data you can collect, the better your assessment will be. Consider what is realistically required financially, academically, and physically. Ask if it is worth your investment in time. Then, decide what you can do.

You remember things better when they have a limbic valence. That is a fancy way of saying that you remember things better when they have an emotional association for you. For example, your roommate asks you to bring home milk. You like milk. So, you agree. You forget it. The next morning there is no milk for your or your irate roommate's cereal. The next time your roommate asks you to bring home milk, you now have an emotional attachment to the idea, and it is easier for you to remember.

If you are studying something and can pin a limbic valence on it, you will be able to remember it better. For example, a nursing student studying high blood pressure would try to associate what she is learning with how it might affect her dad, who has high blood pressure.

You will remember things better if you have had enough sleep and exercise, are not smoking marijuana, are at a healthy weight, aren't eating too many foods high in refined carbohydrates and sugar, and have a normal vitamin D level. Joshua Foer's book, *Moonwalking with Einstein: The Art and Science of Remembering* has more specifics about memory.

Try to build frustration tolerance little by little as you try to last longer at doing frustrating tasks. Imagine how you will swell with pride, knowing that you have been able to avoid making sarcastic comments about your roommate for now up to twenty minutes.

Find friends that will help reinforce your good habits because they do the same things already. Add structure and boundaries to your life to help strengthen your good habits. For example, brush and floss your teeth early each night so you will be less tempted to eat a late-night snack.

Realize that confidence correlates with success. Work on things that build your confidence, one of which is knowing you are competent.

THINK CRITICALLY. Colleges like to stress the importance of critical thinking. Your brain learns to entertain thoughts critically without accepting them at face value. This article is a good start on understanding what critical thinking is: https://collegeinfogeek.com/improve-critical-thinking-skills/

Constructing Effective MindSets

Homicide detectives use critical thinking when they develop a working theory about a murder. They ask themselves about the reliability of the historical data the suspects have given them. They are critical of the explanations the suspects offer and look for inconsistent data. They make observations about how the suspects acted in the interrogation. They look at the objective findings of the autopsy report of the victim's stomach contents and deduce the victim couldn't have eaten when a suspect said they did. They deliberately use their reasoning to make connections between the subjective information the suspects give them and the objective findings of the autopsy. They try to draw logical conclusions from the data they have and evaluate all the information critically. The end of this careful process is that we have a more accurate working theory about the murder.

You will be asked to write essays and to answer essay questions on tests. Then, you will use critical thinking to apply the ideas you have learned from your study during the course.

Chip Heath and Dan Heath in their cutting-edge book, *Decisive: How to Make Better Choices in Your Life and Work*, also talk about the nature of critical thinking in the decision-making process. In making decisions, they suggest you use the *WRAP* process: *W*iden your options. *R*eality Test your assumptions. *A*ttain distance before deciding and *P*repare to be Wrong.

(W) They discuss how thinking of a decision as "either-or" narrows the decision-making process when you should be looking at more options. (R) They note that asking yourself disconfirming questions helps with reality testing them. (A) Sometimes consulting others who have solved your situation can be helpful. In your case, that could be a mentor or an upperclassman. They note the importance of knowing and referring to your core priorities as you make decisions. (P) They ask you to be vigilant about whether your choice is turning out to be correct. (Heath 2013 Chapter 1)

Chip and Dan Heath also suggest you set up the equivalent of a "tripwire" to go off if your decision begins to look wrong. For example, you decide to stay with your partner despite their seemingly always staring at other eligible partners. When you "accidentally" see one of those people's names on your partner's phone the following week, your tripwire goes off, and you reconsider your original decision. (Ibid 2013 Chapter 11)

BE CURIOUS. When it comes to an academic mindset, this is key— <u>Don't just study for the test</u>. Be curious about the subject. Try to have an orientation of being curious about everything. The point is to learn something, not just get a grade from some test scores. Imagine yourself as part of generations of humankind who seek truth and learn from those before them. This attitude may help you as you move out of your comfort zone to confront the uncertainty of the unknown and transform your life. See college as a challenge and your mistakes as opportunities to learn. In that way, you may grow in wisdom as well as knowledge.

REMEMBER TO USE MINDFULNESS Being mindful helps you with your resilience and keeps your priorities in order. As was mentioned in chapter 3, mindfulness can pull you back to what you are doing and refresh a mind worn with worry.

Next: Strategy 9/10—Sharpen the needed skills.

9
Tweaking your Academic Skillset

FINDING POTENTIAL HELPERS

Being self-reliant does not mean refusing needed help. As Michelle Obama said, "everyone at one time or the other needs help." (Obama, Michelle unknown date)

Colleges know this. Colleges usually have resources to help you with studying or career planning, but they assume you will seek them out. There are a finite number of available resources. There may be a flood of demand for them at peak times during the semester, such as before midterms. Make appointments. Avoid the crowds by going early. Ask for academic help as soon as you feel you need it. If you know, going into the class, that you need some accommodation or have neurological vulnerabilities, consider scheduling a meeting with your professor, the counseling office, or the disability office before the first day of class. Bring a nonparent advocate with you.

Some states have laws that specify a particular battery of psychoeducational tests to determine if a student requires legally required educational accommodations. If your state has such laws, you will need to find the centers that offer these tests and schedule them early. Avoid the crowd of students who find out about this only after seeking help after getting failing mid-semester grades. Your campus disabilities office may be able to help you with this and let you know if there are any sources of funding to help you pay for the testing. Expensive though it is, testing may be much cheaper than losing your scholarship because you have attention deficit hyperactivity disorder or another learning problem that makes it hard for you to study.

Look to see if study groups are forming in your class that you can join. If not, consider starting one.

Many colleges require their professors to post office hours where you can drop by and ask questions. Go! Going will open the door for you to get to know your professor. By visiting with your professor and asking questions, you show interest in their subject. Don't abuse the privilege by going all the time. You may risk coming across as lazy if the questions you ask can quickly be answered elsewhere, like by reading the syllabus or going online. Because your professors expect you to act like a responsible adult, they count on you to seek their help if you need something explained or need their help in finding a tutor.

Don't overlook upper-class students in organizations to which you belong. They may have just taken the course. They can help you get insight into how your professor approaches the material, what the professor values in it, and what surprises to expect.

DISCOVERING HELPFUL APPLICATIONS AND WEBSITES

You will develop independence and self-confidence as you acquire grammar skills, improve your vocabulary, and sharpen your math abilities. As you know, you can augment your efforts by using apps.

Some college professors enhance their courses through digital learning environments, like Pearson Higher Education's *Revel* app, which offers your teacher ways to enrich your learning experience while providing you the portability to use it on multiple devices. If you are not already familiar with this approach from your high school classes, go to https://www.pearsonhighered.com/revel/index.html Your professor will give you a link if your course uses it.

Tweaking your Academic Skillset

Remember that Steppingblocks (https://www.steppingblocks.com/) can be used as a digital career counselor and is discussed in the chapter entitled 'Deciding Whether to go to College' in the appendix.

When a primary source ostensibly malevolently obfuscates the cardinal tenet of its treatise via vocabulary alien to you or through wantonly esoteric pedantic language, it is tempting to try to understand it in context and not look the words up. Don't.

When you find a word you don't know, go to a dictionary app on your phone or use a more comprehensive dictionary in print where you study. Google it. You never know for sure the nature of the thing you don't know that people have written or said in class.

In addition to the thesaurus and spell checker in Word or Google Docs, there are thesaurus apps for your phone. You may not be allowed to use *Grammarly* or other grammar tools in your academic work—but using *Grammarly* exclusively on your emails will help you improve your grammar as you find yourself correcting your daily emails. There are software programs for you to scan your papers for plagiarism, the same ones your professor may use to check on you.

We don't have to tell you that there are also apps for particular college subjects, a graphing calculator app, language apps, flashcard apps (like Quizlet), math apps like Mathway, Microsoft Word, apps on writing papers, time management apps, and educational apps like Kahn Academy:

https://play.google.com/store/search?q=educational%20apps%20for%20college%20students&c=apps&hl=en

There are several app stores from which to choose. A few others are the Apple App Store, Slideme, Amazon App store, 1 Mobile Market, and the Samsung Galaxy Apps. You may find some other apps on these platforms.

If you are in the school of nursing, you may want to link to this website that details ten useful nursing apps. https://www.capella.

edu/blogs/cublog/10-apps-for-nurses-in-online-nursing-programs/

You can use Google's Wunderlist To-Do List & Tasks to stay organized, make to-do lists, make grocery lists, track projects, and collaborate. https://www.microsoft.com/en-us/p/wunderlist-to-do-list-tasks/9wzdncrdfxzs The play store lists other organizing apps as well.

GETTING AT THE MECHANICS

The more adept you are at using the features of Microsoft Word or a similar word processing program, the smoother paper writing will be. If you think you are getting "text neck," you might want to buy an ALEX N5 Posture Tracker & Coach at https://alexposture.com/. If you find yourself having wrist pain, you might consider getting an ergonomic keyboard and examining your chair and monitor positions. If you are experiencing eye discomfort, get into the habit of reminding yourself to blink, and readjusting your screen brightness and font size. Look for sources of glare. Don't make your eyes look through dirty lenses at a dusty screen.

Make sure you have your computer set to backup often. Consider buying a separate backup drive or using a backup program—like Carbonite. Losing your work on a paper at the last minute can be hard. You might write documents on Google Docs or Microsoft OneDrive to get around crashes. Having a computer crash can almost sink a semester. In an emergency, if your old computer starts to act up and you fear a crash—and you don't have an external hard drive backup—you can put your paper in a zip file and email it from your school account to your personal account as an attachment. You could also buy an inexpensive flash/USB or thumb drive to save your files for each semester. Some schools will rent you a laptop if yours crashes.

You will be taking online courses at times that require a computer with specific capabilities to use the software program associated with the class. Ideally, it would help if you asked about this before you buy your computer. When you consider all the time you will spend on the computer, you will probably want to get a laptop with the fastest processing speed and the most memory you can reasonably afford.

If you would like to brush up on your Microsoft Office skills and more, you might try GCFLLearnFree. According to the Goodwill Community Foundation Global website, "For almost 20 years, the GCFLearnFree.org program has helped millions around the world learn the essential skills they need to live and work in the 21st century. From Microsoft Office and email, to reading, math, and more—GCFLearnFree.org offers more than 200 topics, including more than 7,000 lessons, more than 1,000 videos, and more than 50 interactives and games, completely free." https://edu.gcfglobal.org/en/.

If you see yourself using a backpack for all four years, it might be worth buying one with your back and shoulders in mind. You might also consider one with wheels. Best Buy, Walmart, and Amazon offer backpacks. These two sites identify backpack features that minimize back pain:

http://outdoorkeeper.com/best-backpacks-for-back-pain-and-shoulder-pain/

http://nymag.com/strategistarticle/best-backpacks-students-and-back-pain-2017.html

BUYING TEXTBOOKS

Buy textbooks in time for the first class. The college bookstore should have the required books and supplies listed on their website for every course by professor. The course syllabus will also identify the textbook. Think about whether you need the textbook for future use. Some texts might be useful to keep, say a math book if you are taking more math since math builds on itself. If you don't want an e-book and you are quick enough, you might find that some college libraries have textbooks for current courses. You may ask your professor if you could use a cheaper, older edition of the same textbook. Your professor might give you the names of students who have just taken the course who would be happy to sell you their old text.

You may save money by renting an e-textbook, but it expires after a specific time. It could be a problem if you are taking a two-semester course. Let's say you fail Spanish 1 first semester and pass it second semester. Your Spanish 1-2 e-book will expire at the end of the second semester, and you will have to repurchase it before you can take Spanish 2.

Several sellers will buy back your used college textbooks. As a buyer or seller, you need to beware. USA Today discusses several vendors at http://college.usatoday.com/2016/05/06/4-places-to-sell-back-your-books-at-the-end-of-the-semester/ . Another seller is at https://www.sellbackyourbook.com/

MAKING THE MOST OF THE CLASSROOM EXPERIENCE

In high school, your teacher may have spent classroom time teaching you the new material. In college, the teacher may expect you to learn the new content outside class. The teacher then uses the classroom experience to have classroom discussions of the learned material. They expand on it with other new materials. They may even relish the clash of ideas that comes from class discussion. Your professor likely expects you to read the assigned content before the lecture.

Some professors base their tests on their class lectures. That makes it particularly important to go to class and take good notes.

Tweaking your Academic Skillset

From their experience in their field and their expertise, they may feel they have a better idea of what is essential to know. You are more likely to be tested on that critical information.

Sometimes you cannot tell from the material itself what is most important to know, because the textbook covers everything. A nursing textbook may devote as much time discussing Schnitzler Syndrome as they do high blood pressure. Your professor knows that you will see patients with hypertension frequently and may seldom see someone with Schnitzler Syndrome. Pay attention to what your professor emphasizes as most relevant.

Some professors will spend a few minutes in the last class before a test discussing in a general way what areas they are emphasizing on the test.

Pick a place in the class where you can best see and hear the professor but aren't so close you frequently get singled out to participate. Avoid having to look at other students using their laptops by sitting where they can be seen only out of the corner of your eye. You want to look directly at your professor and make a conscious effort to stop talking to yourself in your mind about other topics. You can help yourself stay more involved with what your professor is saying by asking yourself what are they driving at and trying to repeat bits of it to yourself that they have just said. The more actively involved you can get your brain to be, the better you will be able to listen.

Taking thorough class notes is difficult because you are trying to listen closely enough to comprehend a new idea and record it at the same time. You could type on your laptop as the professor talks and then correct mistakes later. That would require you to be able to type quickly as well as to avoid the temptation to surf the internet.

Recording class lectures may help you avoid missing something if you are not familiar with your professor's accent. If you are a college commuter, it might be worth using your smartphone to record classes and play them to yourself in the car when you aren't in traffic. Otherwise, recording lectures will cost you an hour to listen to an hour of talk.

Some iPhones have a dedicated recorder app built in that would allow you to quickly turn on the recorder app when you notice you are too busy writing down what is on the board to listen to what is being said.

Some students search for Quizlet note cards for the particular chapter being covered in class or bring blank note cards to write on during class so that they don't have to make cards up later.

Agree to compare or share notes with a classmate. You might do this on an occasion when the lecture was particularly confusing or fast, when your mind has drifted more than usual, or when you have missed a class. Note sharing is just one example of how important it is to network with your classmates. Talk with them before the lecture starts and exchange email addresses if you are sure they are trustworthy. It comes in handy when you need to clarify some directions the professor has given or get stymied by course software. Having connections to classmates is even more critical if you are a commuter and campus is less accessible. You might go so far as to create study groups with students in your class and include friends who took the class earlier with that teacher and did well.

In an ideal world, you would know in advance if you have to miss a class and explain why to your professor and ask if there is something you could do to get the handouts you will be missing. Go to every class. Demonstrate to the professor you care about their class. Some students are reluctant to participate in class because they are not caught up with the readings and believe they will reveal their ignorance. You can avoid this by keeping up and not missing class. Ask questions early when you don't understand something. You aren't attending college to demonstrate what you already know. The professor understands you don't know things.

If you are too shy to ask in class, ask afterward. If you tend to hog class time by asking too many questions in class, set a limit on yourself and ask the rest after class or by email.

You may want to look at www.MindMeister.com to explore how you might use 'mind mapping' to take better notes, or brainstorm, or project plan. You could also download the miMind-Easy Mind Mapping app to organize thoughts, develop concepts, brainstorm, or make visual maps that you could then share with other members of a team. You might enjoy listening to 'Maximise the Power of Your Brain - Tony Buzan Mind Mapping' at https://www.youtube.com/watch?v=MlabrWv25qQ. Mr. Buzan makes a compelling argument for the importance of mind mapping and shows you how to do it. He makes the point that your brain thinks in images and not in the linear mode of language. He believes that drawing a mind map of the ideas your professor is discussing helps your brain imagine what is being said better than using the linear medium of the written word.

You may have had experiences that make receptively listening to what an authority says feel like you are being asked to give in and surrender a part of yourself. This poem describes such an experience.

Obey

Drying throat chokes.
Jaws tighten.
Ears, having warned,
Fall defenseless at the opening volley:

"Now, you listen to me!"

Muscles stiffen
As if to say,
"We will hear but not listen.

We will look but not see."
Admonishing arrows fall,
shot from those 'who know better.'

"Listen to common sense.
Listen to reason.
Listen to your elders."
They say.

Little eyes refuse
To tear-mark damage,
As backbones brace
For the final volley—
"Because I say so!"

If Dr. Duffey's poem resonates with you, you may want to ask yourself whether you have difficulty with listening receptively. Learning involves, in some sense, 'surrendering' your past way of seeing things to a new approach that incorporates what you have known already with the new information. If you have suffered verbal abuse or had authoritarians in your life, not letting yourself be influenced by what is said to you can feel like an unconscious victory for the survival of your self. Even if it is more challenging to listen, you are a growing, learning person and can change this with effort. You don't have a fixed set of skills that will not change. You can develop new skills and use any mistakes as opportunities to learn and grow.

Some things are more laborious to listen to than others. You may have come from a close-knit group where agreeing with the group's beliefs and complying with their rules lead to a deep sense of acceptance and belonging. When your primary rewards have come for complying, having a teacher encourage you to think for yourself, even if those thoughts risk not complying, may make the teacher's remarks frightening. You may also feel your teacher is unwittingly undermining your sense of security.

Similarly, if you hear the teacher say something different from your group's belief, you may feel the teacher is disrespecting or dishonoring you and your group. Your feelings may get in the way of your considering the different idea's value on its merit.

It is essential to be conscious of your need to listen because nothing is more frustrating to a professor than students who don't listen to and follow their instructions, or the written instructions they have spelled out in the course syllabus about course requirements, deadlines, and how to do things. When you hear a professor start to give an instruction, your ears should perk up like a dog hearing his name. Write the instruction down immediately and ask questions if you aren't sure you understand them.

Like every other human, professors can become overscheduled, burned-out, and less approachable. When you approach them, remember that they often deal with students who see them as servants and feel entitled to exceptions being made that excuse their irresponsible behaviors. Put yourself in their shoes. Many of them have accepted less money than they could have made in the private sector because they have a passionate interest in their field and want to teach. Even though they make the tests, they are on your side. They are your partners in learning.

READING

The problem with not doing your homework or studying just enough for a test is that sometimes you get away with it. You may still make a good grade, but you are standing in your way when it came to learning something. It's not about the grade. By getting away with not studying enough on one test, it becomes easy to assume that you don't have to study thoroughly. Also, you need to read with the idea in mind that you need to know the material for the final exam and not just for the unit test.

Textcerpts: Mastering College Textbook Reading is explicitly designed to help you learn how to read college textbooks. Go to https://www.amazon.com/Textcerpts-Mastering-College-Textbook-Reading/dp/0321364708

When you read about a new concept, and you comprehend it, and it makes sense to you, that does not mean you know it. You need to go over the information multiple times until you can explain it to someone else and still remember it after time has elapsed. By going over it repeatedly, you memorize it. You have not reached the highest level of learning until you can take that concept, relate it to other ideas, and apply it. It is this level of understanding your professor may be asking of you.

What follows is an oversimplified description of how your brain works. It may be helpful to imagine your brain as a computer that has a cache that can keep just under fifteen minutes' worth of new data in random access memory. Your brain then has to take the data in that random access memory and put it on the hard drive and label it. Otherwise, the newest learned memories push the more recently learned memories out. So, take a break after fifteen minutes of learning new things and relate what you have learned to what you already know. You might want to use the *Brain Productivity* app or the *Focus* app to help with tracking and reinforcing your studying.

Be as active as you can when you study. You are likely already familiar with using the SQ3R study technique of surveying, questioning, reading, reciting, and reviewing when you study. When you are reading, keep asking yourself what conclusions can you draw from the information you are reading. Try to make the information relate to you in an emotionally meaningful way.

If you memorize that Ralphie Underwood holds the world record for minutes swimming while wearing a football helmet, you have learned a stand-alone fact. You won't have to apply that knowledge to do the problem in the next chapter. If you learn a math concept, you are learning a principle you have to apply later. The math concept requires you understand it well, but Ralphie Underwood's achievement—not so much. Not everything you read is of equal value. Prioritize what you spend time learning.

Ask your friends who have previously had your professor whether the professor will put just anything and everything on a test. The only way to be assured of a good grade—in that case—is to know pretty much everything. Don't waste time thinking this is unreasonable.

By talking about getting good grades or doing well on tests, we don't want to give you the impression that you should study for the test only. Wishing is no substitute for your effort. Many college graduates will tell you that getting a degree is hollow if you don't have the real learning because you have a focus on grades rather than genuine skill development. They will tell you they later realized they had sacrificed the opportunity to become competent for the appearance of competence. They talk about feeling worried they will be found out by employers to be phonies and how they lack confidence and hate having to pretend.

10

Enhancing Relationship Skills and Relationships

CONSIDERING FAMILY

Talk with your family before you leave for school and reach some compromise about how often you will come home. Help them get an idea of how you see your frequency and methods of contact changing so that they can understand your expectations. Finding a workable new rhythm involves taking time and dancing around sensitive topics. Set a goal for yourself to be exceptionally patient and kind. You are trying to balance your need to launch into independence against their sense of loss of the child they have nurtured for eighteen years as well as their anxiety for your well-being.

This description may not fit your family. It may be hard to accept that you don't have such a nurturing family. You may even feel like they sent you out unfinished and unprepared. The good news is that, like you, family members can grow and your family is not a fixed entity. Accepting your family is part of accepting your life.

If you anticipate going somewhere besides home on holidays or spring break, letting your family know ahead of time keeps them from getting their hopes up. Offering to come on another holiday or alternative time may help lessen their disappointment.

Some married couples believe they should stay together until the last child is in college. As a result, some students find they leave for college, and, by Thanksgiving, the home they left is fundamentally different because their parents have separated.

If you are a child of divorce already, you may be familiar with the tug-of-war for your time. This situation makes it even more critical to plan holidays and discuss plans early with all parties.

If you find college is a more functional place to live than the home you left, going back home may not be something you relish. It may help to brainstorm options with a mentor, roommate, or counselor, and work out possible responses, and limit setting behaviors. Try to avoid having to rely on someone else for exit transportation. You might consider reading *Emotional Blackmail: When the People in Your Life Use Fear, Obligation, and Guilt to Manipulate You* by Susan Forward and Donna Frazier.

If the pandemic delayed your plans for living away, take that time to get to know your parents as people by sharing family pictures.

To paraphrase the quote sometimes attributed to Mark Twain, you may go home and find yourself surprised at how much your parents have learned in the interval since you last saw them. That happens when you have had college experiences that confirm things your parents have told you. You might also discover your parents enjoyed being a couple again and having the house to themselves.

A situation you might find too complicated to discuss with friends is living away from home when you feel you are leaving a younger brother or sister unprotected from your dysfunctional family. You may be more worried about a depressed parent than your siblings. Most colleges have a counseling center with counselors who are familiar with student concerns like these. Why not give them a try?

Being away from your family can be surprisingly hard when you haven't had the practice from sleepovers, class trips, going to camp or spending June at Aunt Mary's. Staying in touch with family by phone and some short visits may do until you can make friends and connect with campus and community groups. As your homesickness subsides, you can slowly reduce the frequency of family contact.

If you come from a large family, you could always do something with a sibling. You may not have felt the need to learn how to make friends. It's okay to feel anxious and awkward. Try reaching out until you make some friends. Pursuing an interest or hobby can lead to meeting new people and a spontaneous conversation about your shared interests. You may be able to take advantage of your resident advisor's knowledge of other students' backgrounds and interests.

Recalling your behavior as you left for college, you might be surprised now at how argumentative you were toward your family. Sometimes students actively devalue their family or create a fight as a way of reducing the pain of leaving them. It's a mistake. It's understandable given how attached you might be to your family. Going home can be an opportunity to heal some wounds.

When you go home, think of yourself as a guest. Be considerate to the host by going by the host's house rules. Away at school, you can come in at 2:00 a.m., and your parents don't know. When you go home to visit, they notice and may worry needlessly. Frame going along with the house rules as also helping treat their anxiety. Please don't make it about their needing to see you as more responsible and autonomous. Going along with the rules is not giving in but a kind gesture that recognizes they worry. If you do stay out until 2:00 a.m., tell them you will be out until then, even if you don't do that with your roommate. Their recognizing you are growing up is a long and complicated process that includes dealing with loss.

ADJUSTING TO ROOMMATES

You don't luck into a good relationship with your roommate. It takes building the friendship step-by-step. There is give and take, and you have to establish it over time. Be honest about your leanings like messiness, neatness, loudness, and social interests. Don't get into the habit of criticizing your roommate to others —because it comes back. Settle issues by talking to them quickly, directly, and only when you are calm. Write out what you want to say if you have to, but say it. Make sure you can trust them before you confide much. Show tolerance. Be considerate. Everyone has different views. Be fair. Reciprocate. Set limits on their clinging, but be kind. Set some boundaries. Several websites have templates for roommate agreements. This one has forty templates: http://templatelab.com/roommate-agreement/

In your dealings with roommates as well as friends and family, try to identify the emotions you are experiencing and work at the same time to identify the emotions the other person is feeling. If you can define your emotions and empathize enough with the other person to feel their emotion, then the decision you make as a result will be a better one. Being in touch with yourself and others can help you find your way.

If you are stumped as to what to do about your roommate issues, talking with your resident advisor is a reasonable next step. Who in your family has had to deal with a roommate and might offer some confidential advice? Counseling center staff would help you with roommate issues and give you some different perspectives.

ANALYZING PEER RELATIONSHIPS

Have you found friends that have confidence in themselves and know where they are going but also empower you to be the best you can be, even if it is different from them? Perhaps you find yourself, instead, surrounded by people who are invalidating you or getting in the way of your progress toward your goals?

Maybe they gave you the nickname 'Grumpy,' and now you think that you have some fixed permanent grumpy part of your personality. That's nonsense. Remember, you are an ever-growing work in progress.

If you feel like The Ugly Duckling around a group like this, then you may need to go on a swan hunt to find groups of people more like you who support you at your best. Is there an organization or group of people with goals similar to yours? You could spend time with them and get support. It is up to you to reach your goals. It would be helpful, just the same, to have a group that supports what you value and the person you want to become. It is equally important that you find friends who will tell you when you are acting in a self-defeating way.

> *When you lose your capacity to care what other people think, you've lost your ability to connect. But when you're defined by it, you've lost your ability to be vulnerable.*
>
> (Brene Brown 2012)

Ms. Brown points out the other problem with peer relationships. That is, when you deal with them by trying not to care, you lose your sensitivity if you overdo it.

> *Surround yourself with positive people.*
> –Melanie Fiona, and others
> https://www.brainyquote.com/quotes/melanie_fiona_497269

Melanie Fiona (Hallim) grew up around musicians and became a songwriter and singer. She may have the answer to Brene Brown's dilemma. By finding positive people, you don't have to develop a hard, defensive exterior to be around them. Being able to avoid having to become defensive makes looking for positive people worth the added effort.

The friend that you pick will influence how you think and how you behave. They can be a source of inspiration or continual predicaments. They may get you in trouble by putting you in the wrong place at the wrong time. Picking the right friends is especially important if you are influenced easily by friends. Your initial choices for friends are the most critical picks since those friends may bias your subsequent picks.

> *I used to think that the worst thing in life was to end up alone. It's not. The worst thing in life is to end up with people who make you feel alone.*
>
> –Robin William's character, Lance Clayton, in the 2009 movie *World's Greatest Dad* from the screenplay written by Bobcat Goldthwait

Look at how potential friends treat others. Are they honest, kind, accepting, and loyal? Do they gossip? Do you feel comfortable being yourself around them? Do you think to be acceptable that you have to keep secrets from them? Paul Tournier has said, "Nothing makes us so lonely as our secrets."

You may find the friends you have picked don't share your values, and you can't tell them how you feel. That can make you very lonely, as Paul Tournier, the Swiss physician, and author of *The Healing of Persons*, has said (Tournier 1965). You aren't just picking friends; you are choosing potential influencers. Discovering inspiring friends can be life-changing. So, keep looking until you find the right friends.

As you listen to potential friends, listen for themes in their conversations. Do they seem always to be blaming others and seldom see their role except as being a victim? Do they have agency, or do they see themselves as helpless? Are they able to put themselves in others' shoes? Do they view a circumstance only as it relates to them? Do they care about people or violate their rights? Do they act like they know the difference between right and wrong? Can they hear "no" or make compromises about something they want? Are they honest? Do they bully others? Are they controlling?

Ruby K. Payne, Ph.D. does a masterful job of explaining how different classes of people think, in her book that you can access at https://www.amazon.com/Framework-Understanding-Poverty-Cognitive-Approach/dp/1938248015/ref=pd_lpo_sbs_14_t_0?_encoding=UTF8&psc=1&refRID=4KF6DTFT55JFZQJ6CV9G If you find yourself around people who seem to think differently than you partly because of their socio-economic class, you would find this book well worth your time.

IMPROVING DATING RELATIONSHIPS

The authors have to admit that it takes a lot of nerve to write a book like this. Writing about dating takes even more nerve. Dating is incredibly complicated. So, we urge you to think twice or even more about anything we write in this section.

It may help you to relax about dating if you remind yourself that you are not dating a Martian. Your date is a person, and the people skills you have already learned will help you in dating. Saying that is also our way of suggesting you review the parts of our book meant to improve your people skills: Analyzing Peer Relationships, Manners, Socializing, and Staying Safe.

That said, this person you are dating may have added expectations. Fun, romance, sex, and mate selection could be just some of the things on their mind. We hope to add to what you already know about these areas.

To get some ideas of things to do on a date, review the paragraph on *Doing things that are entertaining but also free* in the section *Saving Money on Expenses*. A word to the wise—free activities on the first date might suggest you are cheap.

Pre-college educational programs vary in the adequacy of their sexual education. Some students will choose not to be sexually active, and that's a legitimate option. If you are sexually active, sexual ignorance can be dangerous to your health and future. You may be both uninformed and misinformed. As you try to become informed, make sure your sources are reliable ones, like the CDC and ACOG.

https://www.cdc.gov/healthyyouth/sexualbehaviors/index.htm
https://www.cdc.gov/sexualhealth/
https://www.acog.org/Patients

Imagine having a partner who knows you, accepts you, and loves you as you are —so their love is not dependent on your giving up self-possession. Imagine that when you have sex, you are comfortable and relaxed because you know, whether tonight is fantastic or disastrous, there will be a tomorrow and a tomorrow after that. Imagine that you know that having sex is like everything else; it can get better with practice. Now, ask yourself, what kind of "state" would make this possible. If you said, a state of genuine intimacy, you're right.

Now, ask yourself a second question—what kind of environment is most likely to make genuine intimacy possible. If you said "anywhere if you have enough beer," you just won *Family Feud*. However, you would be wrong because you are confusing sexual intimacy with emotional intimacy. Emotional intimacy flourishes with work and time. It needs an emotionally secure environment. In his book, during the process of teaching readers how to prolong desire in their relationship, Joseph Nowinski does an excellent job of describing how to work toward emotional intimacy. The book's title is *A Lifelong Love Affair: Keeping Sexual Desire Alive in Your Relationship*.

Someone who acts like a jerk once will likely keep acting like a jerk— because they <u>are</u> a jerk. Use your values as a compass from the very first date. Ask yourself, does this person resonate with my values?

When you think seriously about it, would you feel comfortable telling your future partner that you have been part of the hook-up culture or someone's friend with benefits?

You might want to frame dating in a way that takes some of the pressure off. It's one more of many things you are learning to do. Think of a date as an opportunity to practice dating skills. You can learn things even on bad dates. Dating gives you a chance to get a better idea of what people are like and what is reasonable to expect. You might see dating as if you had the typical box of chocolates, and you were trying to decide which ones you like the best. As you sample more and more, the more accurate and realistic your deductions about the chocolates become.

If you have clinically significant social anxiety, you will save yourself much grief by getting it treated now. Otherwise, it is tempting to settle on a mate hastily rather than go through the stress of continuing to date. You are then more likely to end up divorcing. If you get treatment, you will be able to date and sample enough people. You will feel confident enough to keep at it until you find the best match.

If you are dating and in a committed relationship, you will find yourself, at times, attracted to other people. When someone catches your eye, notice when it happens, and consciously avoid lingering. At this point in the sequence, you have the most control, so exercise this control. Avoid lingering, and don't start fantasizing. Get back into the task you were doing. You may be in daily contact with this person because they are in your class, workplace, or organization.

Don't fall into the mistake of over-trusting your self-control by entering into "innocent situations" where you may be tempted. Many good people have made bad errors by underestimating temptation and the lure of the forbidden, especially while drinking, tired, lonely, irritated at their partner, or in close physical contact.

When you are out of the tempting situation, ask yourself why you desire the person, and if you are missing something that could be addressed within your existing relationship.

MEMORIZING A MNEMONIC DEVICE FOR ASSESSING YOUR DATE—THE EIGHT PS

The authors have adapted parts of this section from Dr. Duffey's book *Exploring Your Unplanned Pregnancy: Single Motherhood, Adoption, and Abortion Questions and Resources*.

The ideal partner will be passionate, permanent, partner-ready, problem-solving, productive, personable, protective, and parent material. When you date, keep these eight Ps in mind.

Partners are just human, and your partner understandably may not do as well in some areas as others. You will need to decide which qualities are essential to you.

PASSIONATE Do you love your partner? Does your partner love you? Are you a priority in their life?

PERMANENT Can you count on your relationship to be permanent? Does your partner have a dangerous future occupation that could result in their death? Is your partner in good health? Do they have a history of being unfaithful in past relationships?

PARTNER-READY Is your partner ready to be an active partner in solving the problems of daily life? A good partner accepts advice

Enhancing Relationship Skills and Relationships

from their mate. Can you think of examples where they have taken advice from their parents or their boss? Can they receive guidance from people regardless of their sex?

Do they look at life the same way you do? Do you believe the same things? If you want to raise a child, could you agree on how to parent? Do you have the same dreams?

Partnership ordinarily involves a sexual partnership. Are you and your partner sexually compatible?

PROBLEM-SOLVING Is your partner a problem solver? Have they shown intelligence, persistence, and the ability to tolerate frustration when they try to solve problems? How have you worked together to solve problems?

PRODUCTIVE Do they have the skills and personality that they need to keep a job and be a productive joint provider for you and your child if you want to have or adopt a child? If they have difficulty taking responsibility for their mistakes and always blame their boss, they may have problems keeping a job. Do they have a legal history that will hold them back?

PERSONABLE When you are in love, it is easy to overlook faults in your partner or think you can change their personality with your love and care. After all their years of being a certain way, it may be quite difficult for your partner to change their views and approach to daily life.

Are they usually happy and satisfied with life, or are they always down on themselves? If they view themselves as a victim, will they start to blame you for holding them back?

Does your partner think about others? Are they self-centered? If you have a child and your partner is demanding, will they become like a jealous child when you show attention to your "other child"?

What evidence do you have that your partner can trust?

Is your partner honest and trustworthy? For example, do they tell you what you want to hear to avoid conflict? If you have talked about having a child in the future, did they say to you only what you wanted to hear?

Does your partner exercise self-control by saying no to themselves or their friends when necessary? Do they have healthy boundaries? Can they say *no* to requests in order to prioritize you and your relationship? Would your partner make impulsive decisions that would affect you or your future child, if you want to have one? Do they think about the future and live in the present? Do they take care of their health, responsibilities, and things properly? Do they manage alcohol and medicines in healthy ways? Are they too judgmental?

PROTECTIVE Is your partner looking out for you? Have they been protective of you, or do you feel worried about being protected from them? Have they been violent toward you? Have they isolated you from your friends, shown unjustified jealous, or bullied you? Would they bully a future child if you had one? Will living with your partner place a future child around unpredictable people who make your child feel insecure? Would you be living in an unsafe neighborhood? Would you have to live with a partner or their relatives who are unstable because of their addictions or mental illness? If you wanted to adopt a child, do they have a history that would disqualify them?

PARENT-MATERIAL Many normal people choose not to have or adopt children, but, if you decide to in the future, will your partner be able to be close to your child?

Enhancing Relationship Skills and Relationships

How have they done at child-care experiences like babysitting, working with campers, or taking care of brothers and sisters? Are they a responsible pet owner? How do they respond in situations around other people's loud, needy, messy children?

Some partners step up to parenthood while others aren't ready. Can you make a clear decision about their potential passion for being a parent?

What examples of them making sacrifices for others might make you think they would make sacrifices for a future child? Will they put you and a future child first? Do they have other obligations that make you and any child you would have a lower priority? If you already have a child, is your child a priority as well?

How they treat others, especially people like their parents and those in a service role—like store clerks, secretaries, or waiters—may give you a clue about how they will treat you and your child. Have you seen them be kind, considerate, helpful, and loving to their parents in various situations over a long period?

If your partner is suspicious of you despite your efforts to earn their trust, they might also have trouble having a close, trusting relationship with your future child.

If you want to have children eventually, the essential question for you is: Does your partner pass enough of these questions for you to bring a child into the relationship?

COPING WITH STALKERS AND UNWANTED ATTENTION

If you find yourself being stalked, consult with your community professionals and authorities, because each case is unique. Your resident advisor may have been briefed on the procedures you might follow. Take a look at The Stalking Resource Center: http://victimsofcrime.org/our-programs/stalking-resource-center/help-for-victims

Unwanted attention occurs in several situations and warrants your concern. On his website *Be Irresistible* in an article entitled *How to Handle Unwanted Attention from the Wrong Guy*, James Bauer suggested that when creeps are around, you should "keep friends close and make brutal honesty and strong boundaries your policy. If he doesn't respect your verbal request, pick any guy standing nearby and ask him to intervene on your behalf." They note that "Notice a guy you are not attracted to looking at you? Don't make eye contact. Deliberately look away or down. Turn your body away from him. For guys who are undeterred and approach anyway, shut them down quickly. Be polite, but firm."

https://blog.beirresistible.com/how-to-handle-unwanted-attention-from-the-wrong-guy/

When telling them you don't want to date them does not stop them, consider implying you are already partnered. Besides not being true, this has some other drawbacks. It could be taken to mean that you might otherwise be interested. It also might be a complication if you want others there to see you as available.

Sometimes a situation gets worse quickly. Aggressors may be getting into your physical space. Size up how intoxicated, impulsive, irrational, or assaultive they might be. Trust that creepy feeling or the discomfort in your stomach. If pursuers have these risk factors for violence, you need to get away from them and quickly leave the scene <u>with friends</u>. Do not leave alone since they may follow you. You need not give them an explanation or any information about yourself. If you have to, say something short and nonrevealing, like, "I don't want to talk to you anymore." Please don't assume they are going to act rationally. You don't need a reason to leave, and you don't owe them an explanation.

If things are getting out of hand and you are inappropriately touched, then you have to be more drastic. If you have enough people around you in public, exclaim your disgust at being touched and describe what they just did to the crowd. Then move away immediately while the crowd shames them and leave with friends.

Many bars have a "bad date" code. After you have asked for an "angel shot" or whether "Angel is working tonight," staff will know you need their help. Bartenders will call a cab, distract the pursuer, and may even sneak you out. Bars differ, so ask the bartender in advance about the procedure and code word. If you have forgotten to ask, make eye contact with the bartender to indicate your distress.

If you can't avoid being in the same room, ignore them. Keep a look on your face like you just smelled a skunk. Stay occupied on an activity like reading the program. Even if there is nothing you need to do, it is vital that you appear preoccupied with your attention obviously turned elsewhere. Have a quiet conversation with friends. Keep your body turned away. When possible, walk quickly away as soon as you can. Survey the room and stay out of their line of sight by putting yourself next to taller people or furnishings. Do not become a sitting duck by sitting down. Make sure they are not between you and the exit, so you don't have to walk past them to get out.

If you are in a situation in which you have to interact, show no interest in what they say. Don't initiate conversation. If you must say something, make short statements in response that are ordinary, superficial, and offer no opening for them to continue the conversation. Use that cold tone of voice you ordinarily save for irritating telephone sales associates you want off the phone. If they start to get pushy, be clear but stop just short of being mean to avoid giving them a story to tell. All these maneuvers work better when you have friends with whom you have strategized before the occasion. They can be free, on your signal, to phone you from across the room or grab you to go to the bathroom with them.

Sometimes the person coming on to you lives around you. To avoid bumping into them or other creepy neighbors, it may be worth changing your routine and leaving early, taking a long way around, dropping common friends, walking places in groups, wearing clothing that helps you blend in with the group, or eating at different restaurants.

If you must walk alone, walk briskly, keep your distance from others, wear earbuds, have an expressionless face, and look around only enough to be safe while avoiding catching anyone's eye. Tell anyone who approaches you that you have to get somewhere—preferably using a second language you know, but they likely don't. Never look lost. Walk into a public place or women's room if you need to.

These avoidant approaches have the advantage of not risking others seeing you as mean. There are times when simple conflict avoidance is not enough, and you should notify someone. Your resident advisor may be an excellent place to start.

When you do know the person coming on to you and think they are sweet but uninteresting, then being kind is a dilemma. You know what it is like yourself to feel rejected, and you would like to be kind, but being kind may be taken the wrong way. They may think you are ambivalent, and they need to redouble their efforts. They may not hear what you are saying because they are too self-centered in their self-consciousness about being rejected. They may assume your continued kindness and tone of voice is saying one thing and your words another. They may be in denial about their shortcomings and disbelief about your rejection. Your ambivalence opens the door for them to ask questions about what they can do differently to change your mind, what they did wrong, and other things. If your initial rejecting statement is confident, clear, firm, and has no wiggle words to leave doubt, you may help them get over it more quickly. While you don't need to point out their faults, you aren't responsible for making it a teaching moment for them either.

Enhancing Relationship Skills and Relationships

If a close friend is starting to show unwanted interest in you, it can be even harder to be clear. If you think they are sensitive and together enough to get what you are saying the first time, you might comment about how much you enjoy just being platonic friends. You might think about asking them for dating advice about someone else you say you like who is strikingly different from your friend.

If your close friend does not get it, or you suspect they have some everyday problems with their thinking, then you will need to think about ending the friendship and all contact. If they don't seem to be taking your wishes seriously for the relationship to be not romantic, you need to be firm in stating those wishes and then consider the need to be kind by not dragging the relationship on despite their being a good friend.

Breaking up with someone you have been dating is, in many ways, quite different from the situations we have just described and may call for different responses, even though some of the avoidance behaviors might still be useful.

When you are the person making a sexual advance:

If you are the suitor, guy or girl, you don't touch someone without their consent. It does not matter if one or both of you are drunk, what their appearance is, or how friendly they have been. If you want to kiss someone, tell them you would like to and see what they say. You don't go touching someone to see if they like it. It may seem stupid but ask them. They may even appreciate your being considerate. If you hear "no," listen to it the first time. You also need to understand that they may try to soften the rebuff by making a joke. They aren't joking—they are not interested, and you are about to be publicly shamed if you persist. They have clearly not said *yes*. Without a clear *yes*, the light is always red.

As the suitor, you need to understand that the object of your advances may be reluctant to say *no* because of repercussions, doubts about whether they might have misread your behavior, self-doubt about how they came across, simply not wanting to reject anyone, and their fear of you.

You may overlook the physical signs of their distress. When they become distressed, they may have sweaty hands or foreheads. Their hands may be slightly shaky or colder. Their fists may be closed. They may fiddle with their hands. You may see their face or neck flush, and the blood vessels in their neck seem to be beating prominently and quickly. They may be breathing faster like they can't quite catch their breath. When they talk, they might have more trouble getting the words out because they are choked up in their throat, and they are trying to be careful with their words and can't seem to think straight. This not evidence they are in awe of your charm. They are on their way to being panicked.

When they become distressed, you may see signs they are closing up. Their facial muscles may tighten, making their facial expressions look cold and constricted. They may wrap their coat tightly, pull their arms closer in toward their body, and possibly cross them. They may inch away from you to create more distance between you. They lean back on their chair away from you. They try to cover their lap and pull their legs in tighter. Their speech becomes more constricted, too, with words that are fewer, more measured, and careful. You may notice they can't look at you directly, or they are looking past you for help or at the clock.

Their closing up may progress to closing down as they feel paralyzed, little, immobilized, and their brain seems to freeze like a deer in the headlights. Please do not take their inability to object as consent. This statement is especially true if they are intoxicated, and their ability to understand and respond by objecting is further limited. Drunk people are unable to give consent.

Their distress could also show up as their looking uncomfortably restless and suddenly announcing they have to go to the bathroom. Let them go. Take the opportunity to exit inconspicuously in another direction.

It may seem to guys that it is typical male behavior to pursue all attractive women on the off chance someone will say *yes*. College women tell us that these guys would eventually have more and better chances by being gentlemen.

GETTING SERIOUS OR BREAKING UP?

If things are going well in your relationship and you want to move it to more permanent status, take a look at this helpful book by Susan Piver— *The Hard Questions: 100 Questions to Ask Before You Say "I Do."* The questions uncover hidden assumptions like expecting you will have weekly dinners with your parents or set up a joint checking account.

On the other hand, you may think you are with the wrong person. No one wants to think of themselves as a poor mate selector, but mistakes happen. Do your friends agree with you that you have taken the reasonable actions that they would take to make the relationship work? Have your friends told you that they would not put up with something your partner did? Then, maybe it's time to think about whether to end the relationship.

If you decide you need to break up, you may find that the way people view the world may make breaking up with them more difficult and even potentially dangerous. If you think you are breaking up with a narcissist or a sociopath, the following articles should be just the beginning of your planning. You should bounce some ideas off a counselor and get some advice from an expert to do everything you can to minimize the potential danger. Each situation is unique. These articles are a good start:

The article "21 Warning Signs of an Emotionally Abusive Relationship" first appeared on Your Tango and can be found now at www.psychcentral.com/blog/archives/2014/10/13/21-warning-signs-of-an-emotionally-abusive-relationship/

https://thoughtcatalog.com/kim-saeed/2016/07/7-sneaky-things-narcissists-say-to-get-you-back/

https://www.businessinsider.com/dating-a-narcissist-phrases-to-know-2017-3

https://www.health.com/relationships/how-to-break-up-with-a-narcissist

https://www.mindbodygreen.com/0-27078/what-its-really-like-to-break-up-with-a-narcissist.html

https://www.truelovescam.com/leaving-a-sociopath-5-break-up-musts/

If you have just broken up with someone, you will see in the appendix a list of possibly helpful things you might use as affirmations.

Next: Strategy 11—Make course corrections.

11

Strategizing to Meet the Challengse that Arise as the College Years Unfold

ENTERING THE MIDDLE PHASE-THE 4 SS

First-year students are a varied group. Students starting their first year of college may have just completed a summer program to fill in gaps in their knowledge. Others may enter their first year of college having taken AP courses in high school. Still others may be a high school student in a dual enrollment program.

The senior class is even less uniform because students transferring in may not get full credit for their previous courses. They take longer to graduate. Other seniors have missed semesters because of illness or finances. Others have changed majors or repeated courses. Still others have taken heavier loads and gone summers to finish early.

Rather than use school class, we will arbitrarily divide college into a beginning, middle, and ending phase. A good portion of what we have written so far concerns the start of college.

After winning a tennis match, Stefanos Tsitsipas— a professional tennis player— wrote, "It never gets easier. You just get better." He could have been talking about college. You get better at being a student as college progresses. The coursework, however, usually does not become less demanding.

As you enter the middle phase, you go from feeling uncertain to feeling like you have some idea of what to expect. Returning to school after your first year can make you feel like a college football coach who was not sure what his players were going to do in the first game. As he plans for the second game of the season, he has the advantage of being able to look at the first game film for mistakes his players made in the first game. He uses the mistakes to help him target areas to correct in practice. He looks at the strengths his players have shown and the things they have done right so he can capitalize on them. When he looks toward the second game opponents, he looks for potential mismatches at positions where his players may not be as strong as the opponents, and then he adjusts. Like the coach, you may feel like reviewing the progress, the stumbles, and the future courses where your skill may not currently match the course's difficulty.

When you enter the middle phase, it's natural to take stock of your goals. You move from seeking reassurance to seeking a clearer understanding of your reality. When you take stock, ask yourself what progress have you made in the areas of the four Ss: Study, Support, Selfhood, and Spirit. After all, the first year tested your mettle— and you survived.

STUDY What study habits have worked for you? What can you learn from mistakes? What tricks did you use to keep up with the pace of study and still work? What did you like about how the structure you created for the previous year worked?

SUPPORT What have you learned about how to network on campus? Think of the examples of how your determination paid off in various ways, like forming relationships. Who are the people who energize and inspire you? Whom have you learned to avoid that drain you with their drama and views? What activities have you found nurturing? What did you discover that you thought would be worthwhile, but now seems like self-sabotage? What place or situation makes you feel the safest and secure?

Strategizing to Meet the Challengse that Arise as the College Years Unfold

SELFHOOD Your first year was likely about launching yourself into a process toward independence. In what areas do you feel competent in taking care of things? In having had to express your opinions in papers and defend positions and explain concepts, do you have growing confidence in your ability to communicate?

By the middle part of college, you may belong to several service organizations and take part in volunteer activities that distract you. Please be aware of the long-term. Don't devote so much time to them that you neglect your studies. Realize that, by going to school, you are training to be more effective in helping others. Don't be shortsighted. Keep your eye on the long-term goal. Like the person in the airplane putting the oxygen mask over their face before helping their child— you should prepare yourself first.

On the other hand, only chasing your pleasure leads to a feeling of emptiness and wish for more stimulation. Extrinsic motivation is not as lasting as intrinsic motivation. Take time to focus on your learning. It will lead to having more skillsets to help others in the future. Your time to study is precious. You don't want to let others distract you from studying.

With this phase comes a recognition of the ever-present grade point average (GPA) matters and is inescapable. Part of the middle stage is accepting that your hard work is required to progress in school and then committing yourself to do that hard work. Seeing other students having to study more is a clue.

When you know your major and see the necessary core and advanced courses, it makes the path more real and concrete. You start breaking it down into smaller steps. You realize you have to grin and bear it. You are happy to be finishing the core courses. If you don't know your core, you start to get antsy about it. If you have to change your major, it could set you back. That does not necessarily mean changing your major was a mistake.

> *We tap into something when we're honest about what's going on in our lives.*
>
> **—Sheryl Sandberg, Chief Operating Officer of Facebook**
>
> Retrieved from https://www.brainyquote.com/quotes/sheryl_sandberg_835072

SPIRIT What is going on in <u>your</u> life? Have you figured out that getting and having stuff can make you feel secure and give you a sense of permanence for only so long? How has the process gone of understanding things bigger than you? How do you now see yourself fitting into the universe and life? What has helped you when you felt alone, lost, or excluded last year? You mastered uncomfortable feeling-states in your first years, how did you do it? What were the techniques you used—like getting busy, entertainment, getting together with friends, or just sitting with the experience—that helped you?

WANDERING IN THE WISDOM WILDERNESS

> *Why do I talk about the benefits of failure? Simply because failure meant a stripping away of the inessential. I stopped pretending to myself that I was anything other than what I was, and began to direct all my energy into finishing the only work that mattered to me.*
>
> –J.K. Rowling
>
> Retrieved from https://news.harvard.edu/gazette/story/2008/06/text-of-j-k-rowling-speech /

Somewhere in the middle phase of college, a strange thing happens that seems like a paradox. Just as you sense a growing belief in yourself and connectedness to those around you, you are more able to admit to vulnerabilities and failures. You begin to benefit from how your failures crystalize things for you—as J.K. Rowling suggests. You can accept that, to tough it out, you have had to pretend to be unafraid and overlook some of your limitations. That denial that helped you get through so much starts to show signs of wear. Have you, for example, sampled some courses and found you had made some missteps and learned you didn't like the subject or it wasn't your strength after all?

As the middle phase of college progresses, you become comfortable enough to become more aware of a bigger picture. A combination of exposure to more of humankind's knowledge and some new life experiences may make you feel rather small in the face of the vastness of it all. You start to realize that knowledge is incomplete without wisdom. Lacking the clarity that comes with wisdom can make you feel like there is no clear path on your journey, and you are lost in a wilderness wandering around.

You may notice that you seem to be engaged in several parallel struggles, each with a similar theme.

When you first came to college, you worked through becoming more independent from your parents. You resented them telling you what you should do and at the same time, worried they might be right. You wanted to have the freedom to make your own decisions even if some might be mistakes. You had to believe in yourself even though being on your own felt new, and you missed others taking care of you.

When you were with your friend groups, you worried about losing your individuality by conforming, but you feared exclusion.

Dating, you found a conflict within yourself between wanting to maintain self-possession and a desire to surrender yourself in blissful oneness to the wishes of your beloved partner.

Growing trust and self-belief will help you with these parallel conflicts having to do with becoming a separate integrated individual and still having a connectedness with other different individuals.

Having developed a base of supportive friends and having survived the ups and downs of college life may give you the self-assurance to risk trusting others as you strive for more closeness with them.

You may have been lucky enough to have wise, accepting, and supportive parents. That would make it easier to imagine that authority figures unselfishly also want your self-fulfillment, and you are more apt to see the situation as a win-win.

Over the first years of college, you may have had interactions with your parents where you felt your parents respected your differentiation even though your views did not always match theirs. They acknowledged your right to free will. You might have seen them watch anxiously as that resulted in your making choices that led to suffering. They made themselves just watch because they knew it was necessary for you to learn. You might have experienced their gracious forgiveness when things you did cost them in different ways. You might have seen them believe in you even when you didn't.

Having experiences like these with your parents may allow you to envision a similar relationship with authority, whether that authority is your fraternity, sorority, professor, college administration, or religious organization. For example, experiencing a professor's concern for you as a person might lead you to want to do well in their class—not out of fear of making a bad grade, but out of positive feeling toward them. Your professor stops being seen as an opponent and becomes a partner in your eyes.

Experiencing the middle years of college without having such parents makes it harder to trust. It makes it easier to view the world as filled with opponents. You may expect people not to validate you, not to have your best interest at heart, and to discriminate against you. Allowing yourself to observe some goodness in others might be considered an unaffordable luxury since you would fear overlooking their ill intent and becoming vulnerable. This thinking can lead to a stance in the world which is defensive and constricting rather than open.

At these times, it is worthwhile for you again to remind yourself of how courage expands life and fear constricts it. Remember your heroes as you search more widely for the *wondrous* in life and grapple with the meaning of suffering. Share your ideas with friends and teachers. If you can, cultivate an attitude of hopeful persistence and expectation that something will show itself more clearly. Take a conscious stance of openness. Let your thirst for more information and experience lead you to a more profound truth. Refuse to see yourself as a victim or the world as loveless.

REFLECTING ON THE END PHASE

In the end phase, suddenly, you are supposed to be well into your major courses. The prospect of leaving college and finding a job may jolt you like a noisy roommate the morning after a night out. You hear yourself talking about how much time you have left in college, rather than how long you have been there. You swing between being tired of college and wanting to go and feeling comfortable being a student. You know how to be a student. You have been doing it for over twenty years. You realize you don't yet know how to perform the work of the actual career. Your attention turns to internships, practicums, completing the cohort, and interviewing for jobs or grad school. You may have buyer's remorse about your major. You wonder if your partner will stick with you when they move to a different city. You find that seemingly every employer wants one to three years of experience, and you realize you need a chance at something to get that.

A few years ago, you left high school to go to college. Now you are about to go into an even bigger world. You did this once before when you graduated from high school, and you went off to college. College, however, did have some structure that life after college may not. In college, if you made a 98, you knew you would get an A— in life, not so much.

So, stop for a minute. This task can be broken down in steps, just like all the other things you have accomplished before. Get your information together. Look at your options. Consult with knowledgeable people. Look for others who have solved similar problems. Seek out others who might provide thoughtful, constructive criticism of your options. Plan your steps. Then, reassess. Take another look at chapter 6 in the section "Working" to remind you of how to act in interviews. You have been competing for things all your life. This competition is just one more. You know you might have to make multiple tries at it and get past early unsuccessful attempts. Prepare to be wrong and improve on the next try. Do you have alumni networks or major professors that can be of help?

If you have your choice of several work locations, you might weigh each's cost of living. Bank rate offers a cost of living calculator at https://www.bankrate.com/calculators/savings/moving-cost-of-living-calculator.aspx

Don't forget the federal government has named some job positions as eligible for loan forgiveness for certain loans. To get an idea of which ones, go to https://studentaid.ed.gov/sa/repay-loans/forgiveness-cancellation/public-service#qualifying-employment

Steppingblocks (https://www.steppingblocks.com/)is discussed in the chapter entitled 'Deciding Whether to go to College' in the Appendix. It uses big data analytics to tell you where graduates from each school in specific majors are likely to work and what their first job most likely is. It identifies how much it might pay and how long it may take for them to pay off a student loan at that salary.

Next: Strategy 12/13—Realize your self-efficacy and attend to your own needs.

12

Recognizing What Helps First-Generation College Students Will Also Help You

About one in five college students have parents who did not finish college. These first-generation college students are a varied group, making generalizations about them often inaccurate. As you read this chapter, keep in mind that you may have a different experience. These descriptions may fail to resonate with you. Some of the suggestions are widely applicable and may still be helpful. We ask you to consider each. Even if you are not a first-generation college student, you may struggle with similar issues.

The Counseling Center at U. Illinois offers a general discussion of first-generation college student issues at this site. https://counselingcenter.illinois.edu/brochures/first-generation-college-students.

If you don't get out of the box you have been raised in, you won't understand how much bigger the world is.

–Angelina Jolie

Retrieved from https://www.brainyquote.com/quotes/angelina_jolie_644397

Educators talk about families wanting to pass down, from generation to generation, specific acceptable work roles that fit with the family, religious, and community traditions. Taking Angelina Jolie's advice to get out of the box will threaten that. When a student breaks with tradition to go to college, family members may lack an understanding of why. They feel it reflects a rejection of the past. This break with tradition can lead the student to feel a shift in their own identity and a sense of loss.

The first-generation student may feel what others have called 'breakaway guilt.' Having decided to go to college, the student finds it hard to talk with the family about subsequent difficulties they are having with school and feels some added pressure to succeed. They may feel added pressure to come home more often than is reasonable. Sometimes first-generation students feel like they have abandoned younger siblings whom they have previously parented or protected and for whom they feel responsible.

Sometimes they are commuting to college and are reminded every day of others' needs. All of these different role demands make it harder for the first-generation college student to feel they have an identity as a college student. Link to this article by Linda Banks-Santilli at the Washington Post for more about guilt and the first-generation college student: https://www.washingtonpost.com/posteverything/wp/2015/06/03/guilt-is-one-of-the-biggest-struggles-first-generation-college-students-face/?utm_term=.0d73f4186beb

> *My mother had bought a sewing machine for me. When I went away to college, she gave me a sewing machine, a typewriter, and a suitcase, and my mother made $17 a week working as a maid 12 hours a day, and she did that for me.*
>
> –Alice Walker, author of *The Color Purple*
>
> Retrieved from https://www.brainyquote.com/quotes/alice_walker_625878

Some families make sacrifices and encourage their children to go to college. Students may feel guilty as though they are taking needed resources away. They may feel the responsibility to take care of the family despite being distant. They might feel they are called on to take on the burden of being a savior or hero to the family. While they may feel proud to bring honor to the family by being the first to attend college, the family's expectation is stressful.

Even with a sympathetic family, members may have little experience to share about how things are done in college and don't have first-hand knowledge of college culture. Families may want to but can't offer their student their knowledgeable guidance or map the path because they have not taken it themselves.

Students may experience a lack of familiarity with college life and academics that can lead them to feel like they are different, don't belong, and are unwanted there. They may feel unqualified despite their outstanding achievement in high school.

It is not unusual to feel like you are an imposter and will sooner or later be found out. It feels like the admissions office slipped up and let you in by mistake. The main job of the trained professionals at the admissions office is to pick qualified students. If they did not think you could do it, they would have admitted someone else instead. They went to some trouble to determine you deserve to be here, can do the work, and belong here.

This article explains imposter syndrome in more detail and offers some solutions. https://www.collegexpress.com/articles-and-advice/student-life/articles/living-campus/youre-not-fake-you-just-have-imposter-syndrome/

This article from the American Psychological Association talks about how imposter syndrome can also be seen in graduate students and suggests additional solutions. https://www.apa.org/gradpsych/2013/11/fraud.aspx

Valerie Young, Ed.D. has written a book about imposter syndrome — The Secret Thoughts of Successful Women: Why

Capable People Suffer from Imposter Syndrome and How to Thrive in Spite of It (Young 2011)

> *People's beliefs about their abilities have a profound effect on those abilities. Ability is not a fixed property; there is huge variability in how you perform. People who have a sense of self-efficacy bounce back from failure; they approach things in terms of how to handle them rather than worrying about what can go wrong."*
>
> –Albert Bandura
>
> Retrieved from https://www.verywellmind.com/albert-bandura-quotes-2795687

The sense of unfamiliarity, a fragility of support, and feeling of being different set the first-generation college student up to doubt their ability to succeed at college. You can overcome this doubt.

Carol S. Dweck, Ph.D., wrote *Mindset: The New Psychology of Success*. Albert Bandura wrote Self-*Efficacy: The Exercise of Control*. Much of what follows in this section is based on a combination of their ideas.

> *Whether you are a first-generation college student or not, it is crucial that you believe in your ability to grow and learn and master things you may not currently know how to do.*
>
> *Before you can do that —if you have a fixed mindset— you need to question it. Dr. Dweck would say that a person with a fixed mindset believes that who they are and what they can do is fixed and unchangeable.*
>
> *The idea of a fixed mindset might sound okay to you if you have been told you are smart or you have some excellent high school grades that did not take you much effort to get. This belief is a source of great misery. You may believe smart people don't have to study. Perhaps you didn't study in high school because you*

would look dumb for having to study. You may think you can get by in college without studying. You can't.

Believing that you are a fixed entity can lead to suffering as you continually attempt to prove you are not wrong about what you think of your abilities. If you fail a test, you are apt to see yourself as a failure. This experience is an emotional event that can lead to blaming other things, denial, and avoiding studying as a way of not being reminded you failed. It can make studying more distressing because it becomes about proving yourself rather than learning.

Don't confuse insisting you are a fixed entity with maintaining integrity or being stubbornly strong. Understanding that you are growing and changing is not a loss of honor or a sign of weakness. Strong people of integrity embrace growth.

Sometimes you have a growth mindset, but you suspect others will discriminate against you because of your background, and so you keep it a secret. This secret can cut you off from others' support and make it harder for you to see your status as a source of inner strength and resilience. Each situation is different and requires you use your best judgment in weighing the risks and benefits of disclosing.

You become more concerned with what your mistakes reveal about you than with how your mistakes could be used to learn and do better the next time. A low test score can feel like a stain forever rather than something from which you can learn. You fall into saying that a lousy spelling test means you are a bad speller, rather than someone who can learn to spell better with effort. You turn the act of misspelling into the state of being a bad speller. You can practice spelling, but being a lousy speller implies you will be one all your life, and there is nothing you can do about it.

You can change and adopt a growth mindset. If you have a growth mindset, your failures don't define you. You believe that change and growth will expand your abilities. How you are now is not

> *permanent. You know that practice improves performance, and you don't buy into the idea that to be accomplished, you have to do things effortlessly. If you know you can learn and grow, you are more likely to keep trying and persist through adversity. You are more likely to bounce back on the next test, having taken the time to study your mistakes and do things differently. You are more likely to see setbacks as a challenge or a signal to do something differently.*

A first-generation college student who believes in a growth mindset does not let their lack of familiarity, sense of fragile support, and feeling of being different get in their way. Instead, they see it as a starting point from which to grow.

They become familiar with financial aid by learning about their financial alternatives from student services. They find out about how student health works, and they study syllabi and catalogs and ask their resident advisor or professor when they cannot find the answer.

They don't buy into the idea that they will not do well because they did not get the right academic preparation in high school. Instead, they go about studying extra hours or change their priorities and drop activities. They ask for help and directions from classmates. They seek out tutors. They look into remedial courses. They identify any knowledge deficits they have about critical thinking and sharpen their skills. They go to find out what resources are available at Student Educational Services. They explore any help they might need with a learning disability or attentional problems with Student Disability Services. They find out at Student Disabilities whether they are eligible for accommodations, such as extra time on tests, early registration, special note pens for note-taking, and being allowed to take tests in the quiet of a testing center.

They may recognize they lack the support that other students have, but they don't see that as permanent. They resist labeling themselves or buying into others' labels of them. Instead, they look for groups that might be supportive, such as campus ministries, counseling services, and clubs that have similar interests. They get to know their teachers by going to their office hours. They go to the study center. They find out what the college does to support diversity. They become a coffeehouse regular. They volunteer with what little spare time they have.

They also realize that their family members are not fixed entities, and they can learn and change as well. They may decide to ask their family to come to campus and show them around and help them discover what the college experience is. In that way, they help family members make connections and reduce misunderstandings. The family may feel less abandoned and also more aware of the stressors with which their student is coping.

Students with a growth mindset actively seek out ways to manage their time and money better. When they overspend or find they have mismanaged their time and are overwhelmed, they examine where they went wrong. They use that information to devise better ways and then practice them. They don't say that they are irresponsible with money or time. They remind themselves that they are learning and will get better. They tell themselves that they can do it.

> *And if you are at home, and you're sitting on your couch, and you're watching this right now, all I have to say is that this is hard work. I've worked hard for a long time, and it's not about, you know...it's not about winning. But what it's about is not giving up. If you have a dream, fight for it. There's a discipline for passion. And it's not about how many times you get rejected, or you fall down, or you're beaten up. It's about how many times you stand up and are brave, and you keep on going. Thank you!*
>
> **Lady Gaga**

Here is Lady Gaga's full acceptance speech transcript https://www.elle.com/culture/celebrities/a25740522/lady-gaga-oscars-2019-acceptance-speech-transcript/

Students with a growth mindset deal with their lack of knowledge and fear of the unknown by seeing each as an opportunity to stretch themselves and grow from the challenge. They expect to stumble, but they also know they will get back up. They don't have anything to prove. They know they are learners and human. They fail but aren't 'failures.'

You will find some of the ideas mentioned above, as well as some excellent tips on making your college experience as a first-generation student a positive one, in this Marquette University Counseling Center website pdf: https://www.marquette.edu/counseling/documents/1stgenerationcollegestudents-websitematerials.pdf

Samantha Fitz-Gerald wrote her doctoral thesis for the Philadelphia College of Osteopathic Medicine Department of Psychology on *Stress, Coping, and Academic Self-Efficacy in First-Generation College Students*. She found that students coped with handling their feelings about going to college when their parents did not receive college degrees by spending time with friends and family, talking to a mental health therapist, and joining groups and organizations to relate to others about their experiences. Fitz-Gerald found that some had problems adapting due to their unrealistic expectations for college. https://digitalcommons.pcom.edu/cgi/viewcontent.cgi?article=1424&context=psychology_dissertations

Sometimes trying to do things perfectly to overcome your self-doubts works against you. This excellent article explains perfectionism and how you can overcome it. https://www.brown.edu/campus-life/support/counseling-and-psychological-services/index.php?q=perfectionism

Recognizing What Helps First-Generation College Students Will Also Help You

It is vital that you believe in your ability to meet the challenges ahead of you and complete the task of going to college. This belief, which is called 'self-efficacy,' makes it more likely that you will succeed. It makes it more likely that you will be motivated, expend enough effort, and thrive. You can influence the events in your own life, and it is crucial for you to believe it. According to Albert Bandura, the David Starr Jordan Professor Emeritus of Social Sciences in Psychology at Stanford University, this belief can improve your ability to cope with stress, to help you stick with it longer, and work through it on your terms and gain the positive experience that success provides. You can increase your skills.

The place of control in your life is within you.

On the other hand, you aren't responsible for everything and should not blame yourself for everything. You work for excellence, not perfection. You can develop more and more coping techniques with practice. Actively engage with others in the creative process of learning. Use the give and take to get reinforcement and constructive criticism. Get your professors to buy into your efforts at success by engaging them in discussion as you learn their material. Ask questions. Keep positive expectations of your results. It is critical that you accept yourself as you are but also that you see yourself as a changing, growing person. You can solve severe problems if you try hard enough and enlist other people and resources. You can stick to your aims and deal with the unexpected. You can make the needed effort. You can grow with effort. You can learn the coursework. Your studies may be harder than you expected, but you can persist. Hard work pays off. A firm belief in your abilities has the potential to boost performance.

You can boost your belief in yourself by attempting to do small things first. Your early successes at small first steps will build your confidence to do more. What steps have you already made that you might have overlooked? Give yourself credit. Also, look around you for models of success in other students and notice their techniques and habits. While your parents may not have finished college, perhaps you have members of your extended family who have and would be willing to mentor you.

Your mentor can serve as an early warning system to alert you quickly to behaviors you are using to avoid the anxiety of studying, like procrastination behaviors, marijuana use, and partying.

Imagine your success in vivid detail as a way of having something to look forward to experiencing. Celebrate others, like Senator Sinema, who have overcome similar obstacles to succeed and realize if she can, so can you.

> *I lived for two years in an abandoned gas station with no running water and no electricity after my parents got divorced and my stepdad couldn't get a job. So, I think a lot about families like mine who were middle class and struggled. So that experience drives my philosophy.*
>
> –Senator Kyrsten Sinema
>
> Retrieved from https://www.brainyquote.com/quotes/kyrsten_sinema_638800

13

Improving Your Well-being

These next sections will offer some specific coping techniques, identify healthy habits, and provide resources to explore particular symptom complexes. We will talk about some common misconceptions about emotional problems and look at resources for students with suicidal thoughts. Finally, we will look at impediments to well-being. None of what we say is meant as the treatment of physical or mental health issues. As a way of avoiding even the appearance of offering treatment, we have instead referred you to quality sources of information about mental and physical health and treatment.

LEARNING MORE ABOUT MENTAL HEALTH

We have already mentioned some of the elements that contribute to wellness like sleep, proper nutrition, a realistic routine, and connections with supportive people. We have discussed other elements, such as a sense of direction and purpose, personal safety, and some degree of financial security. A less obvious element of wellness is staying informed about mental health. If you feel like you are having a problem with your mental health, it is vital that you seek help early because such problems make everything else harder.

One of those resources to help connect you with supportive people who offer this education is *Active Minds*. *Active Minds* uses the student-to-student model to increase awareness of mental health issues and suicide prevention. Check to see if your college has a chapter on campus: https://www.activeminds.org/programs/chapter-network/

IDENTIFYING SPECIFIC COPING TECHNIQUES

OVERCOMING DISTRESS College can be a remarkable opportunity, but it can also be overwhelming at times between exams, finances, relationships, and family. Gloria Whelchel is a licensed professional counselor in Tempe, Arizona, whose writings can help you when you are feeling overwhelmed. In her *Improve the Moment Work Sheet,* she offers advanced distress tolerance skills. We strongly recommend you go to https://www.dbtselfhelp.com/html/improve_the_moment_worksheet.html. The www.dbtselfhelp.com website is a useful service for people wanting to learn more about Dialectical Behavior Therapy (DBT).

Perhaps, you counted on parents and teachers having your back and keeping you on the right track by reminding and guiding you. In college, you have much less structure. If you coast and take things as they come up, you can get pretty far off track before you get a wake-up call. No one is there to ask you what you are doing with your days. As the one who is now responsible for your structure, you need to be intentional about how you spend your time. Ask yourself each morning, "Where am I going, and what do I need to do to get there?" Knowing your direction helps you formulate your path. Feeling like you are on a planned path can free you up to notice things along it as well. You can be spontaneous without having to be haphazard.

ONE-WORD MINDFULNESS TECHNIQUE As you go through the day, ask yourself, "Is my experience of this moment vivid?" Then specifically look at the colors, smells, interactions, internal emotions that are going on in the present. You might overlook the joy of pursuing the positive if you are as devoted to the idea of preventing bad things as this book is. It would help if you shifted from playing not to lose to playing for the win. Playing has its place.

ORIENTING YOURSELF TOWARD THE POSITIVE Each day, ask yourself, "What have I seen today that surprised me, and what have I seen today that moved me?" Then during the day, look for those things, knowing you will ask that question of yourself each night. These exercises help orient you to the present and may increase your enjoyment of the present. It helps to turn your mental focus toward looking for positives. Remember that your unconscious does not know whether or not your pessimism about the weather is warranted but is putting its raincoat on just the same. It does not know you are saying it without really thinking realistically about the weather. Don't be carelessly negative when you talk to yourself.

Dr. Seligman notes that pessimists see negative situations as personal, pervasive, and persistent (Seligman 1994). You can assess how likely you are to look on the pessimistic side by taking "The Learned Optimism Test" adapted from Dr. Martin Seligman's book, *Learned Optimism*. https://web.stanford.edu/class/msande271/onlinetools/LearnedOpt.html

CULTIVATING SERENITY Learn the Serenity Prayer (https://www.chronicle.com/article/Who-Wrote-the-Serenity-Prayer-/146159) and ask yourself repeatedly about whether you can control something or not. Will Muschamp says to the University of S.C. football players he coaches, "Control the controllable." When you realize something is not controllable, try to have some serenity about it. Make peace with the *presently possible*, knowing something more might be possible in the future. Muddle when you need to but don't give up or fall into seeing yourself as a helpless victim. In college, it is essential to understand failure, and that not everything you want to happen will.

LEARNING TO BE DELIBERATE Earlier, we mentioned the STAR interview technique. Another meaning of the acronym STAR refers to the cognitive process you likely were told about in high school: S̲top, T̲hink, A̲ct, and R̲eview. Don't let the simplicity of this fool you. Deliberately and consciously using this can be a powerful habit.

DEVELOPING HEALTHY MENTAL AND PHYSICAL HABITS

Without thinking much about it, we routinely accept negative things we tell ourselves. Cognitive-behavioral therapists teach people to identify and question these and other self-defeating thoughts. Cognitive-behavioral therapists have recognized that there is a connection between what we tell ourselves and how we feel. You might like to learn more about how thinking with your feelings, all-or-none thinking, labeling, mindreading, blaming, and the other automatic negative thoughts can be identified and reduced. Take a look Serenella Ferraro's video, *Life Coaching: How to recognize and get rid of ANTs (Automatic Negative Thoughts)* https://www.youtube.com/watch?v=54UzbWx2ZFE

Getselfhelp.co.uk is a website that offers worksheets, videos, self-help" for distress now," and self-help ideas for specific problems. Find the new site at https://www.get.gg/index.html.

Notice what you are saying to yourself and then begin to question whether it is accurate and makes sense. Ask trusted others if they share your opinion.

Try to realize that you are the locus of control of your life. You are the hero of your life, not a bystander or victim. For that reason, it is essential to take responsibility for your actions and look before you leap.

If you make a practice of putting your thoughts and feelings into words each day in a journal, you will have a better chance to find patterns and see things more clearly.

When you find yourself worried frequently about being abandoned, take the worry energy and focus away from finding the person who will never leave you and put it on learning to be more self-reliant. Then, when you get into a future relationship, you will feel less vulnerable, have more power, and not settle for a person that does not want you to be your best self.

Make a point of scheduling fun activities and identifying recreations that renew you and affirm you.

Sometimes your friends will notice something they like about you that surprises you. Remember? What were some of those?

When you experience tragedy, is it possible for you to use your particular personal skills to express what you are feeling in words or by what you create? As Carrie Fisher said to Meryl Streep, "Take your broken heart, make it into art."

If you are feeling a sense of being demoralized, chapter A-10 offers resources to help nurture an openness to wonder rather than despair.

The exponential change that is taking place in the brain sciences field is another cause for hope. Henry Nasrallah, MD., in the September 2019 issue of Current Psychiatry, described these: He noted that eventually the current diagnoses of mental illness will be replaced with neuro-science based names. Medications will be renamed based on their mechanism of action on the brain. These impending changes reflect progress in more precisely matching medication with brain pathology. He said that genetic researchers are identifying risk genes in psychiatric disorders and learning to replace them using CRISPR technology. Neuro-immunologists are studying neuroinflammation and working with immune cells in the brain in hopes of preventing the neurodegeneration associated with some disorders. New approaches to treatment that take advantage of better understanding of mitochondrial dysfunction, the microbiota, the microbiome, and biomarkers are on the near horizon. Because of the use of artificial intelligence, advances in machine learning, and neuromodulation techniques, new treatment options are opening up. He noted we are beginning to use methods that reverse mental conditions more rapidly by means of IV infusions, inhalation, or intranasal means of administration(Nasrallah 2019 pp 10-12).

FEELING SUICIDAL

Sometimes there are warning signs you can look for in yourself or your friends that can alert you to there being a risk of suicide. These signs may come up even before you or your friend experiences a thought of suicide. The presence of these signs makes the risk of a sudden suicidal act more likely.

If your friend has had a recent break-up or sees themselves as failing at school, or losing their friend group, they may feel intense emotional pain and believe they are stuck and cannot get out of what feels like an unbearable situation. You may observe that they seem to be working hard at pretending they are okay and having fun, but you realize your friend is watching what they say more. When you ask them things, they seem to be avoiding answering your questions and avoiding you. When they do talk to you, they seem to be going over and over their sad situation and what could have caused it. You can't get them to see the positive side of things, and they can't stop thinking about it. Sometimes your friend holds their head like there is something wrong with their brain, and they can't make everyday decisions. You notice they are keeping you awake with their problems sleeping, and you are getting agitated yourself by their edginess and irritability. Igor

Glaynker, MD Ph.D., describes your friend's symptoms as a feeling of "frantic hopelessness" (Moran 2019). These symptoms of suicide crisis syndrome justify getting help immediately, before the crisis comes to a head.

Taking some medications can result in suicidal ideas. If you have suicidal ideas, speak with your health provider about the medications you are taking. Remember to tell them about non-prescription substances as well. Let them know about any medications you have stopped recently.

One of the assumptions in suicidal thinking is that life is not going to change. Have you ever had the experience of needing to cross a busy street and predicting that there would never be an opportunity? After some time went by, you were surprised that traffic did slow down. Your assumption of it staying busy was based on a narrow segment of time. When you feel suicidal, you are predicting your entire future based on how you feel right now. It is hard in the middle of an unbearably painful emotional state to believe that it will pass, but it will eventually. Read more about this below and investigate the resources.

If you are feeling suicidal, remove pills, rope, and weapons so that when you have the impulse to use these items, they are not there, and you have time to change your mind. It is particularly important that you get rid of your gun. The majority of gun deaths in the US are suicides. If you can't do that, then buy a trigger lock for your gun and give the weapon, lock, and ammunition to a trusted person who does not live with you and will agree to keep it for an extended period. Having access to a gun makes even brief suicidal impulses potentially lethal. Look at the statistics on this site: https://everytownresearch.org/firearm-suicide/

The National Suicide Hotline is staffed twenty-four hours a day. 1-800-273-8255. The website is http://www.suicidepreventionlifeline.org/.

The Crisis Text Line: Text to 741741 (http://www.crisistextline.org/texting-in/)

The Transgender Suicide Prevention Hotline is 1-877-565-8860. There are several other diversity-specific suicide hotlines noted in the section on diversity resources in the appendix.

You may want very much to live but feel trapped and can't see your way out. You may notice you are incredibly moody, feel hopeless, are taking risks not usual for you, are pulling back from friends, are drinking more, feel irritable or uncontrollably angry, and have difficulty finding a reason to live or purpose for your life. If so, you should immediately seek effective treatment. These suggestions are no substitute for treatment. These suggestions are meant only to be educational and to help you find treatment.

> *The way we experience the world around us is a direct reflection of the world within us.*
> —Gabrielle Bernstein, founder of a social networking and mentoring website for women

Please stop and question whether your perception of your situation is being distorted because of your depressed world within you. Depressed mood and persistent difficulty enjoying anything are risk factors for suicide, but the various forms of anxiety can lead to a mood state that can feel almost unbearable. That makes anxiety, agitation, and panic dangerous. Like insomnia and psychotic thinking, all three of these manifestations of anxiety are very treatable. Relief from their urgent discomfort can be lifesaving. The treatment works if you persist at it.

You can learn ways of making the emotional pain more tolerable until you can escape it. You have been able to tolerate negative feelings before. You can learn ways of escaping the pain other

Improving Your Well-being

than by ending your life. There will be a pain in life from loneliness, sadness, anxiety, and anger, but it does not go on forever. Think about the times when you felt bad before, and the feeling eventually passed. What did you do to get yourself out of the pattern of avoiding dealing with the situation and into using your active, problem-solving skills to get through it? Did you get busy with something? Did you call someone? Did you listen to music or distract yourself? Did you get out and try to be around others? Did you use your Virtual Hope Box app, or call a helpline? Whom can you contact that will remind you that you won't feel this way forever, that you can and will be able to tolerate it, and you can do things to get out of feeling this way?

If at all possible, speak with your family and friends about how you are feeling and give them a chance to help you. In your hopelessness, you may find it difficult to believe they will respond. Reach out and give them a chance. You don't have to deal with these thoughts alone.

Choosing to Live: How to Defeat Suicide Through Cognitive Therapy by Thomas E. Ellis can be found at https://www.amazon.com/Choosing-Live-Suicide-Through-Cognitive/dp/1572240563 This book speaks to those thinking about suicide and their treaters. It is a nonjudgmental self-help guide that gives readers tools to help them determine risks. It teaches them about the factors that lead to suicidal thoughts and behaviors. It provides a sequenced plan for change so that the reader develops other problem-solving abilities and positive beliefs.

Colorado State University has an awesome website that has several national emergency hotlines for people having suicidal thoughts to call. It provides a list of warning signs, assessment tools, and links to other resources. It is https://health.colostate.edu/suicide-prevention/

Look at the American Association of Suicidology website in detail at https://www.suicidology.org/. It offers a free handbook download of *A Journey Toward Health and Hope: Your Handbook for Recovery after a Suicide Attempt* in which survivors share their experiences and strategies.

The Jed Foundation states it "exists to protect emotional health and prevent suicide for our nation's teens and young adults." Their website addresses some questions about emotional health and suicide at https://www.jedfoundation.org/who-we-are/.

Besides providing resources, The American Foundation for Suicide Prevention discusses the warning signs for suicide at https://afsp.org/about-suicide/risk-factors-and-warning-signs/.

Suicide Prevention Resource Center also looks at risks and protective factors in suicide and provides resources as well at https://www.sprc.org/resources-programs.

This website is helpful to people who have attempted suicide and survived and are coping with having tried to kill themselves. https://www.suicidology.org/suicide-survivors/suicide-attempt-survivors

Suicide Anonymous is a peer-run support group with groups in Tennessee and California at http://suicideanonymous.net

Ask your provider about the possibility of using low dose lithium for suicidal thinking. Lithium has been shown to reduce suicidal ideas in two-thirds of the people who take it, regardless of their diagnosis.

If you are a health care provider, you may find the book that Dr. John Chiles co-authored, *Clinical Manual for the Assessment and Treatment of Suicidal Patients,* helpful.

We have heard some ministers paint such an idyllic picture of heaven that we wondered why we were waiting to go. Then we realized— if we rushed dying—we would have died an unlived life. We remembered the poem found in Dawna Markova's book *<u>I Will Not Die an Unlived Life: Reclaiming Purpose and Passion</u>*.

Improving Your Well-being

"I will not die an unlived life.
I will not live in fear
of falling or catching fire.
I choose to inhabit my days,
to allow my living to open me,
to make me less afraid,
more accessible;
To loosen my heart
until it becomes a wing,
a torch, a promise.
I choose to risk my significance,
to live so that which came to me as seed
goes to the next as blossom,
and that which came to me as blossom,
goes on as fruit."

Retrieved from https://www.goodreads.com/author/quotes/180600.Dawna_Markova

Dawna Markova is asking us to choose to live wholeheartedly and risk our significance. She is saying that —when we do— life will open us, make us more accessible to life and reflect our essence. In that way, we will live our lives and not just merely exist.

In her book, Dawna Markova said, "When you have the courage to shape your life from the essence of who you are, you ignite, becoming truly alive. This requires letting go of everything that is inauthentic." I Will Not Die an Unlived Life, by Dawna Markova - Awakin.org. http://www.awakin.org/read/view.php?tid=552

SURVIVING A LOSS BY SUICIDE

Our words cannot begin to describe the agony of losing someone to suicide. If you have lost a loved one to suicide, we are sorry for your immeasurable loss. We know there is no magical way to take away your suffering, but we do so wish there were. We know that we can't truly understand what it feels like unless we have ourselves experienced it. Sue Chance has experienced it, and her book has resonated with others who are surviving a loss by suicide. Perhaps it could speak to what you are experiencing. https://www.amazon.com/Stronger-than-Death-Suicide-Touches/dp/0393335615/ref=sr_1_fkmrnull_1?keywords=Stronger+than+Death+by+sue+chance&qid=1549830724&s=gateway&sr=8-1-fkmrnull

Beyond Grief: A Guide for the Recovery from the Death of a Loved One by Carol Staudacher offers insights into what it is like to experience different kinds of losses, including losses from suicide and murder. https://www.amazon.com/Beyond-Grief-Guide-Recovering-Death/dp/0934986436

http://www.suicidology.org/suicide-survivors/suicide-attempt-survivors deals with lesbian and gay suicide attempt survivors.

The American Foundation of Suicide Prevention offers help for suicide loss survivors https://theactionalliance.org/sites/default/files/the-way-forward-final-2014-07-01.pdf

GETTING HELP

One step on the path to getting help and finding meaning is becoming more educated about what you are experiencing. If you skip to the appendix and study some of the resources listed there, it may help you know better what kind of help you need. Then, come back to this section for more ideas about how to find that help.

Improving Your Well-being

Having determined your situation does not require you to go immediately to the emergency room, you may have started the process of looking for help by turning to your phone book or the Internet.

If your initial efforts have not been fruitful, here are some other ways to find a provider. Call the number for behavioral health on the back of your insurance card. Your insurance company may have a list of preferred providers in your area. You may go to the website of your state medical board or another licensure board for a list of providers near you. Professional societies, like the American Psychological Association or the American Psychiatric Association, have websites that may help you locate providers who are members. Call the number on the back of your insurance card to find out who the preferred providers are in your area. Your local hospital's website may list the members of its staff with their credentials.

Some organizations often refer people to mental health providers. Usually, in a family medical practice, the office manager or the doctor's nurse can tell you whom they like to use. You may call your past pediatrician, your gynecologist, or your family's physician for recommendations. Such organizations might include local religious organizations, the Department of Children and Family Services, school counseling centers, and support groups. For example, if you are grieving, you might call a grief support organization and ask about providers they use who specialize in grief and loss. You may find your school's women's center very helpful.

While psychologists, licensed professional counselors, social workers, family therapists, drug and addiction counselors cannot provide medication, they do provide therapy, and they can also help you in deciding about taking medication or not.

There may be a community mental health center or clinic near you that provides a range of services, including an intensive outpatient program. Many medical schools have associated clinics.

There are some psychiatrists and other providers who do telemedicine, and you would see that listed on their website. In that case, you might make the trip to meet your provider in person for evaluation, and after you have seen them enough to feel comfortable, then meet with them using telemedicine. Your provider would have to have a license in your state.

Next: Strategy 14—Survey where you have been and how you got there.

14
Summing It Up with an Equation and Final Mnemonic

The authors have relied on Mike Rutherford's *Equation for Change* in writing this book. Mike Rutherford— Rutherford Learning Group https://www.rutherfordlg.com/ —has said that dissatisfaction alone is not enough for someone, or some group, to make changes and overcome their natural resistance to making changes. A person needs to feel a heightened sense of dissatisfaction and then be introduced to a compelling vision of what things would be like if they made changes. That is not enough. He feels that helping them make the first successful small steps towards change is a crucial part of the equation. From a talk we were able to hear, here is his equation:

Dissatisfaction + Compelling Vision + Successful first small steps > Resistance = Change

The authors hope that they have shown you a compelling vision and how to make the first small steps in your college journey.

One of the themes in this book is the importance of having your brain at its best and your mind open. You have read about how having a clear notion of why you are going to college and what your long-term goals are is essential to keeping yourself motivated to do the necessary hard work. You became more aware of the pitfalls of college and the need to be alert for them, in the same way, a dog might perk up its ears when it senses danger. Repeatedly you read about the importance of developing relationships that empower you to be the best person you can be and provide connectedness and emotional support. You recognized that building a foundation of personal belief about the world, your life, and your life's purpose that considered what you had already been taught was a necessary task. As you saw the need to do all these things to succeed in college and avoid getting into trouble, your growing sense of self and confidence in yourself allowed you to claim responsibility for your future.

Wouldn't it be great if you could quickly remind yourself of these things in certain situations? We hope you will look past the use of these trite clichés as we suggest our way. Imagine your body from head to foot and associate these phrases with different body parts.

To master college and life, keep your

Mind — open

Eyes — on the prize

Ears — alert for pitfalls

Arms — outstretched to connect with others

Butt — out of trouble

Feet — grounded in your foundation of belief

Moreover, don't forget to have some fun now and then.

Next: Strategy 15—Learn where to reach out for extra help along the way.

APPENDIX OF RESOURCES

A-1

Resources to Help You Plan What to do for a Living

If you are hesitant about going to college because you don't feel prepared, then consider going away to a preparatory school or taking remedial courses at a community college first. Look at online courses you might take on your own to polish the skills you need. If you don't feel mature enough to go to college, take some time to discover yourself. Work on your frustration tolerance. Maybe you feel like you need to get yourself feeling better mentally before going off to school. Taking time to do some work in therapy while earning money is better than going to college and falling behind. The fast pace of assignments becomes a problem if you are too depressed and anxious to focus or too addicted to be able to manage your life.

Being able to get into college is not the same as being mature enough to go. Some students lack the life experiences that would have helped them develop the self-control and ability to take responsibility for themselves that going to college requires. Having some time to work at a "starter" job can teach you responsibility and self-control and help you understand more about managing money. Living in a nearby apartment can give you experience in managing time and taking care of yourself.

If you are a parent reading this book, you might want to read Dr. Louis Prefeta's article "A Very Dangerous Place for a Child is College (Profeta 2019)." https://www.linkedin.com/pulse/very-dangerous-place-child-college-louis-m-profeta-md/?fbclid=IwAR0SCvUZVy9klyvmBfK5HgpC_IHD0tX8nz93uz5fSmyHyTTE_9DLgC_3q3k

You may be tired of your parents, teachers, relatives, and friends repeatedly asking you, "What's your plan?" You may even be able to laugh about them always asking it. But it's no laughing matter. Whether or not you feel you are in charge of your life, you will bear the responsibility and consequences of your decisions. Having a long-range plan is like having a map that allows you to know if any particular thing you do leads you in the direction you plan to go or away from it.

You may have heard that picking the right life partner and the right occupation may determine whether you are happy when you are thirty. Finding the right life partner is a long process. Spending time getting to know well a wide variety of people helps you in understanding the people you date. From that understanding, you avoid dating people that you would not consider marrying. That protects you from setting yourself up to fall in love with someone who is not a good match. This process takes time and trial-and-error. Fortunately, you have time.

With choosing the right occupation, your decision-making process needs to begin sooner— with a plan of approach.

Minnesota State Careerwise divides all careers into sixteen clusters. These clusters include: Agriculture, Food, and Natural Resources; Architecture and Construction; Arts, Audio/Video Technology, and Communications; Business, Management, and Administration; Education and Training; Finance; Government and Public Administration; Health Science; Hospitality and Tourism; Human Services; Information Technology; Law, Public Safety, Corrections, and Security; Manufacturing; Marketing, Sales, and Service; Science, Technology, Engineering, and Mathematics; Transportation, Distribution, and Logistics.

Go to - https://careerwise.minnstate.edu/careers/index.html This website, developed by the Minnesota State Colleges and Universities, will allow you to explore all of the careers and jobs in each cluster. You will find careers, pathways, and majors. Each cluster includes a video description and link to related careers. You will be able to complete a 'Career Cluster Interest Assessment' to determine your areas of career interest. In the sixteen clusters, there are eighty-one pathways. Additionally, not only does this site give you information on college majors, but also information on certifications, short-term training, and apprenticeships if you choose not to go to a four-year college. By spending time exploring these careers and pathways, you will be able to set goals and design plans for your future.

If your plan does not include a four-year college, there are other ways to plan a career. Everyone does not need to go to a four-year college. However, everyone needs some training after high school.(see below) There are success stories concerning individuals who do not complete a college degree. The stories aren't always about individuals having a big salary since money is not the only measure of success. But let's face it, you have to have some money to afford a place to live, food, and the 'good life' as you define it. Many young people who graduate from college have made poor decisions about a major. Just completing a college degree won't help you if there are limited jobs in that area of study. Some of these poor decisions come from the individual not having sufficient guidance in careers. But honestly, you are in charge of your decisions. Have you explored the economic climate before you advance into a major career? Do you know if there are jobs available? Where are those jobs? Do you know about the starting salary? Can you live on that salary? You must be your advocate for your own life.

In politics and social media, Americans debate the necessity, purpose, and value of college education. From all sides, influence and pressure are brought to bear on colleges and college-age students.

Ill-informed opinions and misinterpretations of facts and data innocently lead to incorrect misconceptions. Other times the truth is intentionally twisted. Acting on such misinformation risks damaging your chances for success even before you begin. Depend on little else but the most verifiable sources of information to research your decisions. This added effort will make a difference in your ability to determine the truth and discard biased self-serving publicity.

Watch for sweeping generalizations like these: Students don't need more than a high school education. College is not important. College is an absolute necessity and the only option after high school. College is the only form of post-secondary education. People who don't go to college will not succeed.

SOME STATISTICS ON THE ADVANTAGES OF COLLEGE

"The Bureau of Labor Statistics reports that only about one-third of all jobs require education beyond high school. (Parker 2016)

The Good Jobs Project looks at where good jobs are that don't need a BA or BS. Check it out at https://goodjobsdata.org/

So, it's essential to distinguish the facts of what a post-secondary education can do for you, and for all to understand that obtaining a four-year college degree isn't always the best strategy for succeeding in today's job market. Two of the options that don't include a college degree are an associate degree at a technical college or studying for a certificate in a continuing education program in a needed field of work. Check out the technical colleges in your area. Numerous programs will prepare you for a life's work in some area you may enjoy.

Another option might be observing or working in a small business to determine if this is something that you would like to do. There is a story about a young man who left Harvard University after his first year because he wanted to work in a woodworking business. He had spent some of his time during high school working in the company with the owner. Even though his parents had both graduated from Harvard, he knew that he wanted to own a woodworking business. There are some opportunities to work your way up in a small business, but it requires a passion and much hard work.

> "...according to the most recent US Census, about one-third of Americans have bachelor's degrees- and the Bureau of Labor Statistics show that only about one-third of all jobs require education beyond high school. Moreover, the bureau predicts that the biggest growth in the next decade will be in the number of jobs that require a bachelor's degree or more. According to the Pew Research Center, the disparity in earning potential between high-school graduates has never been bigger," ... (which contradicts claims that one's) ...parents did better with a high school diploma than they've done with a four-year degree." (Parker 2016, p3-4). That is a possible scenario, of course, but usually, that is not the case, and the majority of data and statistics continue to outline the numerous benefits of higher education. According to Pew research, "college grads earn $17,500 more than high school grads. Those with college degrees are more likely to be employed full-time and less likely to be unemployed." (Ibid p 4)

The benefits of receiving a college education can be numerous. For generations, college graduates have enjoyed their economic and social advantages over those who were less-educated. In recent years, studies done by the Centers for Disease Control and Prevention National Center for Health Statistics clearly indicated that more education tends to lead to healthier lifestyle choices and better access to healthcare. (Cardillo, Online blog entitled, "Can a College Degree Make You Healthier and Happier?" by Donna Cardillo, RN, MA.)

Graduates with a bachelor's degree or higher are even recorded to live longer, and approximately nine years longer than those who do not graduate from college (Cardillo). As indicated by current trends, college-educated workers will likely continue to enjoy most of the new jobs and be the recipients of the highest pay gains (Cardillo). In other instances, a college education has been shown to strengthen people's fortitude and better equip them to handle stress in their daily lives. Data shows that the college experience tends to increase people's confidence levels and encourage communication skills (Cardillo). A college graduate is more likely to be up-to-date on current issues and more apt to engage on global ones. They are more likely to marry and to own a home, and the home they own is more likely to be in another place than the town where they were born and grew up, or in other words, a college graduate enjoys more geographic mobility. Enrico Moretti, an economist at the University of California Berkeley said, "College graduates are essentially in a nationwide labor market." According to data collected by the Economic Policy Institute in 2015, college graduates were earning more than 56 percent in comparison to those with just a high school education, which is the largest gap on record with the EPU, dating back to 1973 (Printed Article entitled: "Workers with no college degree fall further behind than ever.") All in all, the benefits are clear, but the market is currently demanding educated workers.

People commonly make the mistake of assuming college is the only option. They believe that college is the only way to get a meaningful job that pays well and has benefits. The misconception that "college" equals "the good life" is not always reality. It's not true for the many college dropouts, who, for various reasons, couldn't follow through and finish their degrees. It's also not true for a large number of college graduates who are struggling to pay off student loan debts or struggling to find jobs with degrees that aren't in demand within the job market. College doesn't equal "the good life." It comes with no guarantees, and without the proper strategies and motivation to see it through, the result can be a waste of time and money.

College is not always the "right" or most productive path for everyone, and that has no bearing on whether or not they are capable of succeeding. Explore your options before you make a decision.

Secondary education refers to high school instruction. After earning a high school diploma or equivalent, many students choose to pursue post-secondary education, such as college, university, community colleges, junior college, career school, technical school, or vocational/trade school, public vs. private schools, and special interest. One path might lead to an 'associate degree.' This degree is a two-year degree, which includes the core curriculum of the four-year degree. This degree is accepted as a package for admission to many four-year colleges.

College isn't the only option, because interests and abilities vary. People don't need years of classroom experience to be successful. Some pathways and job opportunities don't require post-secondary education. Some people have extraordinary gifts and abilities that go beyond academics. You can not only survive without a college degree, you can thrive, but it all depends on what you want to do, the market value of your endeavor, and how well you have assessed your ability to do it. Knowledge is power, but skills are power too. Experience and skills can be acquired, and this is often not always done within a classroom. When assessing yourself, you should seek to define the skills and abilities that are better suited to build upon, before researching the careers that are best suited for you. Sometimes the general listings will not include the most compatible opportunities. If you don't know what's out there, then you can't understand what's possible.

The same could be said of other possibilities, like whether you're eligible for grants or scholarships. It is another misconception to assume that post-secondary education is simply unaffordable for you. In truth, there are a variety of ways to achieve further education without breaking a bank account or spiraling into debt.

Attending college is not an end in itself. Simply going to college does not ensure success in your life or work. College is a means to an end. It is an institutional tool to help you succeed.

College is not the key to your success—you are. Just like a key has to match with a lock, you have to find the locks that the ridges on your key will fit. Imagine trying to force the wrong key into the wrong door lock, again and again, and all the while expecting a different result. You'll then have some idea of what so many people are doing wrong at the start of their journey to seek post-secondary education.

For a key to fulfill its purpose and unlock whatever thing was previously closed or denied, it must first be molded to do so. In other words, compatibility, more than the key or lock alone, is a critical factor for success. Otherwise, a key is of no use to anyone, and it might as well gather dust in a desk drawer than be waved around for show. Now imagine you're the key, and it's imperative that you find the right door to fulfill your life's purpose. If you don't fit from the start, your efforts, no matter how willfully undertaken, will likely prove futile in the end. We do not suggest that education is ever without benefit, but, if not correctly applied, its usefulness will lessen, along with opportunities for success.

What if you don't finish high school? You can still get work if you are willing to work hard. You may even need to complete a training course for many jobs. Some of the best-paying jobs for a high school dropout include the following examples: general manager (restaurant), executive assistant, truck driver, welder (cutter, solderer, or brazer), automotive service technician or mechanic.

Examples of the highest-paying jobs for high school graduates include: transportation, storage and distribution managers, elevator installers and repairers, detective and criminal investigators, first-line supervisors of non-retail sales workers, transportation inspectors, postmasters and mail superintendents (Georgetown Center on Education and the Workforce- https://cew.georgetown.edu/wp-content/uploads/2014/Recovery2020.ES_.Web_.pdf)

If you don't know what to do with your life, there may be less expensive ways of figuring it out besides going straight from high school into college. Instead of investing money in going to college to find what you want to do with your life, you could invest in some of the career guidance programs below to help you decide. Taking the time and effort to find out what you want to do, or at least get into the ballpark, can save the money you would waste in taking unnecessary courses or having to change your major.

You might consider first acquiring a higher-paying skill in a field that would not be your final career.

If later you are going to school and working at the same time, you may not have to work as many hours if you earn more per hour. For example, the International School of Bartending offers a forty-hour course that will qualify you to tend bar. Bartenders make more money than you might make as an untrained undergraduate looking for a job while they go to school. Saving up some money before starting school might allow you to study without having to work so much while you are in school.

Maybe your real passion would lead you to a culinary arts school, a school for dramatic arts, or an art academy. Does your family's alma mater offer these courses? Should your life choices belong to you, especially if the educational debt you will be acquiring belongs to you?

Our culture would have us believe that everyone has to go to college and that making a good living requires it. This notion is just not correct for everyone. Often, technically trained workers earn more than college graduates, and their training may be shorter and much more appropriate for their interests and talents.

Some employers will tell you they don't care that you graduated from college if you have no job skills, even if it was a prestigious one. In some parts of the country, you could join the other overqualified college graduates doing menial jobs.

If you are worried you might have learning problems such as a reading disability, language disability, math disability, hearing disability, attentional impediments, math disability, or an intellectual impairment from brain trauma, you should get your family to have a psychologist do a psycho-educational test battery. A psycho-educational test will give you a better idea of where your strengths and weaknesses are, and this will help you in deciding about your career. If you are weak in math, you may not want to be a rocket scientist.

As a way of brainstorming about possible technical careers, go to the Central Georgia Technical College website and glance through their many courses of study. You will find jobs you have never heard of before. Notice that there are over fifty courses that you can do online. http://www.centralgatech.edu/programs-of-study/

Steppingblocks (https://www.steppingblocks.com/) describes itself as a digital career counselor. It gives you the Myers-Briggs Personality test and matches you with suggested careers and educational paths based on your results. You then can follow a recommended path or do a custom career search of various career paths. Using their tuition analyzer, they can auto-populate estimated tuition for a school you pick. They have a tool that searches for scholarships from diverse sources and matches you with scholarships based on your demographics. They identify internships. They can use big data analysis to tell you what graduates in a particular major from a specific school typically end doing and what their first job is likely to be and pay. Consult the website for the costs of different packages, and this video for more information: https://www.youtube.com/watch?v=0Fx1rKFwBfU. The career counselors in your school may already use a version of Steppingblocks. Consider consulting your school before buying the individual packages.

https://unigo.com is a helpful site for picking college situations and searching for scholarships. It has articles on textbooks, jobs, internships, and has a review of colleges, in case you might have picked the wrong one.

As mentioned earlier, on the website Wait But Why, in his article *How to Pick a Career (That Actually Fits You)*, Tim Urban offers a thoughtful discussion of career choice. The article works you through the path toward finding a career that reflects both you and your current realities. https://waitbutwhy.com/2018/04/picking-career.html

Self-Directed Search: The Self-Directed Search test matches your personality type with the occupations and types of work environments that fit it best and are most likely to satisfy you. Your results show a summary code that lists the three personality types that match your activities and interests the most out of six personality types- realistic, investigative, artistic, social, enterprising, and conventional. The summary code is then matched to give you a list of occupations to consider with some description of each. You get information about whether your fields are new or emerging high growth industries. There is a personalized list of programs of study associated with your Summary Code and a list of careers organized by career clusters. You can pay the ten-dollar cost with a credit card or Pay Pal. http://www.self-directed-search.com/

If you want to gain employable skills but think you cannot afford to go to college, you might want to explore how you could benefit from MOOCs (Massive Open Online Courses). By completing some of these courses, you gain the skills to demonstrate specific competencies to potential employers.

"As traditional institutions struggle to innovate from within and other education technology vendors attempt to plug and play into the existing system, online competency-based providers release learning from the constraints of the academy. By breaking down learning into competencies—not by courses or even subject matter—these providers can cost-effectively combine modules of learning into pathways that are agile and adaptable to the changing labor market." (Weise, Michelle 2014)

Michelle Weise, of Southern New Hampshire University, has written an eye-opening paper, *Hire Education: Mastery, Modularization, and the Workforce Revolution*. For a free pdf, go to https://www.christenseninstitute.org/wp-content/uploads/2014/07/Hire-Education.pdf

Other universities that are exploring new approaches include Capella, Western Governor, and Wisconsin.

A-2
Resources Concerning Diversity

The following resources may help you or add to your understanding of diversity.

Best Colleges lists some resources for diverse and multi-cultural students:
https://www.bestcolleges.com/resources/diverse-and-multicultural-students/

The following remarkable website not only contains support resources but describes assistive technology available for students with autism, cognitive deficits, hearing deficits, ADHD, and other physical disabilities. https://www.affordablecollegesonline.org/college-resource-center/resources-for-students-with-disabilities/

SACNAS indicates it is "an inclusive organization dedicating to fostering the success of Chicanos/Hispanics and Native Americans, from college students to professionals, in attaining advanced degrees, careers, and positions of leadership in STEM." Web source: https://www.sacnas.org/who-we-are/mission-impact/

Here are some resources for undocumented students. https://www.affordablecollegesonline.org/college-resource-center/undocumented-college-student-resources/

The National Black Student Union encourages black student unions to pursue graduate and professional study, and to network with other student unions in pursuit of employment, and increase campus curricular and co-curricular activities participation. http://nbsu.org/about/

The National Society of Black Engineers is a sizeable student-run organization that seeks to provide personal and professional opportunities for success by improving the recruitment and retention of Black and other minority engineers. http://nsbe.org/home.aspx

The Steve Fund is dedicated to the mental health and emotional well-being of students of color. You can text 741741 to talk to a live, trained Crisis Counselor. They have a Knowledge Center as well. Look up www.stevefund.org

Canadian Association of Muslims with Disabilities is an association of Muslims with disabilities whose vision is an inclusive society that realizes the principles of accessibility. American Muslim Health Professionals indicates they are concerned with Advocacy, Health Education, and Career Development. Moreover, they are an empowerment organization. They note they have an outreach of 7,000 health professionals and students working to leverage the educational background and skills of Muslims in the health care sector to improve the health of Americans.

At NAMI's website, you will find leads to multiple resources https://www.nami.org/Find-Support/LGBTQ and a discussion of the stressors facing members of the LGBTQIA community. The site can help you if you want to locate an LGBTQIA-inclusive provider.

The site mentions the Trevor Project, and it toll-free twenty-four hour national suicide hotline for LGBTQIA youth, which is 866-488-7386. The Trevor Project site is http://www.thetrevorproject.org/, and they have online chat and confidential text messaging. To chat, you link to http://www.thetrevorproject.org/pages/get-help-now#tc or text "Trevor" to 202-304-1200 for confidential text messaging.

Trans Lifeline is a national crisis hotline for transgender people in the United States staffed entirely by other trans and nonbinary people. Their number is 877-565-8860.

The NAMI site also mentions the LGBT National Help Center, which also has a hotline (888-843-4564) and youth chat line serving youth through age twenty-five (800-246-7743). Their link is https://www.glbthotline.org/. Note that the link letters are different.

Campus Pride is a national nonprofit organization for student leaders and campus groups. It works to develop a safer college environment for LGBT students. https://www.campuspride.org/

Gender Diversity provides education and support services and can use Skype for individual consultations. http://www.genderdiversity.org/individual-support/

PFLAG's website notes PFLAG offers support, education, and advocacy to unite LGBT people with family, friends, and allies and advance equality. https://pflag.org/

If you would like more knowledge about the LGBTQ community and help with being an ally for the community, check out *Straight for Equality* at http://www.straightforequality.org/about

Everything You Ever Wanted to Know About Trans (But Were Afraid to Ask)* by Brynn Tannehill is as comprehensive as its title suggests. https://www.amazon.com/Everything-Wanted-about-Trans-Afraid/dp/1785928260/ref=sr_1_1?ie=UTF8&qid=1543338148&sr=8-1&keywords=everything+you+ever+wanted+to+know+about+trans

Many colleges offer SafeSpace training programs to students and faculty who want to learn more about the transgender community, available resources, and how to best be an ally.

Lost-n-Found Youth is an organization that assists homeless LGBT youth and is based in Atlanta, Georgia.

According to their website, "Lambda Legal, a 501 (c)(3) nonprofit, is a national organization committed to achieving full recognition of the civil rights of lesbians, gay men, bisexuals, transgender people and everyone living with HIV through impact litigation, education, and public policy work." Retrieved from https://www.lambdalegal.org/about-us Lambda Legal.

The Center for Global Education: An international Resource Center lists programs available for international students on different campuses. http://globaled.us/internationalization/mental-wellness-support-for-international-students.asp

The Asperger/Autism Network (AANE) indicates they "work with individuals, families, and professionals to help people with Asperger Syndrome and similar autism spectrum profiles building meaningful, connected lives." Find more at https://www.aane.org

The College Autism Network puts together people who are working to help college students on the autism spectrum have a better college experience and improve their access and success. Investigate at https://collegeautismnetwork.org

The International Student Organization in the USA offers students education on a wide array of topics to help them learn the practicalities of going to school in the US. See http://www.intlstudent.org/

A-3
More General Resources for Wellness

NAMI gives a good overview of the warning signs of mental illness and provides some resources as well at https://www.nami.org/Learn-More/Know-the-Warning-Signs

If you are concerned that any medication you might need for physical or psychological problems would be too expensive to afford, you should go to the goodrx.com site and put in the name of the medication and your location. https://goodrx.com You should also look at the website for a particular drug to see if there are coupons.

While the authors are not in a position to vouch for the competence of the 'listeners' involved in the 7 Cups of Tea Program, an online emotional support service, it's refreshing to see people caring for each other in a creative online program that might fit a subset of the student population and possibly might be used to augment treatment. To find out if the benefits outweigh the risks for you and whether it fits your needs, go to

http://blog.time2track.com/a-psychologists-honest-review-of-7-cups-of-tea.

Therapyforblackgirls.com is dedicated to encouraging the mental wellness of black women and girls and includes a podcast by Dr. Joy Harden Bradford, an online community, and a therapist directory. https://www.therapyforblackgirls.com/

Latinxtherapy is a weekly podcast that discusses mental health topics related to Latinx individuals. https://latinxtherapy.com/ This site has a therapist directory, as well.

The Asian Pacific American Nursing Student Association (APANSA) at the University of Pennsylvania indicates it "exists to explore and resolve the unique challenges, obstacles, and responsibilities specific to APIA nursing students, nurses and the communities from which they come." https://www.nursing.upenn.edu/apansa/ Perhaps your college has a similar organization.

According to their website, The Asian American Women's Alliance (AAWA) "seeks to create opportunities for mutual learning & nurturing, mentor relationships, career & leadership development, personal & group support, and engagement in community services." While this is a group for women of all ages, the group offers mentor relationships. http://new.aawalliance.com/

The books listed in this book's bibliography may help you gain additional information.

A-4

Symptom-Targeted Resources

At the Google Play Store, download the Virtual Hope Box app, which is very encouraging and helpful when you are feeling down and anxious. It has inspiring elements, entertaining and distracting elements, and calming elements and can be personalized to fit you precisely. https://play.google.com/store/apps/details?id=com.t2.vhb&hl=en_US

If you are having sleep difficulties, Stanford School of Medicine, with the help of the VA and DoD, has developed the CBTi Coach app to help. It gives you the tools to quiet your mind and create new sleep habits. It includes guided imagery and sleep tips. With your help, it develops your sleep prescription. https://play.google.com/store/apps/details?id=gov.va.mobilehealth.ncptsd.cbti&hl=en_US

New approaches to helping with sleep, like the Dodow and weighted blankets, speak to how people continue to explore different possible solutions for such a prevalent problem. https://www.mydodow.com/dodow/en-us/home

Several states have dedicated apps that offer the chance to chat or text or call caring professionals to help you deal with problems or access additional help. For example, the MyGCAL App is sponsored in Georgia and available for free at the Apple App Store and the Google Play store. At MyGCAL, supportive professionals are available twenty-four-seven to talk with you confidentially about being bullied, and about family, school, self-harm, suicide, a new first job, or other crises.

The Depression Center Toolkit is available to the public for free at *www.depressioncenter.org/toolkit*. Besides offering information about depression and treatment options, it also has links to other useful sites and assessment methods. It provides practical tools for dealing with problems with anxiety and mood.

You can use the Coach.Me app to track your progress in changing or establishing fitness, sleep, mindfulness, eating, and other daily habits. https://www.coach.me/

Moodgym notes that it "is an online self-help program designed to help users prevent and manage symptoms of depression and anxiety. It is like an interactive, online self-help book that teaches skills based on cognitive behavior therapy." http://moodgym.anu.edu.au

John Faulk, in his book, *Hello To All That: A Memoir of Zoloft, War, and Peace,* was able to capture the experience of depression in a way that makes it remarkably vivid to the reader and may resonate with your struggles if you are depressed. After reading his book, you may feel less alone. https://www.amazon.com/dp/B00EX07ZKQ/

The SMI Advisor app can be downloaded to your smartphone at http://SMIAdviser.org/app . It was developed by the American Psychiatric Association and SAMHS. You can find more about what the app offers at https://smiadviser.org. You can search topics, find resources, find treatment, and learn more about bipolar illness, major depression, and schizophrenia.

A-5

Resources to Help you Size Up Impediments to Well-being and Success

Before we completed this book, we asked students to read it and make suggestions. They asked us to point out what we thought were the most significant mistakes students made in college that lead to their getting side-tracked. We were reluctant to offer what is our subjective opinion because our experience may not be truly representative. They insisted. So, here are our ideas about what sandbags students the most, in no order:

CHOOSING THE WRONG CAREER PATH Advising college students about their careers is complex and not straightforward. There is a considerable variation in the quality of advice given by college teachers who have students assigned to them for advisement. Most college teachers do their best because they care about what happens to their students. You cannot count on your advisor being one of these. The college may expect them to do this without any specific training or education about career advisement. They may not be up on changes in curriculum, coursework requirements, major graduation requirements, or the workplace. They may overestimate the role of the career center. If you want them to take your advisement seriously, you have to take it seriously. If you passively go through the motions of being advised, you likely will get out of it just what you put into it.

Failure to persist until you get adequate academic advice from your college advisor may result in your pursuing a major or career path that fails to motivate you. Without a sense of going in the right direction, it is easy to feel like what you are doing lacks purpose and meaning. Changing majors, recognizing you may not graduate with your class and have wasted effort taking the wrong courses is demoralizing and expensive. It is worth double-checking their advice, talking to others, and exploiting the full resources of the career center. Change advisors If you must.

UNDERESTIMATING HOW ALCOHOL CAN MAKE YOUR LIFE UNMANAGEABLE Drinking too much alcohol seems innocuous at first but leads to such poor decision making about sex, dangerous driving, suicidal behaviors, thrill-seeking, worsening depression, and to acts people regret like being involved in a sexual assault, DUI, or an ER trip for alcohol poisoning. Here is a link to an excerpt from *Reducing Underage Drinking: A Collective Responsibility* by the National Research Council (US) and Institute of Medicine (US) Committee on Developing a Strategy to Reduce and Prevent Underage Drinking; Bonnie RJ, O'Connell ME, editors. Washington (DC): National Academies Press (US); 2004. https://www.ncbi.nlm.nih.gov/books/NBK37591/ It discusses the different consequences of underage drinking.

As common as binge drinking is, you are not likely to have been educated about the damaging effect it has on the brain and your ability to study. Here is a very readable article about binge drinking. https://pathwaytohope.net/blog/binge-drinking-side-effects/#

This TED talk is a heads-up for college women: Drinking and how it changed my life: Ann Dowsett Johnson https://www.youtube.com/watch?v=LqtZjpI1oVQ

UNDERESTIMATING HOW HARD COLLEGE IS Failure to recognize that college is not high school and you have to work at it because no one saves you can put you in hot water. Procrastinating to avoid doing your assignments and missing class leads to a vicious cycle when you become too embarrassed to return to class or

Resources to Help you Size Up Impediments to Well-being and Success

seek help so late. It turns into more avoidant behavior that leads to more shame and then more avoidant behavior and self-loathing. It is dangerously miserable. When you put things off, you are putting everything on your ability to quickly do a task you are having trouble doing right now when you have plenty of time to do it. That is much pressure to put on your future self.

OVER-EXTENDING YOURSELF It is excellent if you have the enthusiasm and are interested in many things. You can, however, overestimate your ability to do it all. You only have so many hours in the day, so much energy in your body, and so much money in your pocket. Lack of adequate funding can sandbag you because you are working too much at your job instead of studying. You can find yourself not wanting to disappoint your boss, your friends, or your organization members by taking time to study. Studying is less fun. The book does not insist on your reading it, and tests might be in the distant future until they aren't. Trying to make it all fit by short-changing your sleep and diet can be other factors that result in your burning out by exam time.

DRAMA Preoccupation with relationship drama with partner, roommate, or friends based on the belief that acceptance by the individual or group is crucial to your happiness can get you nowhere. A belief that your worth is dependent on how others see you will sandbag you. Instead of doing the studying you need to do, you will be doing things others want you to do so you can meet their expectations. When you do study, you may be plagued with intrusive thoughts about your peers' opinions.

IGNORING YOUR HEALTH Poor sleeping and eating habits from lack of a healthy routine impair your ability to study. Failure to ask for help soon enough from family, professors, friends, or counselors can allow untreated depression, anxiety, or substance abuse to derail you. Untreated depression with episodes of unbearable feeling states requires immediate attention.

Untreated ADHD can lead to feeling uncomfortable around people who aren't struggling, habitual procrastination, restless sleep that impairs memory, impulsive behaviors, blurting things out socially, feeling awkward socially due to difficulty mastering names and processing stimuli, motor-vehicle accidents, and difficulty with self-control and planning. Bright students study long hours in high school and do very well until they hit a wall during their second college year when the material becomes complicated, and the pace picks up. By the time their parents approve of them taking medication, they have already lost their scholarship and made some poor judgments.

ISOLATING YOURSELF Isolation has many spin-off problems, including self-doubt, discounting your ability, and worries about identity and depression. It is very risky because it allows you to get worse without others realizing it.

REFUSING TO GROW UP Irresponsibility and passivity will sandbag you, especially if they stem from a sense of entitlement, an unwillingness to accept responsibility for your life, and a magical belief you will be rescued and saved from having to tolerate anything frustrating or laborious. Avoiding responsibility and difficulties, in the long run, is not easier than facing them. It is not inevitable that your early childhood experiences must govern you and your feelings.

REMAINING CONVINCED MARIJUANA IS HARMLESS Marijuana subtly saps motivation, impairs memory, eventually leads to sleep disturbance, and makes procrastination worse. It can lead to failure to go to class, falling behind in assignments, ineffective studying, and not realizing how bad it is until the wake-up call at the end of the semester.

BRUSHING OFF YOUR PARENTS Underestimating your parents' ability to be a source of support, shared values, acceptance, and help will lead to a failure to reach out and a sense of alienation and demoralization. Feeling alienated from your parents is worth working hard to overcome because it is a significant risk factor for suicide, in our opinion.

GAMBLING THAT WHAT YOU DON'T KNOW WON'T HURT YOU

One of the problems with hearing so much in the media about drugs, alcohol, and smoking being impediments to well-being is that you tune it out or fail to acknowledge the consequences that will affect you. You can begin to think that everyone has their agenda and is exaggerating the problems. You likely know ordinary people who have done some of these drugs and don't seem to have harmed themselves much. You may have done some yourself without much ill-effect and concluded that people are making too much fuss over it all. However, have you studied in detail the risks and benefits based on scientific research from respected sources? Even if you know you aren't going to do drugs and alcohol, you need to know more about how they are affecting your fellow students. It requires more than just knowing when to hide your Cheetos from hungry marijuana users. It may require knowing how to administer Narcan (naloxone) for opiate overdose.

TOBACCO

It is not a coincidence that every smoker wishes they had never started. Ask them. Listen to them. The temporary thrill is not worth the addictive craving it instills.

We know you already know that cigarettes are dangerous to your health, but did you know they can significantly limit your dating pool? https://bigthink.com/dollars-and-sex/why-smokers-cant-get-a-date

ALCOHOL

In some ways, college sets you up to drink because deprivation leads to entitlement. All week you have made yourself get up and go to class, study when others wanted you to hang out, do homework, and sit through long classes You have deprived yourself. When the week is over, you feel entitled to stop delaying gratification. Partying seems like your reward. Oddly enough, many students don't enjoy it but don't feel able to say they don't until later in college.

Planning might help out here. Look at times in your study week when you can take short breaks to do something gratifying for yourself that might lessen your sense of deprivation. Are there ways you can make weekday tasks more enjoyable or less tedious? Before the weekend comes, create some plans for activities that might have less risk, like going to a campus play or musical performance.

You may be surprised at just how many ways alcohol can affect you and your friends.

https://www.cdc.gov/alcohol/fact-sheets/alcohol-use.htm

https://www.collegedrinkingprevention.gov/specialfeatures/interactivebodytext.aspx

https://www.mayoclinic.org/diseases-conditions/alcohol-use-disorder/symptoms-causes/syc-20369243

Resources to Help you Size Up Impediments to Well-being and Success

This website has a most comprehensive, well-documented discussion of the effects of alcohol on the body and is from New Zealand. https://www.alcohol.org.nz/alcohol-its-effects/body-effects/effects-on-the-body

There are several books in the bibliography that concern themselves with growing up in an alcoholic family. It is widely known that alcohol intoxication increases suicidal risk. Alcohol is both a cortical depressant and a chemical that lowers your ability to control impulses, including suicidal ones.

Here are some links to excellent summary articles on other substances of abuse.

MARIJUANA

Marijuana can lower your motivation and impair your concentration and memory. Some people experience depersonalization and psychotic symptoms. Taken with SSRI antidepressants, it can cause hypomania in some people. It also diminishes the effectiveness of antidepressants. Here is an overview of what research shows about marijuana: https://www.ncbi.nlm.nih.gov/pmc/articles/PMC4827335/

KRATOM

Kratom is a mind-altering drug that is still available despite its potential to cause hallucinations, psychosis, and other dangerous effects. The FDA has not approved it for any medical use. The DEA lists it as a Drug of Chemical Concern. Find more at https://www.drugabuse.gov/publications/drugfacts/kratom or https://www.dea.gov/sites/default/files/2018-06/drug_of_abuse.pdf . This same website also discusses the hallucinogenic drugs, like LSD.

PSYCHOSTIMULANTS

Adderall (a mixture of the two amphetamine isomers), Vyvanse (lisdexamfetamine), and Ritalin (methylphenidate) are psychostimulants. They are prescription drugs that are used in appropriate doses to treat Attention Deficit Hyperactivity Disorder and other illnesses. People who have attention deficit disorders and take the medications as prescribed have a paradoxical reaction to them and feel calmer and more focused. When these medications are taken in high doses, or by people who don't have attention deficit disorders, they provide a sensation of being speeded up. That is why they are called speed and are diverted for illicit use. Please don't ask your friends for their Adderall or Vyvanse or Ritalin to use at exam time. You are taking a health risk and also asking them to commit a felony by giving it to you. Here is an overview: https://www.drugabuse.gov/publications/drugfacts/prescription-stimulants

METHAMPHETAMINE (METH)

Isopropyl alcohol and ethyl alcohol are two different drugs, even though both belong to the alcohol family. You use isopropyl alcohol to clean your arm before you get a shot. They serve ethyl alcohol at bars. You would not want to confuse them. Neither would you want to confuse methamphetamine and other amphetamines. Methamphetamine is a very different chemical even though the name sounds similar, and it is in the amphetamine/psychostimulant family. Meth has devastating effects on the brain.
https://www.drugabuse.gov/publications/research-reports/methamphetamine/what-are-long-term-effects-methamphetamine-abuse

While this article is more technical and challenging to read, it documents the specific ways that meth affects the brain and leaves no doubt about how harmful it is. https://neuro.psychiatryonline.org/doi/full/10.1176/jnp.15.3.317

COCAINE

Some severe medical consequences can come from the use of cocaine. This article discusses the short-term use of cocaine. https://www.drugabuse.gov/publications/research-reports/cocaine/what-are-short-term-effects-cocaine-use

This article discusses the long-term effect of cocaine use. https://www.drugabuse.gov/publications/research-reports/cocaine/what-are-long-term-effects-cocaine-use

MDMA

(Molly or Ecstasy) Molly is a derivative of amphetamine and a member of the phenethylamine family. It acts as a hallucinogen and stimulant.

https://www.drugabuse.gov/publications/research-reports/mdma-ecstasy-abuse/what-mdma

The use of MDMA may cause seizures, high blood pressure, hyperthermia, and other serious side effects. https://www.drugabuse.gov/publications/research-reports/mdma-ecstasy-abuse/what-are-effects-mdma

OPIATES

In this article, the Mayo Clinic describes how opioid addiction occurs. https://www.mayoclinic.org/diseases-conditions/prescription-drug-abuse/in-depth/how-opioid-addiction-occurs/art-20360372

HEROIN Heroin is an opiate drug made from morphine. Here is some specific information on it. https://www.drugabuse.gov/publications/drugfacts/heroin

FENTANYL Fentanyl is a synthetic opiate that is ordinarily used as an anesthetic or to control pain. People abuse it with dangerous results. For more go to https://www.webmd.com/mental-health/addiction/news/20180501/fentanyl-what-you-should-know

If your circumstances temporarily prevent you from escaping an environment where others are abusing opiates, you may want to discuss having Narcan (naloxone) on hand in case someone accidentally overdoses. Look at http://stopoverdoseil.org/assets/naloxone-fact-sheet.pdf A kit might cost you from $20-40 and could save a life. You can get Naloxone without a prescription over the counter in many states. Here is CVS's website with a mechanism for finding a pharmacy. https://www.cvs.com/content/prescription-drug-abuse/save-a-life

Many colleges have a policy that allows the campus police to help you without getting you into trouble for calling. They don't want you not to call for fear of getting into trouble. Check out your campus policy in case you need to call for a friend who needs help.

DESIGNER DRUGS

Designer drugs are synthesized to get around existing drug laws. Here is an article by Inspire Malibu that gives an overview of designer drugs. https://www.inspiremalibu.com/blog/drug-addiction/7-types-of-designer-drugs/

Remember, no one ever knows what they get from a dealer because a dealer can't know either.

A-6

Resources to Give You an Overview of Some Symptom Complexes

If you access the following websites and articles, you will find more comprehensive overviews of the symptom complexes than could be adequately written about here. Our book is meant to add to your education and encourage further learning about these subjects. It is not a substitute for you seeing a professional.

These are a few of the more frequent complexes of symptoms experienced by college students.

THE SELF-EVALUATOR

The *self-evaluator* was developed for Ulifeline by Duke University Medical School and is described as "screening for thirteen of the most common mental health conditions that college students face". Go to http://www.ulifeline.org/self_evaluator. We do not warrant this to be accurate and are suggesting it for your education only.

Please remember that you are a work in progress and that any psychological symptom complex you have may or may not be transient and reflect how you are at a particular time. You are not the diagnosis. You are having symptoms that providers lump into clusters and label to make decisions about treatment for the present. You are growing and changing like everyone else. For that reason, diagnoses may lack predictive power, and doctors may change some diagnoses over time.

NORMAL GRIEF

https://healgrief.org/actively-moving-forward/ Actively Moving Forward is one part of Healgrief.org that connects actively grieving college students. There are also resources for those mourning the loss of their pets.

http://hopeagain.org.uk/ is a website in the United Kingdom that offers education about grief for young people in particular.

Sheryl Sandberg, in her commencement speech at the University of California at Berkeley, May 2016, spoke candidly about her grief. She said, "after spending decades studying how people deal with setbacks, psychologist Martin Seligman found that there are three P's — personalization, pervasiveness, and permanence — that are critical to how we bounce back from hardship. The seeds of resilience are planted in the way we process the negative events in our lives." Her speech explains these critical ideas and much more. https://www.entrepreneur.com/article/275924

Multiple factors make Lesbian and Gay Bereavement more complex as discussed in this article by Katherine Bristowe, Steve Marshall and Richard Harding: *The bereavement experiences of lesbian, gay, bisexual and/or trans people who have lost a partner: A systematic review, thematic synthesis, and modeling of the literature.* Retrieved from https://www.ncbi.nlm.nih.gov/pmc/articles/PMC4984311/

The Wendt Center for Loss and Healing https://www.wendtcenter.org/ also has helpful information for those who have had a loved one murdered. You may find parts of the Support After Murder and Manslaughter organization (SAMM) site useful, even though the organization is in the UK. https://www.samm.org.uk/

Resources to Give You an Overview of Some Symptom Complexes

ADJUSTMENT DISORDERS

https://medlineplus.gov/ency/article/000932.htm discusses adjustment disorders, which usually are not long-term disorders and may involve overreacting behaviorally or emotionally to an identifiable stressor. This website also discusses adjustment disorders:https://www.webmd.com/mental-health/mental-health-adjustment-disorder#

Depression Central offers information about the various forms of depression, including bipolar depression. https://www.psycom.net/depression.central.html

The Anxiety and Depression Association of America not only provides information about depression and anxiety, but it also offers screening tools, ways to find help, and information about support groups. http://www.adaa.org/

MAJOR DEPRESSIVE DISORDER WITHOUT PSYCHOTIC FEATURES

https://medlineplus.gov/ency/article/000945.htm has an article from the NIH National Library of Medicine about major depression and its treatment. https://www.nimh.nih.gov/health/topics/depression/index.shtml#part_145397 is from the National Institutes of Mental Health

www.ConnectingMDD.com offers information about the role of synaptic connections and glutamate signaling in Major Depressive Disorder.

MAJOR DEPRESSIVE DISORDER WITH PSYCHOTIC FEATURES

Some subtypes of major depression are severe enough that some form of psychosis can occur. As a college student, you may notice the cognitive changes first when you find you cannot think well enough to study. You may find yourself holding beliefs about your worthlessness or being a failure that others do not confirm. You may see you are neglecting your appearance or not bathing. You may find yourself not telling others what you think because you feel the thoughts are illogical, or you don't trust them as you would ordinarily. You may have a sense that a voice is trying to tell you that you are bad or that you should not believe others. You may mistakenly feel very guilty, inadequate, punished, mistreated, or diseased. You may feel very restless and agitated and unable to sleep. You may find yourself preoccupied with your body function, and it may seem like both your bowels and your brain are slowed down. You may experience yourself feeling immobilized and unable to get out of bed.

It may be hard to talk about these things because you feel strange about experiencing all this, but it is critical to get help for this immediately because it is treatable, and early treatment can make a real difference. It is also dangerous not to get treatment. It can be life-threatening. It is treated differently than other types of depression. Remember, if you are having too much trouble thinking to study, you may be able medically to withdraw from school without your grades counting against you. When you have gotten help and are better, you may be able to return to school.

https://www.healthline.com/health/depression/psychotic-depression

OVERVIEWS OF ANXIETY

https://www.nami.org/Learn-More/Mental-Health-Conditions/Anxiety-Disorders/Overview

https://medlineplus.gov/magazine/issues/summer15/articles/summer15pg6-8.html

Resources to Give You an Overview of Some Symptom Complexes

GENERALIZED ANXIETY

https://www.nimh.nih.gov/health/publications/generalized-anxiety-disorder-gad/index.shtml
   https://adaa.org/screening-generalized-anxiety-disorder-gad

SOCIAL ANXIETY

https://www.nimh.nih.gov/health/publications/social-anxiety-disorder-more-than-just-shyness/index.shtml

PANIC DISORDER

https://www.nimh.nih.gov/health/publications/panic-disorder-when-fear-overwhelms/index.shtml
   https://www.mayoclinic.org/diseases-conditions/panic-attacks/symptoms-causes/syc-20376021?p=1

OBSESSIVE-COMPULSIVE DISORDER

https://www.nimh.nih.gov/health/publications/obsessive-compulsive-disorder-when-unwanted-thoughts-take-over/index.shtml
   http://ocd.stanford.edu/treatment/resources.html discusses resources, literature, diagnosis, and treatments for Obsessive-Compulsive Disorder

POST-TRAUMATIC STRESS DISORDER/ TRAUMA

https://www.nimh.nih.gov/health/topics/post-traumatic-stress-disorder-ptsd/index.shtml
   https://www.ptsd.va.gov/public/PTSD-overview/basics/index.asp is the National Center for PTSD site and covers PTSD from multiple causes.

Look at Yulan Zhang's article *Tetris as Therapy* in the November 2, 2017, Yale Scientific http://www.yalescientific.org/2017/11/tetris-as-therapy/ to find how playing a 'visuo-spatially challenging' game can reduce consolidation of trauma memory in the short-term.

Propranolol is also being used to work with trauma memory. Thomas Giustino, Paul Fitzgerald, and Stephen Maren write about it in their journal article *Revisiting propranolol and PTSD: Memory erasure or extinction enhancement?* at https://doi.org/10.1016/j.nlm.2016.01.009

Doxycycline shows promise, as well. https://www.pharmacytimes.com/news/study-doxycycline-for-ptsd-treatment

The Rape, Abuse & Incest National Network operates the National Sexual Assault Hotline 800-656-HOPE and provides support and information at https://www.rainn.org/after-sexual-assault

If you are an LGBTQ person who has experienced sexual violence, RAINN offers you this resource:

https://www.rainn.org/articles/lgbtq-survivors-sexual-violence

This site provides help managing distress in the wake of a mass shooting. https://www.apa.org/helpcenter/mass-shooting.aspx

https://forge-forward.org/about/ discusses FORGE, a national transgender anti-violence organization

ATTENTION DEFICIT HYPERACTIVITY DISORDERS

https://www.nimh.nih.gov/health/topics/attention-deficit-hyperactivity-disorder-adhd/index.shtml
https://www.cdc.gov/ncbddd/adhd/state-data-hub.html

PSYCHOSIS

Psychosis is an umbrella term and not a diagnosis. A psychotic person has difficulty seeing reality. This article discusses the symptoms and potential causes of psychosis. https://medlineplus.gov/ency/article/001553.htm

EATING DISORDERS

You may find educational information about eating disorders at the National Eating Disorders Association http://www.nationaleatingdisorders.org/ or the Alliance for Eating Disorders Awareness https://www.allianceforeatingdisorders.com/. NEDA offers a hotline at 1-800-931-2237. Consult their site for its hours.

A-7

Affirmations After a Break-Up

Here are some affirmations that may be helpful after a break-up.

1. My self-worth is independent of their opinion of me.

2. I am not a fool for trying so hard. If it had worked out, it might have been worth it.

3. I was not mistaken in seeing something special in them.

4. What someone else thinks of me is none of my business.

5. Grief is a process, not an event, so I will not beat myself up for not being able to get through this all at once.

6. It is not my "lacking" that caused this—it might have happened with anyone. It may be a function of them and the difficulty of their being self-centered.

7. The bad times and good times do not undo each other.

8. The experience has made me stronger even though I don't feel strong now.

9. Some things are worth trying and failing at, and now I know for sure it wouldn't work.

Affirmations After a Break-Up

10. There are many people in the world—not just them.

11. I will find pleasure in things at some point, even though I don't feel it now.

12. Time does heal—if I continue to experience and do things and grow through it.

13. I will fake it until I make it, knowing that I will eventually feel better.

14. It takes time to recreate a personal and social identity independent of them, but I will make a start.

15. If I ever decide to marry, I know that everyone who walks down the aisle has broken up with everyone else but the one they are marrying.

16. I will rediscover extended family, old friends, and people I have not seen much because I was busy with this relationship and will be reminded, through how they see me, of who I am, and not how they pictured me.

17. I will remind myself that in my loving them, I idealized them and gave them the authority to judge whether I am okay or not. They do not deserve to have that authority because they are human too.

18. I did what I could to make the relationship work, and my peers agree that they would not put up with their behaviors.

A-8

Items for Your Safety Kit

Divide the kit into several sections using bags that you can move to where you need them.

CAR SECTION — Get together a bungee cord, rope, heavy coat/gloves/hat, collapsible shovel for snow, fire extinguisher, jumper cables, screwdriver, glow-in-the-night shirt, pliers, small empty gas can for the trunk, maps, batteries for your phone, pop-top canned beans or other food like peanut butter, plastic utensils, blanket, road flare or glow-in-the-night stuff.

Leave a change of clothes at your friend's house if you have a boyfriend from whom you must escape. Get a thin collapsible bag for more stuff. Check the spare tire and make sure the jack works. Do not risk your life to change a tire on the side of a busy highway. Wait for help and stay in the car.

HEALTH SECTION — Obtain a sugar source, water bottle, protein bar, Ibuprofen, Benadryl, Rolaids, cold tablet, alcohol preps, wipes, Neosporin, Band-Aids, bandage tape, gauze, mosquito repellant, two days' worth of your meds for allergy, asthma, etc. which you rotate, sunscreen, Emetrol, toilet paper, surgical gloves.

DOCUMENTS AND INFORMATION SECTION — Assemble copies of insurance documents, driver's license, phone numbers, AAA Car info, car insurance, Vehicle Identification Number (VIN), driver's registration. After assembling these documents, make copies of them and put copies in multiple places.

Items for Your Safety Kit

Prepare to have no cell phone. Write down on paper a taxicab number and numbers you would have wanted to access from your phone. Write down identifying information on paper. Take a picture of this for your phone also. Email the info to a trusted friend who could be contacted in an emergency to give you the information. Better yet, mail it to them. You could leave a safety box at the friend's house too. In that box, you would have money and the phone numbers of friends and family. Assemble stamps, envelope, paper, pen, and two blank checks to put with the documents.

OTHER ESSENTIALS SECTION — Obtain plastic bags, towelettes, water, a cloth, Kleenex, undergarments, flashlights (with batteries separate), a small knife, small change, plastic rain poncho, toothbrush, toothpaste, mosquito bite aides, whistle, personal hygiene items, cash in small and big bills, duplicates of keys, different credit cards, a cheap cell phone, cell phone charger, soap ,deodorant, and a car fire extinguisher, energy bars or food that will keep, seatbelt cutter, scraper, wind-up flashlight, a big flashlight to use as a weapon, a signal light or glow-in-the-night materials. Get your folks to work with you to assemble these items and offer other suggestions.

You may need additional items if you live in an area where there are floods, tornadoes, and hurricanes. Know where to go and have discussed a plan.

A-9
Wilfred Bion's Theories about Groups

In college, you are going to be in many different kinds of groups. You may belong to more formal groups like a sorority, a fraternity, a club, an athletic team, a special interest group, or a campus religious group. You may participate in less formal groups like a social media group, a group of suitemates, a class, a study group, a special project group, or a fan group. This section is meant to give you a way to examine the group processes you see unfold in front of you. If you understand them, you are less likely to be the victim of them.

Theories about group behaviors are as many and diverse as the many fields of knowledge that study groups. The authors have found Wilfred Bion's theories about groups to be useful in their understanding of the group process.

Before his death in 1979, he had written extensively and was an important figure in psychoanalysis. Some of his writings were published by Brunner-Routledge last in 2004 as the book *Experiences in Groups and other papers*. (Bion 2004 p 61-86; 98-113). We hope our analyst friends will excuse how many liberties we have taken with his ideas in trying to simplify them.

Very simply put, Bion believed that groups operate in four modes: The *workgroup* mode and three "as if" modes. A group can shift from one mode to another at any point. The three "as if" modes are the *dependency group* mode, the *fight-flight* group mode, and the *pairing group* mode.

When the group is in the *work-group* mode, members see the group as meeting to solve a problem, and they delegate responsibilities to group members according to their skills, like a housing contractor delegates carpentry to a carpenter, and painting to a painter. They act rationally in a goal-directed manner to accomplish work. A group leader tries to bring a group back to this mode when they stray into one of the "as if" modes. It is in the *workgroup* mode that the group functions most productively.

When the group is in the *group dependency* mode, they act "as if" they have met to be taken care of, and they look to the leader to take care of them. The group has a kind of warm, fuzzy, passive feel about it. They act "as-if" the group leader is the sole possessor of skill, knowledge, responsibility, and leadership. There is the unspoken belief that if members are helpless and compliant enough, the leader will appreciate their neediness and meet their needs. Because they believe they are weak and deserving, members are mad at the idealized group leader if the leader does meet their expectations.

When the group is in the *fight-flight* mode, they act "as if" there is an enemy, and they need to fight the enemy or flee. There is an us-and-them, take no prisoners mentality. There is a sense of unity against the foe, and differences between the group and the enemy are accentuated.

The *pairing group* has a hopeful, optimistic, spring-time air about it "as if" something or someone new is about to be born out of being together. There is a sense that from the associations in the group, there will arise a new leader or idea that will be saving or revolutionary in the future.

A group of people might move from any mode to another. The mode might be brief or lasting.

Sometimes organizations may intentionally emphasize one mode over the other because of their current needs. For example, a political party might encourage a *fight-flight group* mentality by highlighting all the terrible things the other party is doing and how members have to overlook the differences within their party to fight the opponent and win the election. That same party, at another time, might cultivate a *pairing group* and encourage party members to see their candidate as the new leader who will save them.

Bion believed you could rank group members according to their valency (tendency) to act, think, or feel a particular way (Ibid p 116-117). When the group is feeling suspicious, the person with the highest propensity to be suspicious will be the one talking. Other group members who have some suspicion will sit back and let this person speak as if they have no suspicions themselves, or they may indirectly encourage the speaker.

For example, class members talk with each other about how the test question number seven was misleading. The most assertive student with the highest tendency to feel mistreated will speak up about it. When the professor asks the other students if they agree, they pretend that they are content rather than risk disfavor. By understanding valence, you can wait to see if someone else has a higher tendency to speak up and not be the one left out in the cold. Alternatively, you could understand your tendency to hold back and decide to support the protestor instead.

A-10

Resources to Help Nurture an Openness to Wonder

Previous chapters have concerned themselves mostly with the world of facts. They have discussed practical matters like how to do things. In this chapter, written by Dr. Duffey, he will discuss resources that are much more subjective. Dr. Duffey would like you to remind yourself—when you are tempted to take what he says at face value—that he is a man who can't correctly load a dishwasher. He would like you to keep your critical thinking cap on and your mind open.

So much—of what you have read before this chapter— is cautionary. "Do this! Don't do that! Watch out!" You have been reading about determining goals and learning the details to help you reach them. There is an inherent assumption that only if you achieve these goals, will you be happy. Another theory is that if you don't reach these goals, you must be unhappy. Neither is true.

Ezra Bayda wrote," The deeper, more genuine experience of happiness is the natural state of our Being when we are not so caught up in our self-centered thoughts and emotions. It is the experience of true contentment, of being fundamentally okay with our life as it is, no longer so attached to getting what the small mind of ego wants, nor demanding that life be a particular way (Bayda 2011 p157)." In this line of thinking, happiness has no cause. We peel back the ego to find it already there.

At some point in your college experience, you may develop a belief system that is not entirely consistent with your family's. Beginning to question what you believe is a normal developmental process. You may find yourself, over time, coming back to your original beliefs with a renewed faith that comes from having thought deliberately about what you initially had not questioned. You may, however, come to some different conclusions that incorporate new things you have learned.

For example, you may come to confine your beliefs to things that can be proven by science. On the other hand, you may allow that there is an ineffable experience of something beyond science and believe we are like blind men who can't see the sun but feel its warmth everywhere. These are examples of just two of many ways of believing. Whatever you come to believe, the process of examining your beliefs can be anxiety-producing. Anais Nin wrote that "Life shrinks or expands in proportion to one's courage." Exploring your beliefs and listening to others with an open mind takes courage.

In her book—*The Power of an Open Question*—Elisabeth Mattis-Namgyel talks about the value of cultivating openness. She notes that "The moment we try to wrap our conceptual mind around an experience, we lose it. We reduce the limitless quality of being to a thing." ...She notes that "embracing complexity unlocks the profundity, intelligence, and compassion of our humanness (Mattis-Namgyel 2010)." She talks about the value of direct experience with a mind free of conclusions.

Alice Walker, the author of *The Color Purple*, put it another way when she said, "I think the foundation of everything in my life is wonder (Walker 1982)."

I hope that— with time, openness, and patience—you will be able directly to experience the wonder all around you, any way you conceptualize it. As you do this, it may be helpful to remember that it is not that a warrior has no fear, but that— while having the fear— he remains engaged in the world.

These resources address our struggle to stay open to wonder and remain engaged in the world:

Resources to Help Nurture an Openness to Wonder

Doubt: A History: The Great Doubters and Their Legacy of Innovation from Socrates and Jesus to Thomas Jefferson and Emily Dickinson by Jennifer Michael Hecht

Finding Your Strength in Difficult Times: A Book of Meditations by David Viscott

I Will Not Die an Unlived Life: Reclaiming Purpose and Passion by Dawna Markova

Pathfinders: Overcoming the Crises of Adult Life and Finding Your Own Path to Well-Being by Gail Sheehy

The Places That Scare You: A Guide to Fearlessness in Difficult Times by Pema Chodron

When Bad Things Happen to Good People by Rabbi Harold S. Kushner

Bibliography

The authors do not endorse the content of these books or provide any sort of guarantee that they are accurate, timely, or complete.

Adult Children of Alcoholics by Janet Geringer Woititz

Adulting: How to Become a Grown-Up in 468 Easy(ish) Steps by Kelly Williams Brown

A Framework for Understanding Poverty: A Cognitive Approach by Ruby K. Payne

A Journey Toward Health and Hope: Your Handbook for Recovery After a Suicide Attempt by the American Association of Suicidology

A Lifelong Love Affair: Keeping Sexual Desire Alive in Your Relationship by Joseph Nowinski

Beyond Grief: A guide for the recovery from the death of a loved one by Carol Staudacher

Beyond Happiness: The Zen Way to True Contentment by Ezra Bayda

Children of the Self-Absorbed: A Grown-Up's Guide to Getting Over Narcissistic Parents by Nina W. Brown

Choosing to Live: How to Defeat Suicide Through Cognitive Therapy by Thomas Ellis and Cory Newman

Christian Meditation: Experiencing the Presence of God by James Finley

Search: A Guide for College and Life

Clinical Manual for the Assessment and Treatment of Suicidal Patients, by John Chiles, Kirk Strosahl, and Laura Weiss Roberts

Codependent No More: How to Stop Controlling Others and Start Caring for Yourself by Melody Beattie

Decisive: How to Make Better Choices in Your Life and Work by Chip Heath and Dan Heath

Distracted: The Erosion of Attention and the Coming Dark Age by Maggie Jackson

Doubt: A History: The Great Doubters and Their Legacy of Innovation from Socrates and Jesus to Thomas Jefferson and Emily Dickinson by Jennifer Michael Hecht

Dynamics of Faith by Paul Tillich

Eats: Fast, Cheap, Healthy- the Best Tried-and-True Recipes for Students by Rachel Phipps

Eat Well on $4/day by Leanne Brown

Emotional Blackmail: When the People in Your Life Use Fear, Obligation, and Guilt to Manipulate You by Susan Forward and Donna Frazier

Experiences in Groups and other papers by Wilfred R. Bion

Exploring Your Unplanned Pregnancy: Single Motherhood, Adoption, and Abortion Questions and Resources by Jeff Duffey

Finding Your Strength in Difficult Times: A Book of Meditations by David Viscott

First in the Family: Your college years. Advice about college from first-generation students by Kathleen Cushman

Bibliography

Food Rules: An Eater's Manuel by Michael Pollan

Frame Control: Subconscious Conversational Dominance by George Hutton

Healing ADD Revised Edition: The Breakthrough Program that Allows You to See and Heal the 7 Types of ADD by Daniel G. Amen.

I Will Not Die an Unlived Life: Reclaiming Purpose and Passion by Dawna Markova

Learning to Fly: Trapeze—Reflections on Fear, Trust, and the Joy of Letting Go by Sam Keen

Making Ends Meet with a Popcorn Popper by Jacqueline Lucia

Making Peace with Your Parents by Harold Bloomfield with Leonard Felder

Mindset: The New Psychology of Success by Carol S. Dweck

Moonwalking with Einstein: The Art and Science of Remembering by Joshua Foer

Navigating College: A Handbook on Self-Advocacy Written for Autistic Students from Autistic Adults by the Autistic Self-Advocacy Network

Pathfinders: Overcoming the Crises of Adult Life and Finding Your Own Path to Well-Being by Gail Sheehy

People of the Lie: The Hope for Healing Human Evil by M. Scott Peck

Plan to Prevail: A Resource Guide for College Bound Students by Victoria M. Sparks (This book looks promising, but we have not yet read it.)

Reclaiming Your Life After Rape: Cognitive-Behavioral Therapy for Posttraumatic Stress Disorder Client Workbook (Treatments That Work) by Barbara Olasov Rothbaum

Reviving Ophelia: Saving the Selves of Adolescent Girls by Mary Pipher and Ruth Ross

State of Mind 2.0: 11 Lessons of the Most Productive People on the Planet by Christopher A. Pinckley

Stronger Than Death: When Suicide Touches Your Life by Sue Chance

Textcerpts: Mastering College Textbook Reading by Gene Wintner

The Anxiety & Phobia Workbook by Edmund J. Bourne

The Artisan Teacher: A Field Guide to Skillful Teaching by Mike Rutherford

The Courage to Be by Paul Tillich

The Grain Brain Whole Life Plan by David Perlmutter and Kristin Loberg

The Hard Questions: 100 Questions to Ask Before You Say "I Do" by Susan Piver

The Little Prince by Antoine de Saint-Exupery

The Naked Roommate: And 107 Other Issues You Might Run into in College by Harlan Cohen

The Places That Scare You: A Guide to Fearlessness in Difficult Times by Pema Chodron

The Plant Paradox: The Hidden Dangers in "Healthy" Foods that Cause Disease and Weight Gain by Steven R. Gundry

Bibliography

The Power of an Open Question: The Buddha's Path to Freedom by Elizabeth Mattis-Namgyel

The Single Mother's Survival Guide by Patrice Karst

The Willpower Instinct by Kelly McGonigal

Too Good to Leave, Too Bad to Stay: A Step-by-Step Guide to Help You Decide Whether to Stay in or Get Out of Your Relationship by Mira Kirshenbaum

Uncoupling: Turning Points in Intimate Relationships by Diane Vaughn

When Bad Things Happen to Good People by Rabbi Harold S. Kushner

You Can't Say That to Me: Stopping the Pain of Verbal Abuse by Suzette Haden Elgin

References

All our lives, we have been listening to the ideas of others to the point, now, where we don't know whether any of our thoughts are original. This chapter is our attempt to give credit to the other people whose ideas and writings have contributed to this book. We have tried to be diligent about giving people credit and not plagiarizing. If we have credited the wrong source or failed to credit someone, we are truly sorry and hope you will tell us about it so we can correct future editions. It can be challenging to know what is common knowledge or common sense, and what is an idea unique to one person.

Alizadeh, Sonita. 2018. "Newsweek Special Edition: She Persisted." Interviewed and edited by Kaytie Norman

Spring 2017 American College Health Association National College Health Assessment

https://www.acha.org/documents/ncha/NCHA-II_SPRING_2017_REFERENCE_GROUP_DATA_REPORT.pdf

American Psychological Association.2007. "Stress in America." Washington, D.C.

Bayda, Ezra. 2011. *Beyond Happiness: The Zen Way to True Contentment*. Shambhala

BIon, Wilfred R. 2004. *Experiences in Groups and other papers*. Brunner-Routledge

Brown, Brene.2012. *Daring Greatly: How the Courage to Be Vulnerable Transforms the Way We Live, Love, Parent, and Lead*. Avery

Brown, Kelly Williams. Updated 2018. *Adulting: How to become a grown-up in 468 easy(ish) steps*. Grand Central Life & Style.

Brown, Leanne. 2015. *Good and Cheap: Eat Well on $4/day*. Workman Publishing Company

Charney, Dennis. 2019. Speech 14th Annual Amygdala, Stress, and PTSD Conference of April 2019. Psychiatric News, June 12, 2019, p 23

Cohen, Harlan. 2017 7th edition. *The naked roommate: And 107 other issues you might run into in college.* Sourcebooks

Covey, Stephen. 1989. *The Seven Habits of Highly Effective People: Powerful Lessons in Personal Change.* Simon & Schuster

Duffey, Jeff. 2016. *Exploring Your Unplanned Pregnancy: Single Motherhood, Adoption, and Abortions Questions and Resources.* Cairde, Karuna & Hedd Publishing, LLC

Ericksen, Su. 2016. *Self-defense for Women Warriors: A practical approach.* Amazon Digital Services LLC

Fiona, Melanie.BrainyQuote.com, BrainyMedia Inc, 2019. https://www.brainyquote.com/quotes/melanie_fiona_497269 , accessed October 5, 2019

Gundry, Steven. 2017. *The Plant Paradox: Hidden Dangers in "Healthy" Foods That Cause Disease and Weight Gain.* Harper Wave

Heath, Chip and Dan. 2013. *Decisive: How to Make Better Choices in Your Life and Work.* Currency

Hutton, George. 2015. *Frame Control: Subconscious Conversational Dominance.* Amazon Digital Services LLC

References

Jackson, Maggie.2008. *Distracted*. Prometheus Press

Kelly, Jack. 2019. "Predictions for the uncharted job market of the future" https://www.forbes.com/sites/jackkelly/2019/02/27/predictions-for-the-dystopian-job-market-of-the-future/#148fa6186057

Kennedy, Pagan 2018 "The Secret to a Longer Life? Don't ask these Dead Longevity Researchers". The New York Times

Kruger, Justin; Dunning, David. 1999."Unskilled and Unaware of It: How Difficulties in Recognizing One's Own Incompetence Lead to Inflated Self-Assessments". Journal of Personality and Social Psychology. 77(6); 1121-1134

Latimer, Melody et al. Autistic Self-Advocacy Network 2013. *Navigating College: A handbook on self-advocacy written for autistic students from autistic adults.*

Lee, Kai-Fu. 2017. Quoted by Sophia Yan in "Artificial intelligence will replace half of all jobs in the next decade, says widely followed technologist " https://www.cnbc.com/2017/04/27/kai-fu-lee-robots-will-replace-half-of-all-jobs.html

Lucia, Jacqueline.2018. *Making Ends Meet with a Popcorn Popper.* Independently published in print, Audible.com, Amazon Digital Services LLC

Mattis-Namgyel, Elisabeth .2010. *The Power of an Open Question: The Buddha's Path to Freedom.* Shambhala

Mayo Clinic Staff. 2018. "Withdrawal Method (Coitus Interruptus)"(https://www.mayoclinic.org/tests-procedures/withdrawal-method/about/pac-20395283

McGonigal, Kelly Ph.D.2011 *The Willpower Instinct.* Avery

Mellins CA; Walsh K; Sarvet AL; Wall M; Gilbert L; Santelli JS et al. 2017." Sexual assault incidents among college undergraduates: Prevalence and factors associated with risk." PLoS ONE 12(11): e0186471. https://doi.org/10.1371/journal.pone.0186471

Moran, Mark. 2019. "Suicidal Crisis: Frequently Precipitous with no suicidal intent until moments before." Psychiatry News, September 2019 p 9

Myers, Michael F. 1998.*How's Your Marriage? A Book for Men and Women.* American Psychiatric Association Publishing

Nasrallah, Henry A. 2019 "Transformative advances are unfolding in psychiatry" Current Psychiatry. September 2019 pp 10-12

Obama, Barack .2019. https://archive.org/details/archiveteam_videobot_twitter_com_755863391084969985

Obama, Michelle. Michelle Obama Quotes. BrainyQuote.com, BrainyMedia Inc, 2019. https://www.brainyquote.com/quotes/michelle_obama_791418, accessed October 2, 2019.

Ocasio-Cortez, Alexandria. 2018. "The Courage to Change: Alexandria Ocasio-Cortez." Published on YouTube May 30, 2018, https://www.youtube.com/watch?reload=9&v=rq3QXIVR0bs

Parker, Ben. 2016. "Nearly 64 percent of jobs don't require college education, but wait - there's more." June 13, 2016. https://www.thecollegefix.com/nearly-64-percent-jobs-dont-require-college-education-wait-theres/

Peck, M. Scott.1983. *People of the Lie: The Hope for Healing Human Evil.* Simon and Schuster

References

Perlmutter, David, and Kristin Loberg. 2016. *The Grain Brain Whole Life Plan: Boost Brain Performance, Lose Weight, and Achieve Optimal Health*. Little Brown and Company

Perry, Tyler. 2010. "Sheryl Garratt Interview: Tyler Perry" August 2, 2010

Phillips, Andrew J.K. 2107." Irregular sleep/wake patterns are associated with poorer academic performance and delayed circadian and sleep /wake timing" Scientific Reports 7, Article number: 3216

Phipps, Rachel. 2017. *Student Eats: Fast, Cheap, Healthy-the-Best Tried-and-Tested Recipes for Students*. Ebury Press

Pinckley, Christopher A. 2016. *State of Mind 2.0: 11 Lessons of the most productive people on the planet*. CreateSpace Independent Publishing Platform

Pollan, Michael. 2009. *Food Rules: An Eater's Manual*. Penguin Books

Rice, Condoleezza. 2010. Transcript NPR Author Interviews, "Condoleezza Rice Details Her Civil Rights Roots," Morning Edition, October 13, 2010, Renee Montagne, host

Roosevelt, Theodore.1910. Citizenship in a Republic Speech at Sorbonne, France on April 23, 1910

De Saint-Exupery, Antoine. 2015. *The Little Prince*. Seaburn World Classics

Seligman, Martin E.P. 1994. *Learned Optimism*. Random House

StatCrunch™– Data analysis on the Web. 2017-2019 "Pets owned in College." Pearson Education, https://www.statcrunch.com/5.0/viewreport.php?reportid+54831&groupid+3897

Swirsky, Danny. 2015. How to graduate college early: Save thousands of dollars and years of time by deciphering the college credit system. Amazon Digital Services

Thoreau, Henry. 2004. *Walden: A Fully Annotated Edition* (Kindle Edition). Edited by Jeffrey S. Cramer. Yale University Press

Tournier, Paul. 1965. *The Healing of Persons.* Harper and Row

Turner, James C.; Leno, E. Victor; Keller, Adrienne. 2013 "Causes of Mortality Among College Students: A Pilot Study." Journal of College Student Psychotherapy. 27:1,31-42, DOI: 10.1080/87568225.2013.739022. https://doi.org/10.1080/87568225.2013.739022

University of Rochester Medical Center Health Encyclopedia 2019 reviewed by Fetterman, Ann RN BSN, Campellone, Joseph MD, Turley, Raymond Kent BSN MSN RN (https://www.urmc.rochester.edu/encyclopedia/content.aspx?ContentTypeID=1&ContentID=3051)

Walker, Alice. 1982. *The Color Purple.* Published by Harvest Books in 2003

Ware, Corinne. 1995. *Discover Your Spiritual Type: A Guide to Individual and Congregational growth.* The Alban Institute

Weise, Michelle R. & Clayton M. Christensen. 2014. *Hire Education: Mastery, Modularization, and the Workforce Revolution.* Clayton Christensen Institute for Disruptive Innovation

References

Weliver, David. 2013."The Annual Cost of Pet Ownership: Can You Afford A Furry Friend?"

https://www.moneyunder30.com › the-true-cost-of-pet-ownership July 2013 Money under 30

Weston, Dan n.d. "29 Powerful and Inspirational Will Smith Quotes". Wealthy Gorilla. https://wealthygorilla.com/inspirational-quotes-will-smith/

White, Kate. 2013. *I Shouldn't Be Telling You This: Success Secrets Every Gutsy Girl Should Know.* Harper Business Reprint Edition

Young, Valerie. 2011. *The Secret Thoughts of Successful Women: Why Capable People Suffer from Impostor Syndrome and How to Thrive In Spite of It.* Crown Business

; Index

Index

A

AANE (Asperger/Autism Network), 212
AAWA (Asian American Women's Alliance), 214
academic skills, sharpening, 127–39
   apps and websites, 128–31
   the classroom experience, 132–37
   dictionaries/thesauri/spell checkers, 129
   and disabilities, 127–28
   ergonomics/mechanics, 130–31
   helpers and resources, 127–28
   listening receptively, 135–37
   note taking, 133–35
   reading/homework/studying, 137–39
   textbooks, 131–33, 138
Academic Skills Center study library (California Polytechnic State University), 27
Active Minds, 179–80
activism, 14–15
Adderall, 71, 224
ADHD (attention deficit hyperactivity disorder), 64, 127–28, 220, 224, 232
adjustment disorders, 229
Adulting (K. W. Brown), 47
advisors, 30, 217–18
alarm clock apps, 65
Alcoholics Anonymous, 122
alcohol use, 16, 37–38, 43, 98, 218, 221–23
ALEX N5 Posture Tracker & Coach, 130
Alizadeh, Sonita, 14–15
allergies, 72
Alliance for Eating Disorders Awareness, 233
American Association of Suicidology, 187–88
American College Health Association, 55
American Foundation for Suicide Prevention, 188, 190
American Psychiatric Association, 191
American Psychological Association, 171, 191
Americans with Disabilities and Fair Housing Act, 55
anaphylactic shock, 72
anxiety, 109–10, 186, 229–31
Anxiety and Depression Association of America, 229
APANSA (Asian Pacific American Nursing Student Association), 213–14
apartment living, 47–50
artificial intelligence, 13, 85, 184
Asian American Women's Alliance (AAWA), 214
Asian Pacific American Nursing Student Association (APANSA), 213–14
Asperger/Autism Network (AANE), 212
associate degree, 203
Autistic Self-Advocacy Network, 92

B

backpacks, 131
The Balance, 75
Bandura, Albert, 177
   Self-Efficacy, 172
bank accounts, 76–77
bankrate.com, 168
Banks-Santilli, Linda, 170
bars, "bad date" codes at, 155
bartenders, 205
bartering, 78
Bauer, James, 154
Bayda, Ezra, 241
Beckett, Samuel, 25
beliefs, examining one's, 241–42
Bernstein, Gabrielle, 186
bestcolleges.com, 209
Beyond Grief (Staudacher), 190
Bion, Wilfred: *Experiences in Groups*, 238–40
birth control, 67–68
body image, 59, 102
brain
   development, 21, 122

and memories, 138
mind mapping, 135
neuron firings, 122–23
neuroscience, 183–84
nurturing, 119–20
unconscious, 122
Brain Productivity app, 138
break-up affirmations, 234–35
breathalyzers, 38
Breath Pacer app, 108
Bristowe, Katherine, 228
Brown, Brene, 92, 145
Brown, Kelly Williams: *Adulting*, 47
Brown, Leanne: *Good and Cheap*, 61
brown noise, 28
bSafe-Personal Safety app, 38
budgeting apps, 76
bullying, 102–3, 117
Bundy, Ted, 44
busywork, 25
Buzan, Tony, 135

C

Campbell, David, 22
Campus Pride, 211
Canadian Association of Muslims with Disabilities, 210
Carbonite, 130
Cardillo, Donna, 201–2
career
  choosing the wrong path, 217–18
  counseling on, 105–6, 129, 206, 217
  milestones, 106
  options, xiv
  planning, 197–200, 206–7
Career and Professional Development Services (Arizona State University), 106
cars
  buying used, 78
  on campus, 53
  drinking and driving, 37–38
  maintenance, 79
  safe practices, 40–41, 52
  safety kit, 236
CBTi Coach app, 215

Cengage, 82
Center for Global Education, 211–12
Centers for Disease Control and Prevention, 201
Central Georgia Technical College, 206
challenges during college years, 161–68
Chamber of Commerce, 84
Chance, Sue, 190
change, equation for, 193
Charney, Dennis, 116
Chiles, John: *Clinical Manual for the Assessment and Treatment of Suicidal Patients*, 188
China vs. US, 118–19
Choosing to Live (Ellis), 187
cigarettes, 222
circadian rhythm, 62–63
classroom experience, 132–37
CLEP (College Level Examination Program), 31, 80–81
Cleveland Clinic, 69
climate change, 13, 73
Clinical Manual for the Assessment and Treatment of Suicidal Patients (Chiles), 188
Coach.Me app, 216
cocaine, 225
cognitive-behavioral therapy, 182, 216
Cohen, Harlan: *The Naked Roommate*, 47
college
  advantages/value of, 199–206
  dislike of, 108–9
  end-phase reflections, 167–68
  as hard for most, 114–15, 218–19
  middle-phase challenges, 161–67
  opportunities provided by, xiii–xiv
  planning for life after, 168 (*see also* career)
  readiness assessment, 1–6
  types, xiv–xv
College Autism Network, 212
CollegeCompass.co, 47
College Level Examination Program (CLEP), 31, 80–81
Colorado State University, 187

Index

community, 87–104
  diversity, 87–89
  manners, 89–90
  social groups, understanding, 92–95, 238–40
  socializing, 90–92
  social media, 101–3
  spring break, 96–101
  systems, 103–4
competency-based learning, 207–8
competition, 118–19
computers, 130–31
ConnectingMDD.com, 229
Consultation Tower, 84
contraception, 67–68, 98
cooking apps, 59
coping techniques for well-being, 180–82
courses
  impractical but stimulating classes, 7
  overloading your schedule, 30
  prerequisites, 30, 33
  selecting and registering, 29–32
  sequence of, 33–34
  summer, 31
  and transferring to another school, 33–34
Covey, Steven: *The Seven Habits of Highly Effective People*, 27
credit cards, 75, 100
Credit.com, 77
credit ratings, 77
Crisis Text Line, 186
critical thinking, 124–26
curiosity, 126
cyberbullying, 103

D

dating, 147–53, 165
DATOM ("Doesn't Apply to Me"), 110
DBT (Dialectical Behavior Therapy), 180
Decisive (C. and D. Heath), 125–26
depression, 186, 216, 229–30. *See also* suicide/suicidal thoughts or feelings
Depression Center Toolkit, 215–16

Depression Central, 229
Dialectical Behavior Therapy (DBT), 180
diet, 59–62
disability
  accommodations for, 34, 127–28, 174
  in language or math, 32
  psycho-educational tests for, 206
  support resources, 209–10
discipline, 22
distress, 180
diversity, 87–89, 209–12
documents/information (for a safety kit), 236–37
dorms (residence halls), 45–47, 60
downtimes, mental (quieting the mind), 121–22
doxycycline, 232
drinking. *See* alcohol use
drugs. *See also* medication
  Adderall, 224
  cocaine, 225
  designer, 226
  drugging of drinks, 39, 44, 100
  educating yourself, 221
  fentanyl, 226
  heroin, 226
  illegal use, 16, 43, 221
  kratom, 223
  marijuana, 122, 220–21, 223
  MDMA (Molly; Ecstasy), 225
  methamphetamine, 224–25
  opiates, 221, 225–26
  overdoses, 221, 226
  psychostimulants, 224
  Ritalin, 224
  Vyvanse, 224
Duffey, Jeff, 135–36
Exploring Your Unplanned Pregnancy, 68, 150
Dweck, Carol S.: *Mindset*, 113, 172

E

eating disorders, 233
eating health, 59–62
ebates.com, 61

Economic Policy Institute, 202
Ecstasy, 225
Eisenhower Matrix, 27
Ellis, Thomas E.: *Choosing to Live*, 187
emergency kits, 39
Emotional Blackmail (Forward and Frazier), 142
entitlement, 112
EpiPens, 72
Ericksen, Su: *Self-Defense for Women Warriors*, 44
etiquette, 89–90
Everything You Ever Wanted to Know About Trans* (Tannehill), 211
evil people, 95
expenses. *See* finances
Experiences in Groups (Bion), 238–40
Exploring Your Unplanned Pregnancy (Duffey), 68, 150

F

FAFSA (Free Application for Federal Student Aid), 75
failure. *See* mistakes/failures
family, 141–43, 171, 176. *See also* parents
FamilyDoctor.org., 69
Faulk, John
  Hello To All That, 216
Feeding America, 77
fentanyl, 226
Ferraro, Serenella
  Life Coaching, 182
finances, 75–86
  bank accounts, 76–77
  credit cards, 75
  credit ratings, 77
  expenses, calculating, 75
  expenses, fixed vs. nonfixed, 76
  expenses, saving money on, 77–80
  managing money, 75–77
  student loans, 80–81, 168
  tuition/room and board, calculating, 75
  working, 80–86
Fiona, Melanie, 145

first-generation college students, 169–78
  as breaking with tradition, 169–70
  family expectations, 171, 176
  fitting in, 2–3
  guilt felt, 170–71
  and imposter syndrome, 171–72
  pressure to prove themselves, 2
  self-efficacy, 172–78
Fitzgerald, Paul: *Revisiting propranolol and PTSD*, 232
Fitz-Gerald, Samantha, 176
Fiverr, 82
fixed mindset, 172–73
flu, 66–67
Focus app, 138
Foer, Joshua, 124
food banks, 77
Food Rules (Pollan), 61
FORGE, 45, 232
forgiveness, 116
Forward, Susan: *Emotional Blackmail*, 142
fraternities, 32, 35, 238
Frazier, Donna: *Emotional Blackmail*, 142
Free Application for Federal Student Aid (FAFSA), 75
Freeman, Justin, 40
friends, 52, 143–47, 157, 165–66
frustration tolerance, 114–15, 122
future
  adaptability to, 13–15
  worrying about, 23

G

GCFLLearnFree.org, 131
Geekly Hub, 29
Gender Diversity, 211
Gen Z (people born 1995–2015), 14
Getselfhelp.co.uk, 182
gig apps, 81
Giovanni, Nikki, 115
Giustino, Thomas: *Revisiting propranolol and PTSD*, 232
glassdoor.com, 84
Glaynker, Igor, 184–85

Index

Goddard, Cathy, 27
Goldthwait, Bobcat, 146
gonorrhea, 67
Good and Cheap (L. Brown), 61
Good Jobs Project, 200
goodrx.com, 213
Goodwill, 77
GPA (grade point average), 163
grades, 107, 139, 163
The Grain Brain Whole Life Plan (Perlmutter and Loberg), 61
Grammarly, 129
Greene, Betty, 22
grief, 190, 228
groups, theories about, 238–40
growth mindset, 113, 173–76
Gundry, Steven R.: *The Plant Paradox*, 62
guns used in suicides, 185

H

habits, 29, 39, 120, 123–24, 182–84
handshake.com, 84
happiness, 23, 219, 241
Harding, Richard, 228
The Hard Questions (Piver), 159
Healgrief.org, 228
health, 59–73. *See also* well-being
  active participation in your care, 71–72
  allergies, 72
  anaphylactic shock, 72
  eating, 59–62
  emergency plans, 65–66
  finding a new doctor, 65
  ignoring, 219–20
  infection prevention, 66–67
  infection treatment, 70–71
  long-term, 73
  maintaining physical health, 65–73
  medical websites, 69
  medication, 69–71, 96–97, 213
  minimizing sick time, 68–69
  proactive behavior, 65–66, 68
  safety kit, 236
  sexual, 67–68
  sleeping, 62–65, 122, 215
  symptom complexes, resources on, 227–33
  tiredness, 73
  vaccinations, 66
health insurance, 10
Heath, Chip and Dan: *Decisive*, 125–26
Hello To All That (Faulk), 216
hercampus.com, 47, 60
heroin, 226
high school dropouts, jobs for, 204
high school graduates, jobs for, 204–5
Hire Education (Weise), 207–8
HIV/AIDS, 67
homesickness, 142–43
homework, 137–39
hopeagain.org, 228
hotlines
  eating disorder, 233
  sexual assault, 45, 232
  suicide, 185–87, 210
  transgender crisis, 210
housing, 37–57. *See also* roommates; safety issues
  at home, 50–52
  off-campus, 47–50
  pets, 53–57
  residence halls, 45–47, 60
  and weapons on campus, 52–53
  what to bring, 45–46
How to Graduate College Early (Swirsky), 80–81
HPV, 66–67
Hutton, George, 105
hydration, 60

I

Imbesi, Tony, 105
imposter syndrome, 171–72
Improve the Moment Work Sheet (Whelchel), 180
impulse control, 122
infection prevention, 66–67
infection treatment, 70–71
instructors, 31–33
integrity, 111, 117

International School of Bartending, 205
International Student Organization, 212
internships, 206–7
intimacy, sexual vs. emotional, 148–49
irresponsibility, 220
isolation, 220
I Will Not Die an Unlived Life (Markova), 188–89

J

Jackson, Maggie, 120
Jackson, Mary, 113–14
Jed Foundation, 188
jobs
   for college students, 80–86
   Good Jobs Project, 200
   for high school dropouts vs. graduates, 204–5
   work-study, 82
Johns Hopkins Medicine Health Library, 69
Johnson, Ann Dowsett, 218
Johnson, Dwayne, 113
Johnson, Katherine, 113–14
Jolie, Angelina, 169–70
A Journey Toward Health and Hope: Your Handbook for Recovery after a Suicide Attempt, 187–88

K

Kahn Academy, 129
Kelly, Jack: *Predictions for the Uncharted Job Market of the Future*, 14
Kennedy, Pagan, 73
Kerr, Clark, 104
kratom, 223

L

Lady Gaga, 175–76
Lahijani, Eve, 59
Lambda Legal, 211
Latinxtherapy.com, 213
Learned Optimism (Seligman), 181
lectures, recording, 133–34
Lee, C. M., 97
Lee, Kai-Fu, 13

Lee, Rebecca, 103
Lewis, M. A., 97
LGBT National Help Center, 210
LGBT students, 210–11, 228, 232
Life Coaching (Ferraro), 182
A Lifelong Love Affair (Nowinski), 148–49
life-purpose development, 17–18
limbic valence, 123–24
listening receptively, 135–37
lithium, 188
loans, 80–81, 168
Loberg, Kristin: *The Grain Brain Whole Life Plan*, 61
lodgings. *See* housing
loneliness, 146
Lost-n-Found Youth, 211
Lucia, Jacqueline: *Making Ends Meet with a Popcorn Popper*, 61
luck, 118
lying, how to spot, 95

M

major
   and career counseling, 105–6
   choosing, 33, 105–6, 163
Major Depressive Disorder, 229–30
Make a Great Grocery List in Minutes, 60
Making Ends Meet with a Popcorn Popper (Lucia), 61
manners, 89–90
Maren, Stephen: *Revisiting propranolol and PTSD*, 232
marijuana, 122, 220–21, 223
Markova, Dawna: *I Will Not Die an Unlived Life*, 188–89
Marquette University Counseling Center, 176
Marshall, Steve, 228
mass shootings, 232
Mattis-Namgyel, Elisabeth: *The Power of an Open Question*, 242
Mayo Clinic, 67–69, 225
McGonigal, Kelly, 107–8
MDMA (Molly; Ecstasy), 225
measles, 66

Index

medical websites, 69
medication, 69–71, 96–97, 213
Medisafe app, 71
Medline Plus, 69
memory, 122–24, 138
meningitis B, 66
mental health education, 179–80
mental illness. *See under* well-being
mentors, 120–21, 178
mercy, 115
methamphetamine, 224–25
Microsoft Word, 129–30
middle class, disappearance of, 14
Million Women Mentors, 121
mindfulness, 22–24, 126, 180–81
mind mapping, 135
MindMeister.com, 135
Mindset (Dweck), 113, 172
mindset, 105–26
    actions' effects on others and yourself, 116–17
    brain-centered, 119–26
    "cold hard realities," 108–19
    competition, 118–19
    critical thinking, 124–26
    curiosity, 126
    entitlement, 112
    fixed, 172–73
    forgiveness, 116
    growth, 113, 173–76
    importance of, 105–8
    luck, 118
    mistakes/failures, 115, 164–65
    moral compass, 110–11
    obeying the law, 118
    perfectionism, 117
    simplifications, 111–12
    victim, 112–13
Minnesota State Careerwise, 198–99
minorities
    discrimination against, 112–14
    and getting pulled over, 119
    resources for, 209–10
Mint app, 76
mistakes/failures, 115, 164–65, 173–74
Molly (drug), 225

money management, 75–77. *See also* finances
mononucleosis, 66
MOOCs (Massive Open Online Courses), 207
Moodgym, 216
moral compass, 110–11
Moretti, Enrico, 202
motivation, extrinsic vs. intrinsic, 163
multitasking, 29, 52, 121
Muschamp, Will, 181
Myers, Michael F., 5
Myers-Briggs Personality test, 206
MyGCAL App, 215

N

The Naked Roommate (Cohen), 47
NAMI, 210, 213
Narcan (naloxone), 221, 226
narcissists, 160
Nasrallah, Henry, 183–84
National Black Student Union, 209
National Center for PTSD, 231
National Eating Disorders Association (NEDA), 233
National Institutes of Health, 69
National Institutes of Mental Health, 229
National Sexual Assault Telephone Hotline, 45
National Sleep Foundation, 62
National Society of Black Engineers, 209
National Suicide Hotline, 185
Navigating College: A Handbook on Self-Advocacy Written for Autistic Students from Autistic Adults, 92
Navratilova, Martina, 35
NEDA (National Eating Disorders Association), 233
negative self-talk, 181–82
Neighbors, C., 97
NerdWallet, 76
Nightware, 64
Nin, Anaïs, 242
Noonlight app, 38
note taking, 133–35

Nowinski, Joseph: *A Lifelong Love Affair*, 148–49
NURX.com, 68

O
Obama, Barak, 25
Obama, Michelle, 127
obsessive-compulsive disorder (OCD), 231
Ocasio-Cortez, Alexandra, 11
openness to wonder, 241–43
opiates, 221, 225–26
optimism, 181
overextending yourself, 219
overthinking, 121

P
panic disorder, 231
parents. *See also* family
  brushing them off, 220
  dependence on, 8
  and the FAFSA, 75
  health problems, 14
  independence from, 165–66
  living with, 50–52
  separation/divorce, 141–42
Payne, Ruby K., 147
Pearson Higher Education, 128
Peck, M. Scott: *People of the Lie*, 95
peer groups, 94–95
perfectionism, 117, 176
Perlmutter, David: *The Grain Brain Whole Life Plan*, 61
Perry, Tyler, 116
pets, 53–57
PFLAG, 211
Phillips, Andrew J. K., 62
Phipps, Rachel: *Student Eats*, 61
Pierson Education, 53–54
Pinckley, Christopher A.: *State of Mind 2.0*, 105
Piver, Susan: *The Hard Questions*, 159
plagiarism, 129
Plan B kits (morning-after pill), 98–99
Planned Parenthood, 43
The Plant Paradox (Gundry), 62

Pollan, Michael: *Food Rules*, 61
pornography, 103
positivity, 181
posttraumatic stress disorder (PTSD), 231–32
The Power of an Open Question (Mattis-Namgyel), 242
Predictions for the Uncharted Job Market of the Future (Kelly), 14
Prefeta, Louis, 197
prefrontal cortex, 21, 122
pregnancy, 68
PrEP (pre-exposure prophylaxis), 67–68
prioritizing, 24–25
procrastination, 21–22, 27, 218–19
propranolol, 232
psychosis, 232–33
PTSD (posttraumatic stress disorder), 231–32
Public Service Loan Forgiveness, 80
PubMed Central, 97

R
rape, 99. *See also* sexual assault
Rape, Abuse & Incest National Network (RAINN), 232
readiness assessment
  differences, 5–6
  strengths, 4–5
  vulnerabilities, 1–4
reading, 137–39
receipthog.com, 61
receiptpal.com, 61
Reducing Underage Drinking, 218
registration, 31
relationships, 141–60. *See also* roommates
  abusive, 159–60
  dating, 147–53, 165
  drama in, 219
  family, 141–43 (*see also* parents)
  friends, 143–47, 157, 165–66
  getting serious/breaking up, 159–60, 234–35
  ideal partners, 150–53
  rejection, 156–58

Index

stalkers, 153
　unwanted attention (creeps hitting on you), 153–59
residence halls, 45–47, 60
resources
　academic skills, 127–28
　advantages of college, 200–206
　break-up affirmations, 234–35
　career planning, 197–200, 206–7
　diversity, 209–12
　internships, 206–7
　mindfulness, 23–24
　openness to wonder, 241–43
　safety kits, 236–37
　scholarships, 206–7
　symptom complexes, 227–33
responsibility, 220
Revel app, 128
Revisiting propranolol and PTSD (Giustino, Fitzgerald, and Maren), 232
Rice, Condoleezza, 10–11
risk assessment, 123
risky behavior on spring break, 97, 99
Ritalin, 71, 224
Rock, Chris, 113
room and board/tuition, calculating, 75, 206
roommates
　adjusting, 143–44
　agreement templates, 144
　apartment sharing, 49–50
　careless, 42
　communication/sharing, 45–46
　gun ownership by, 42, 52
　and pets, 56
　problem-solving, 47
Roosevelt, Theodore, 115
Rover app, 81
Rowling, J. K., 115, 164–65
RuPaul, 114
Rutherford, Mike, 193

S

SACNAS, 209
safety issues, 37–45
　buddy system, 37
　car practices, 40–41
　drinking and driving, 37–38
　drugging of drinks, 39, 44, 100
　emergency kit, 39
　hostage/kidnapping situations, 40, 100
　planning, 39–40
　robbery, 40
　safety habits, 39
　safety kits, 236–37
　safety/security apps, 38
　sexual assault, 42–45, 98–99
　walking at night, 38–39
　weapons on campus, 52–53
　where you live, 41–42
Saint-Exupery, Antoine de, 88
SAMM (Support After Murder and Manslaughter organization), 228
Sandberg, Sheryl, 164, 228
scholarships, 206–7
Scott, Felicia T., 117
Screaming Meanie video, 65
The Secret Thoughts of Successful Women (Young), 171–72
Seeking Alpha app, 85
self-awareness and reflection, 15–17
self-confidence, 16, 128
self-control
　and ADHD, 220
　improving/developing, 108, 197
　reaching goals through, 107
　situations that lower, 122
　on spring break, 97
　vs. temptation, 150
Self-Defense for Women Warriors (Ericksen), 44
Self-Directed Search test, 207
self-efficacy, 113, 172–78
Self-Efficacy (Bandura), 172
self-evaluator (Ulifeline), 227
selfhood, 163
selfmadesuccess.com, 82–83
Seligman, Martin, 228
　Learned Optimism, 181
serenity, 181–82

7 Cups of Tea Program, 213
The Seven Habits of Highly Effective People (Covey), 27
sex
   and consent, 42–43, 98, 157
   contraception, 67–68, 98
   and intimacy, 148–49
   nonconsensual, 98–99
   sexual education, 148
   on spring break, 97–98
sexual assault, 42–45, 98–99
Sexual Assault Hotline, 232
sexual health, 67–68
shopping rebates, 61
simplifications, 111–12
Sinema, Kyrsten, 178
sleepfoundation.org, 62, 64
sleeping, 62–65, 122, 215
sleeping apps, 64
SMI Advisor app, 216
Smith, Will, 4
smoking, 222
Snoozester.com, 65
social anxiety, 90–91, 149
social groups, understanding, 92–95, 238–40
socializing, 90–92
social media, 101–3
social mobility, 12
sororities, 32, 35, 238
spirit, 164
spring break, 96–101
SQ3R study technique (surveying, questioning, reading, reciting, and reviewing), 138
stalkers, 153
Stalking Resource Center, 153
STAR interview technique, 85, 182
State of Mind 2.0 (Pinckley), 105
Staudacher, Carol: *Beyond Grief*, 190
STDs, 67–68, 97–98
Steppingblocks.com, 105, 129, 168, 206–7
Steve Fund, 210
Stoneman Douglas High School (Parkland, Fla.), 15

Straight for Equality, 211
strep throat, 67
stress, 107–8, 120
"Stress in America" (American Psychological Association), 107–8
Student Eats (Phipps), 61
studentloanhero.com, 80
student loans, 80–81, 168
study abroad, 34
studying, 137–39
   in the middle phase of college, 162–63
   SQ3R study technique, 138
   study groups, 134
success in college, importance of
   adaptability to the future, 13–15
   impediments to success, resources for, 217–26
   life-purpose development, 17–18
   mnemonic for, 194
   possessions and activities, ability to acquire, 11–12
   poverty and dependence on others, avoiding, 7–11
   social mobility, 12
   understanding yourself, 15–17
Suicide Anonymous, 188
Suicide Prevention Resource Center, 188
suicide/suicidal thoughts or feelings, 52, 184–90
Sullivan, Harry Stack, 15, 87
summary
Support After Murder and Manslaughter organization (SAMM), 228
support animals, 55
support system, 34, 39, 109, 120, 145, 162
Swirsky, Danny: *How to Graduate College Early*, 80–81
Symptomate-Symptom Checker app, 69
systems, colleges/universities as, 103–4

T

Tannehill, Brynn: *Everything You Ever Wanted to Know About Trans**, 211
teachers, 31–33

Index

technical school, 7
Tetris as Therapy (Zhang), 232
textbooks, 131–33, 138
Textcerpts, 138
Therapyforblackgirls.com, 213
Thoreau, Henry David, 8–9
thrift stores, 77
time management, 21–35
  and busywork, 25
  campus places/distances, 28
  course selection/registration, 29–32
  course sequence, 33–34
  habits, daily, 29
  mental abilities used in, 21
  mindfulness, 22–24
  organizing your time, 25–28
  organizing your workspace, 28
  prioritizing, 24–25
  procrastination, 21–22, 27
  software, 21, 28
  strategic planning for the semester, 34–35
  teacher selection, 32–33
  to-do lists, 29
Time Timer, 28
tiredness, 73
tobacco, 222
to-do lists, 29, 130
Tournier, Paul, 146
Trade Schools, Colleges, and Universities, 84
Transgender Suicide Prevention Hotline, 186
Trans Lifeline, 210
trauma, recovery from, 116
Trevor Project, 210
Tsitsipas, Stefanos, 161
tuition/room and board, calculating, 75, 206
"21 Warning Signs of an Emotionally Abusive Relationship," 159
Tyson, Neil DeGrasse, 18

U

undocumented students, 209
University of Rochester Medical Center's Health Encyclopedia, 21
unwanted attention (creeps hitting on you), 153–59
Upwork.com, 82
Urban, Tim, 105–6, 207
USA College Today Uloop, 32
US Department of Education Campus Safety and Security website, 38
US Embassy, 100

V

vaccinations, 66
Vaughan, Dorothy, 113–14
victim mindset, 112–13
Virtual Hope Box app, 215
Visual Timer-Countdown, 28
Vyvanse, 71, 224

W

wage estimates, 9
Waitbutwhy.com, 105–6, 207
Walker, Alice, 170, 242
weapons on campus, 52–53
Weise, Michelle: *Hire Education*, 207–8
Weliver, 56–57
well-being, 179–92. *See also* health
  coping techniques, 180–82
  distress, 180
  getting help, 185–86, 190–92
  healthy mental/physical habits, 182–84
  ignoring your health, 219–20
  impediments to, resources for, 217–26
  mental health education, 179–80
  mindfulness, 180–81
  positivity, 181
  resources, 213–14, 217–26
  serenity, 181–82
  the STAR technique, 182
  suicidal feelings, 184–89
  suicide, surviving a loss by, 190
Wendt Center for Loss and Healing, 228
Whelchel, Gloria: *Improve the Moment Work Sheet*, 180
White, Kate, 121
Wiesner, Christoph, 28

Wi-Fi, registration via, 31
willpower. *See* self-control
Winfrey, Oprah, 15
work after college, 168, 197–200
work during college, 80–86
workspace organization, 28
work-study jobs, 82
World's Greatest Dad, 146
Wunderlist To-Do List & Tasks, 130

Y

Young, Valerie: *The Secret Thoughts of Successful Women*, 171–72

Z

Zebian, Najwa, 89
Zhang, Yulan: *Tetris as Therapy*, 232
Zika virus, 98
Zipit app, 99

About the Authors

Dr. Barbara Roquemore EdD is an associate professor in the Department of Professional Learning and Innovation at Georgia College and State University. She graduated from Tift College in Forsyth, Georgia. She coached high school basketball and taught high school English. After completing her EdD at the University of Georgia, she worked as an assistant principal and eventually an assistant school superintendent. After completing a career in K-12 education, she started at GCSU over thirteen years ago. She lives with her husband, Dr. Duffey, in Cumming, Georgia.

Dr. Jeff Duffey M.D. is a board-certified psychiatrist and the author of *Exploring Your Unplanned Pregnancy: Single Motherhood, Adoption, and Abortion Questions and Resources.* As the psychiatrist for Georgia College and State University's Counseling Center, he has worked with college students for over thirteen years. He graduated from Davidson College and the Medical College of Georgia before completing his psychiatric residency at the Sheppard and Enoch Pratt Hospital in Baltimore, Maryland. He has been a clinical assistant professor of psychiatry at the University of Maryland, Emory University, and Mercer University Medical Schools. He has worked with young people in his private practice, at a long-term residential center and a psychiatric hospital for adolescents. His first book's website is http://exploringyourunplannedpregnancy.com. His blog is Simply Human Conversations— An invitation to brainstorm about the human condition. https://jeffduffey.wordpress.com/.

Check out Dr.Roquemore and Dr. Duffey's website at
www.SEARCHaguideforcollegeandlife.com

From the Authors

Customer reviews make an incredible difference in how visible this book will be on Amazon and whether other students will think it is worth buying. You can help other students find this book more easily by posting a review of it on Amazon. Please, let other students know if you found it useful. You don't need to write a long or formal review. A sentence or two would be very much appreciated. Thank you.

www.ingramcontent.com/pod-product-compliance
Lightning Source LLC
Chambersburg PA
CBHW030436300426
44112CB00009B/1023